66 The inspiring stories related here are particularly meaningful to citizens of the United States, not only because the movement largely originated here, but also because, in no small measure, the atrocities can be traced right back to Washington—which means to all of us who could act to modify the actions of the power systems, state and private, that are based in the U.S. There are many lessons here of great human significance, if we choose to learn them."

—NOAM CHOMSKY
Professor of Linguistics
Massachusetts Institute of Technology

66 . . . an important contribution in the search for paths and alternatives in extreme and violent situations. These testimonies convey a sense of hope, born of solidarity and ripened through walking side by side with the people."

—ADOLFO PÉREZ ESQUIVEL
1980 Nobel Peace Laureate

66 Mahony and Eguren reaffirm the importance of the noble labor of accompaniment and its contribution to the survival and strengthening of organizations struggling for respect of human rights."

—RIGOBERTA MENCHÚ
1992 Nobel Peace Laureate
(Ms. Menchú used accompaniment
protection frequently in her struggle for
human rights in Guatemala.)

66 This book is a very touching testimony to the courage of the people who provided international protective presence for people in the extreme distress of terrorism, state terrorism, torturism and death squads. With these profoundly humane acts of solidarity they not only saved lives but also shamed many guns into silence. Read them, support them, join them!"

—JOHAN GALTUNG
Professor of Peace Studies and Director
of TRANSCEND, A Peace Network

66 . . . a masterly empirical and theoretical explanation of the power of nonviolent protective accompaniment as a technique for generating safe political action spaces in situations of tyrannical or arbitrary rule. It is a vital source for conflict resolution practitioners, human rights activists, and students of political science."

—DR. KEVIN P. CLEMENTS
Director, Institute for Conflict Analysis
and Resolution, George Mason University
President, International Peace Research
Association

Unarmed Bodyguards

Peace and Conflict Resolution Titles from Kumarian Press

Unarmed Bodyguards: International Accompaniment
for the Protection of Human Rights
Liam Mahony and Luis Enrique Eguren

Multi-Track Diplomacy: A Systems Approach to Peace
Third Edition
Louise Diamond and John McDonald

GAZA: Legacy of Occupation—A Photographer's Journey
Dick Doughty and Mohammed Al Aydi

All Her Paths Are Peace: Women Pioneers in Peacemaking
Michael Henderson

Unarmed Bodyguards

International Accompaniment for the Protection of Human Rights

Liam Mahony
Luis Enrique Eguren

Kumarian Press

Dedicated to Laurie and Nuria

Unarmed Bodyguards: International Accompaniment for the Protection of Human Rights.

Published 1997 in the United States of America by Kumarian Press, Inc., 14 Oakwood Avenue, West Hartford, Connecticut 06119-2127 USA.

Portions of chapters 8, 16, 17, and the introduction were previously published in the monograph *International Accompaniment for the Protection of Human Rights: Strategies, Scenarios and Objectives,* Institute for Conflict Analysis and Resolution, George Mason University, Fairfax, VA, 1996.

Production supervised by Jenna Dixon
Copyedited by Linda Lotz   *Typeset by CompuDesign*
Text design by Jenna Dixon   *Proofread by Ann Flanders*
Index by Elizabeth Kniss
Maps by Laurie Goldman

The text of this book is set in 10/13 Adobe Sabon.

Printed in the United States of America on acid-free paper by Thomson-Shore. Text printed with soy-based ink.

Library of Congress Cataloging-in-Publication Data
Mahony, Liam, 1958–   .
   Unarmed bodyguards : international accompaniment for the protection of human rights / Liam Mahony, Luis Enrique Eguren.
     p.   cm.
   Includes bibliographical references and index.
   ISBN 1-56549-069-X (cloth : alk. paper). — ISBN 1-56549-068-1 (pbk. : alk. paper)
   1. Human rights. 2. Civil rights workers—Protection. 3. Political activists—Protection. 4. Bodyguards. 5. Non-governmental organizations. I. Eguren, Luis Enrique. II. Title.
JC571.M3248   1997
323—dc21   96-37848

06 05 04 03 02 01 00 99 98 97   10 9 8 7 6 5 4 3 2 1   1st Printing 1997

Contents

Prologue

The Girl with the Big Eyes
—Luis Enrique Eguren

HER EYES. I MOSTLY REMEMBER HER EYES, crowning her tiny seven-year-old body. Her eyes, big and black, that followed me about as she trotted on her little legs around that small Salvadoran village of former refugees. In one place or another, each time I turned around, there she was behind me.

Her expression was usually serious, but when I smiled at her, she broke into a broader smile, enveloped in shyness. For days this was our only communication—glances and smiles. At the time, I marveled at how the children seemed capable of keeping a distance from all the suffering around them.

One night, several years before, they had all fled from that same village of Santa Marta, with only their clothes on their backs, running from the thunder of airplanes and falling bombs. They followed dirt trails through the mountains and ravines, finally crossing the Rio Lempa into Honduras. In that river many died—some by drowning, others from the simultaneous bullets of the Salvadoran and Honduran armies.

I'd heard the stories of this ordeal and of their long years in Honduran refugee camps. Now they were home again: only a few months before, these few thousand campesinos* had returned to rebuild their lives on the ruins and memories of the past. The Salvadoran army still threatened them and hampered their every move. We two or three accompaniment volunteers had one aim—to defend the right of these former refugees to live in their own country.

As the days went by, we gradually started to talk, the girl with the big eyes and I. I would ask her something, and she would chat for a while about this and that, before invariably getting lost in thought, playing with small stones or her little torn doll.

It was during one of these conversations that she mentioned her mother and father "from before." I heard it, but I didn't understand. She kept talking, and I didn't interrupt. Later she repeated the phrase. With a weight in my chest, I ventured to ask her why she called them her mother and father "from before." She didn't respond directly. Only a little later, between comments she made while drawing in the sand, I heard her say in an absent voice that she didn't remember her papa and mama from before, but others had told her that they had been left in the Lempa river when everyone else had to leave, and that's why she now lived with her papa and mama "from now."

She kept on talking about one thing or another, as if not knowing what to do with that memory learned from someone else's lips. My eyes filled with

*A Latin American small farmer or peasant.

tears. I couldn't put faces to the "mama and papa from before" of that girl with the big eyes. But her words showed me the dark abyss of her past, and I knew now that she was not distant from the pain all around her; she was just learning how to live with it.

The Wake

—Liam Mahony

THE SUNDAY I ARRIVED IN GUATEMALA CITY to start working with Peace Brigades International (PBI), Camilo García Luis, a farmworker, was abducted by unknown men. On Monday, his twenty-two-year-old wife, Marta Odilia Raxjal-Sismit, came to the PBI house to report the disappearance. The next day, Marta Odilia was called down to the police station. María Esteban Sismit, her mother, was abducted from their home a few hours later.

Marta's and María's mutilated corpses were found on Friday morning, January 30, 1987, in a ditch off the Pan-American highway in Chimaltenango. Friday was my first day of "protective escorting" with the Guatemalan Mutual Support Group for Families of the Disappeared, also known as the GAM. I attended a demonstration in front of the National Palace, where Mariano Raxjal-Sismit publicly accused the army of killing his sister and mother.

As the demonstration came to a close, Nineth de García, GAM's president, took the megaphone and urged everyone there to show solidarity with the family by attending the wake that night in San José Poaquíl. I remember thinking that she couldn't be serious. How could she ask these poor people to drop everything to go to an unknown family's wake, nearly a day's ride away? I then followed as fifty women, with children on their backs, trudged twenty blocks to the bus terminal.

The public bus went only as far as Chimaltenango, halfway to our destination. There we were stranded on a deserted rural street corner, and it was getting dark. Nineth de García headed off with a foreign journalist, saying, "We'll find another bus," as if it were a simple matter in rural Guatemala to find a bus driver who would agree to drive a threatened group to an especially controversial wake in the middle of nowhere—at night.

I stood apart from the group, talking with David, another Peace Brigades volunteer and the only other foreigner around. The Guatemalans seemed barely aware of our presence. It was now pitch dark. Two other women came over to us, saying, "We must find some food for all these people while we wait. Can you come with us?" We both nodded and took a few steps in their direction, when all of a sudden several shouts arose from the group behind us—"No! Solo uno! Solo uno!" (Only one!). David accompanied the two women; I stayed with the group.

So there I was, standing in the dark, incredulous. Did they really think that I could make a difference if soldiers or death squads arrived? There was no light, no phone, no bus, no food, and it was getting cold. I was frightened.

An hour later, we were piled on top of one another in a bus, eating hot tortillas and black beans, bumping over the dirt road to San José Poaquíl. Don't ask me how they did it. By midnight we were at the all-night wake. Around us were sobbing women, stone-faced men, and confused children. The women spent the whole night cooking tamales and brewing coffee. David and I sat in silence or tried awkwardly to make conversation. We stepped outside now and then to look around, since patrols of soldiers had come by earlier in the evening.

In the morning, other villagers came by to pay their respects. I mostly waited out on the street. Four young soldiers in camouflage fatigues came walking up the hill, machine guns in their hands, grenades dangling from their belts. Everyone just watched in silence. Jim, a U.S. photojournalist, took their pictures as they approached. The soldiers surrounded him and started questioning him. Somehow word got passed inside that they wanted to take his camera.

At this moment, Nineth, a tiny woman, stormed out of the house like some sort of self-contained tornado, saying, "Jim, give me the camera." Without a pause she nudged herself between two of the machine guns, took the camera from Jim's hands, and walked back into the house. The soldiers just stared at her—as astonished as I was. I didn't question whether the photo or the camera was really worth such a confrontation. Nineth's display of raw courage and moral authority just froze everyone in place.

After a moment, the soldiers went over and peered in the door. Then one by one they walked inside. I followed them. It was a crowded room, with barely enough space for the two coffins and the rickety chairs against each of the four walls. No one protested the soldiers' presence or their guns. Instead, four chairs were silently emptied, and the soldiers were invited to sit down and take off their hats. An instant later, four women came out of the kitchen with hot tortillas and beans for each soldier. The soldiers put their guns aside to free up their hands.

Fourteen-year-old Carlos Raxjal-Sismit watched them eat. "If looks could kill," I thought. Carlos's father had been disappeared* a year ago. Now Carlos's mother, sister, and brother-in-law were dead, and his brother Mariano was in danger. When the soldiers finished eating, Carlos approached them quietly. One by one he escorted each soldier up to view the faces of his dead sister and mother. The soldiers then left in silence.

* To be disappeared is to be abducted and never seen again. This method of terror became so common in Latin America after the 1960s that it prompted the creation of this new verb.

A few days later, eldest brother Mariano brought the other orphans back to their one-room house in the capital. He was now being threatened by the local army intelligence unit in Chimaltenango. He asked if we could stay with the children—for their protection.

For the next two months, I lived on and off with the Raxjal-Sismit orphans. I spent the days playing games or learning a few words of *Cakchiquel*, their native language. At night I slept on a small flea-ridden cot in the same room as the children. Mariano made himself scarce, since the police kept stopping by, looking for him "for questioning." The children, terrified, would ask me to answer the door. With Mariano absent, fourteen-year-old Carlos was now the man of the family, but it was tiny twelve-year-old Rosa who kept things together. With Justina and Estela—her younger adopted sisters—she supported the family by selling tortillas on their little street corner in a poor neighborhood not far from the center of Guatemala City. They shopped, cooked the meals, and kept the clothes clean. Their one appliance was a television Mariano dropped off for them late one night. We spent the evenings watching *telenovelas*, Latin American soap operas whose drama and pathos paled in comparison to these children's real lives.

Eventually the police stopped coming. The children relaxed a little. Mariano moved the whole family back up to Chimaltenango, explaining that things were calm now and they would no longer need accompaniment. I never learned why such a hell had been visited upon this family.

Preface

THIS BOOK WAS CONCEIVED in a pizza joint in El Salvador in January 1992. San Salvador was celebrating the just-signed peace accords and cease-fire. We had been involved in protective accompaniment work for four years. Inspired by the jubilation around us, and maybe a little proud of having played a small role, the same thought occurred to both of us: someone should write this down. We wanted to share the excitement of having witnessed and supported a valiant struggle.

As we gathered stories together, we got more ambitious. Could we *prove* that human rights accompaniment deters violence? Does it really encourage activists to organize and take risks they would not otherwise have taken? Has international accompaniment contributed significantly to the growth of nonviolent social movements? When does it succeed or fail?

These questions took us back for a closer look at the areas of conflict where we had worked. We visited small villages in Guatemala and Buddhist monasteries in Sri Lanka. We chatted over coffee with Salvadoran generals, and over tea with Sri Lankan union organizers. We interviewed scores of accompaniment volunteers from all over the world. In libraries and human rights centers, we pored over history books, human rights laws, studies of deterrence and social movements, and psychological research on fear and decision making.

In this book, we attempt to draw some lessons from a decade of practice with a new tool in human rights protection, wherein unarmed international volunteers physically accompany those who are threatened with violence. These lessons derive from the experiences of hundreds of courageous human rights activists and accompaniment volunteers. Our analysis is based partly on our own accompaniment work; indeed, our very motivation to write this book cannot be separated from our personal contact with political repression and human rights abuse, nor from the privilege of having witnessed the courage with which human rights activists confront it.

Acknowledgments

OUR FIRST AND DEEPEST THANKS must go to the thousands of local activists around the world who take risks daily in the struggle for human rights and justice. The few stories of courage told in these pages cannot do justice to the countless other heroes facing equal danger—most with no international support—whose stories remain untold. Their commitment brought accompaniment into existence in the first place. The privilege of witnessing their courage inspired us to stick with the five-year process of finishing this work.

The hundreds of accompaniment volunteers who responded to these activists' calls for support and protection also merit recognition, though they are usually the last to claim it. Accompaniment volunteers have taken risks, made sacrifices, and lived out their moral commitments. "No," they protest, "it's the Guatemalans [or Sri Lankans, and so forth] who deserve all the credit!" This is true in large part. But this honest humility is also one of the strengths of accompaniment's offering to the struggle for global justice, an offering whose story deserves to be told.

This study is based almost entirely on primary sources, and our deepest thanks go to all those who consented to be interviewed (see Appendix 1). We secured a broad array of interviews with the invaluable organizing assistance of Jude Sunderland in Guatemala; Carmen Guzman, Esther Domenech, and Luis Perez in El Salvador; and Almut Wadle in Sri Lanka. Rosa García Gutierrez and Winnie Romeril assisted with transcriptions. All English translations of these interviews are ours.

We are also grateful to the organizations and their staffs that made their archives and resources available to us, including Peace Brigades International's offices in Guatemala, Sri Lanka, Halifax (England), and Toronto (Canada); the Guatemalan Accompaniment Forum; the National Coordinating Office for Refugees and Displaced (Chicago); the Seva Foundation (Massachusetts); Amnesty International (London); the Sri Lanka Civil Rights Movement; Human Rights Watch–Americas and the Center for Justice and International Law (Washington); the El Salvador Nongovernmental Human Rights Commission (CDHES), the Human Rights Institute of the University of Central America (IDHUCA); the El Salvador Institute for Juridical Studies; Tutela Legal (San Salvador archbishop's legal aid office); and the Guatemalan Mutual Support Group (GAM).

Our research was assisted by tireless librarians in the New York Public Library, Ottawa University Human Rights Centre, Centro de Investigación para la Paz (Madrid), Guatemalan Human Rights Ombudsman's library, and Provincetown Public Library (Massachusetts). The Harvard Human Rights

Program generously facilitated our access to the Harvard University Libraries. Patrick Coy, Anne Manuel, John Lindsay Poland, Ram Mannikalingam, Clark Taylor, Bill Hutchinson (Marin County Interfaith Task Force), Beate Thorenson (International Council of Voluntary Agencies), Ulli Laubenthal, Jesus Puente, Marie Caraj, Phil Esmonde (Quaker Peace and Service), and many others provided additional documentation and advice.

Transforming our research material into this modest book would have been impossible without the support and advice of Janice Fine, Barbara Scott, Karen Brandow, Curt Wands, Randy Divinski, Yeshua Moser-Phoungsuwan, Mirabai Bush, Sheila Gilroy, Alaine Hawkins, Louise Palmer, Janey Skinner, Carol Baum, Michael Valliant, and many others. Special thanks to Kara Hooper, Ed Kinane, John Mahony, Laurie Goldman, and Linda Lotz for their perceptive, exacting, and tireless editing, and to Donald Irish for his steadfast encouragement. Any errors of fact or analysis are, of course, ours.

Photos were gathered with the assistance of Bjorn Sendel, Karen Brandow, Yeshua Moser-Phoungsuwan, Sheila Gilroy, Edith Cole, Alain Richard, Gilbert Nicolas, Kelly MacCready, Kara Hooper, Lizzie Brock, Alaine Hawkins, Derrill Bazzy, Erika Meier, Joe Gorin, Henrik Frykberg, Didier Platon, Didier Varrin, and Piet Van Lier. We are grateful also to the many anonymous photographers who have donated their photos over the years to the accompaniment organizations, which in turn loaned them to us. Laurie Goldman donated her mapmaking skill and Ed Lyman and Adib Goldmansour assisted with the figures.

The Program in Peace and International Cooperation of the John D. and Catherine T. MacArthur Foundation funded this research. We received additional financial support from the United Methodist Church Women's Office and from Donald Irish. Finally thanks to Trish Reynolds and Kumarian Press for recognizing the value of our work and for publishing it.

Introduction:
Breaking New Ground

WHEN THE MUTUAL SUPPORT GROUP for Families of the Disappeared rose from the ashes of genocidal violence in Guatemala in 1984 to demand respect for human rights, it was considered suicidal. But the organization survived—with the constant presence of Peace Brigades International (PBI) volunteers at their side. When Sri Lankan police abducted and killed noted journalist Richard De Zoysa in 1990, his mother took the unprecedented risk of pressing charges against the chief of police and requested protective accompaniment from international volunteers for both herself and her lawyer. Protected by unarmed volunteers, Nobel Peace Prize winner Rigoberta Menchú risked several visits from exile back to Guatemala. Guatemalan activist Amilcar Mendez, 1990 winner of the Robert F. Kennedy Foundation Human Rights Award, states simply, "Without accompaniment I would not be alive today."

Before returning home from camps in Mexico in 1993, thousands of Guatemalan refugees insisted that the Guatemalan government recognize their right to the protection of international nongovernmental volunteers. Within a year, dozens of foreign volunteers, sometimes hundreds, were living and traveling with the refugees in the jungles that had previously been the army's private war zone.

The accompaniment volunteer is literally an embodiment of international human rights concern, a compelling and visible reminder to those using violence that it will not go unnoticed. The volunteers act essentially as unarmed bodyguards, often spending twenty-four hours a day with human rights workers, union leaders, peasant groups, and other popular organizations that face mortal danger from death squads* and state forces. The premise of accompaniment is that there will be an international response to whatever violence the volunteer witnesses. Behind such a response lies the implied threat of diplomatic and economic pressure—pressure that the sponsors of such violence may wish to avoid.

---

*Death squads (or hit squads in the Sri Lankan context) are paramilitary commando units that carry out anonymous attacks on civilians, usually with political motives. Although they operate with varying levels of autonomy and are sometimes used by private citizens for personal gain, in all the cases we've studied, these squads were developed by the government as part of a counterinsurgency strategy, enabling political killings without the embarrassing use of government uniforms. Death squads can be composed of military or police personnel operating out of uniform, or they may be paid thugs.

Victims of human rights abuse are frequently those attempting to organize social change movements that question their society's powerful elites. An international presence can be a source of hope to these activists. It assures them that they are not alone, that their work is important, and that their suffering will not go unnoticed by the outside world. The volunteer's presence not only protects but also encourages.

There is no guarantee of safety in being a foreigner. The Sri Lankan army deliberately attacked an ambulance of the Doctors Without Borders, and the Salvadoran government carried out a campaign of harassment and expulsion of foreigners. Peace Brigades' volunteers in Guatemala were bombed and knifed. Do such incidents call into question the concept of protective accompaniment, or are they exceptions proving the rule?

Human rights scholars and activists may be inspired by personal experience and convictions, but they must be guided by sober and objective analysis. To presume, without evidence, that accompaniment is effective protection would be irresponsible for the scholar and downright dangerous for the human rights activist. A deeper analysis must comprehend the uncertainties of complex situations and, more importantly, the perceptions and points of view of a wide range of key actors in each scenario.

There are good reasons to trust the veracity and analysis of the victim over that of the attacker. But this bias must be tempered by the recognition that even heroic human rights activists who risk their lives every day may be ill-informed and mistaken in their analysis, and they may lie. A death squad leader or dictator, in turn, might be intelligent and may be telling the truth. An activist for justice may, without contradiction, be quite power-driven, and a military officer quite susceptible to moral persuasion. The accompaniment volunteer, as well as the scholar, without sacrificing any moral convictions, must look beyond the good guy–bad guy dichotomy and comprehend the thinking of all the key players.

We use the term "accompaniment" to refer to the physical presence of foreign volunteers with the dual purpose of protecting civilian activists or organizations from violent, politically motivated attacks and encouraging them to proceed with their democratic activities. Our specific focus is the accompaniment provided by nongovernmental organizations (NGOs). The generic term "activists" refers to those who use accompaniment for protection. Finally, we refer to those individuals providing this service as "volunteers," even though some are paid employees of NGOs.*

An unarmed international presence as protection is not a new concept. An evangelical Salvadoran government official even cited the example of

---

*Obviously, local human rights workers are usually volunteers, and international volunteers are also activists, and accompaniment could be defined much more broadly. The nomenclature is thus not entirely accurate, but it adds clarity and simplicity to the subsequent analysis.

St. Paul the Apostle to us: his clout as a Roman gave him the political freedom to take risks that the other apostles could not. In the early colonial history of the Western Hemisphere, some European missionaries stood up
against conquistadors for the rights and lives of indigenous people. Gandhi
made sure to have foreign journalists in the right places at the right times
to dramatize to the outside world the injustice of the British occupation. In
the United States, "freedom riders" of the civil rights movement of the 1950s
and 1960s provided domestic nonviolent accompaniment, bringing young
white northerners to southern states to take part in, and offer protective
accompaniment to, southern black integration initiatives.

The modern notion of a nongovernmental, international protective presence can be traced at least to the formation of the International Committee
of the Red Cross (ICRC) in 1863, the first NGO to convince warring nations
to honor the moral and symbolic force of an outside neutral party. The bulk
of subsequent international human rights and humanitarian law presup-
poses a deterring effect of international moral pressure.

The formation and growth of NGOs such as Amnesty International in
the 1960s and 1970s broadened this concept by involving everyday citizens
in direct pressure campaigns. By building a network of letter writers, Amnesty
proved that even unknown prisoners in obscure parts of the world could be
protected by the power of international opinion. Whereas Amnesty protects
the rights of political prisoners by exerting pressure with an onslaught of
letters, accompaniment manifests similar pressure much more immediately,
with volunteers risking their lives to stand beside human rights activists—
to *prevent* arrest or attack.

Implementing accompaniment is not easy. Resources are needed to build
organizations, recruit volunteers, and maintain them in the field. Volunteers
must be selected and trained. Each one must confront a certain degree of
fear about engaging in this risky service. Networks must be built to back
up the symbolic nature of the volunteer's presence with international clout.
It is a considerable investment for the direct protection of relatively few
people at any given moment.[1]

Overcoming these hurdles required a confluence of factors and circumstances that were provided by the Central American conflicts of the 1980s.
The institutions pioneering accompaniment brought together strands of
several international movements. The loosely knit nonviolence movement
included activists from around the world, some tracing their commitment
back to Gandhi, others to resistance to military conscription, struggles
against the Vietnam War, or the more recent antinuclear efforts. In addition,
the human rights movement, spearheaded and popularized by Amnesty
International in the 1970s, was growing and diversifying rapidly. Finally,
in the early 1980s, the Central American solidarity movement burst onto

the global scene. International solidarity brought together the socialist tenet, "Workers of the world, unite!" and a global extension of the religious demand to "love thy neighbor." It was not a new concept, but the intersection in Central America of revolutionary resistance movements, liberation theology, and uncontrolled state violence against civilians inspired historically unprecedented international support movements around the world.

From this convergence, two organizations were born in two very different ways. PBI was founded in late 1981 at an international conference on nonviolence held in Canada. From Europe, Asia, and the Americas, the participants brought decades of experience working in a variety of conflicts and organizations: Quakers, Indian activists in the Gandhian tradition, others seeking models to prompt future large-scale initiatives in the United Nations, and many more. What they had in common was an idea: that active nonviolence was a practical and vital tool for confronting violent conflicts. The new organization's statement of principles was simple but ambitious:

> We are forming an organization with the capacity to mobilize and provide trained units of volunteers . . . in areas of high tension, to avert violent outbreaks. . . . Peace brigades, fashioned to respond to specific needs and appeals, will undertake nonpartisan missions which may include peacemaking initiatives, peacekeeping under a discipline of nonviolence, and humanitarian service. . . . [A] brigade may establish and monitor a cease-fire, offer mediatory services, or carry on works of reconstruction and reconciliation. . . . Those who undertake these tasks will face risks and hardships. . . .
> We are building on a rich and extensive heritage of nonviolent action. . . . We are convinced that this commitment of mind, heart, and dedicated will can make a significant difference in human affairs.[2]

The next year was spent building interest and support for the organization. A second meeting in 1982 in the Netherlands approved committees to investigate project possibilities in Central America, Sri Lanka, Namibia, Pakistan, and the Middle East.[3] Seven months later, in March 1983, PBI installed its first team in Guatemala.

Meanwhile, the Nicaraguan revolution had captured the imagination of progressives around the world. A month after PBI started in Guatemala, a delegation of U.S. Christian church activists from North Carolina went to Nicaragua on a fact-finding tour. On a visit to a small village that had just been attacked by the U.S.-backed contras, the U.S. activists asked people, "Why aren't they shooting now?" The answer, "Because you're here." The group was so moved by the experience that some of them considered staying. Instead, they went home to organize a long-term constant presence of U.S. citizens in Nicaragua. Thus Witness for Peace was born.[4]

Unlike PBI, Witness for Peace emerged from a specific shared experience, a Christian solidarity with other Christians in a particular struggle, and a profound sense of responsibility—even guilt—that these U.S. citizens felt about their own country's policies and its victims. They contacted others who had been moved by the Nicaraguan struggle and found that the idea was contagious. In a few months, Witness for Peace began sending hundreds of people, and eventually thousands, to Nicaragua on short-term visits. The organization pioneered a unique integration of community-level accompaniment, guided small-group visits to Nicaragua, and public education and lobbying in Washington. Although one of its tools was protective accompaniment, its broader mission was to educate the American public and change U.S. policy.

It was no coincidence that the two organizations that first succeeded in implementing protective accompaniment were doing their work in Central America. The focus of global attention on this region provided both the potential for interested and inspired volunteers to take on the risk and the necessary network of international support and pressure to back them up. Accompaniment was attempted in regions lacking such international solidarity networks only after the Central American experiments proved that the service was possible.

In the 1990s, accompaniment expanded so quickly that we cannot pretend to offer an exhaustive survey of all the ongoing work in the field.[5] Instead, we focus on extensive experiences in three countries—Guatemala, El Salvador, and Sri Lanka—and add some contrasting analysis of two more recent projects in Colombia and Haiti. We concentrated the majority of our research on the efforts of a single organization, PBI. This allowed a comparative study of several conflicts, since PBI is one of the only organizations providing accompaniment in different parts of the world. PBI also has the longest history of accompaniment, allowing for a study of how the service changed over time. This choice, however, is by no means a statement about the relative value of different organizational efforts. Many important accompaniment efforts have been carried out by other organizations. We touch upon some of these, but space does not allow for the thorough treatment they all deserve.

We used the accompaniment experience in Guatemala as our centerpiece, because Guatemala has the longest available accompaniment history. The extent and variety of accompaniment efforts there provide a wealth of lessons. The accompaniment idea was born at a moment of near-total paralysis of civilian democratic activity in 1984, when PBI helped facilitate the founding of the first human rights organization to survive Guatemalan terror. As the civilian movement grew, accompaniment grew with it, playing a significant role in a protracted national transition. A decade later, the sustained multiorganizational accompaniment of the returning Guatemalan refugees proved that protective accompaniment could be implemented on a large scale.

Other wars presented other challenges. In El Salvador, foreign volunteers lived precariously in a war zone, facing a government that openly hated them. In Sri Lanka and Colombia, accompaniment was started without the benefit of any significant solidarity network, and it operated within multiple conflicts between politically sophisticated government and rebel armies. In Haiti, the accompaniment volunteers lived in terrorized villages where activists dared not work publicly.

Some analysts categorize accompaniment using the conflict-resolution terminology of "third-party intervention." Others speak of multitrack diplomacy, where "track 1" is between governments and "track 2" involves NGOs. The field of international humanitarian intervention has broadly embraced the classifications of "peacemaking, peacekeeping, and peacebuilding."[6] In this breakdown, *peacemaking* interventions are those that serve to bring about an immediate cessation of hostilities, such as facilitating a negotiation process. *Peacekeeping* efforts serve to keep hostile parties separate, to prevent the conflict from erupting again immediately—for example, a UN armed buffer force. *Peacebuilding* works toward long-term stability, establishing institutions and understandings addressing the root causes of conflict. Galtung distinguishes peacekeeping as *dissociative*, keeping the conflicting parties apart, whereas peacemaking and peacebuilding are *associative*, bringing the parties together. Lisa Schirch, emphasizing the primary goal of preventing a hostile attack, categorizes accompaniment within this scheme as peacekeeping.[7]

Although accompaniment is certainly a third-party intervention, it is more fundamentally a *tool* used by actors in the conflict. As such, it traverses all the above categories. It is not solely dissociative peacekeeping, since its protection allows the victims to confront, communicate, and negotiate with their attackers (peacemaking). The act of encouragement and empowerment, overcoming internalized terror, is in itself a key aspect of long-term peacebuilding. Whereas many existing models and examples of international humanitarian intervention rest on the often unarticulated assumption that external actors can solve problems, accompaniment helps local civilian activists become protagonists in their own search for peace.

Accompaniment is still a young practice: ten years of experience in a limited number of countries. Before accompaniment, the projection of the human rights movement into the field of conflict was largely limited to brief fact-finding missions or lone field-workers collecting data. Now, more and more international organizations are using accompaniment. This analysis of recent experience should help guide future accompaniment efforts in other conflicts. Meanwhile, it is our hope that the story of accompaniment will educate and inspire the public at large to further support and protect the efforts of courageous human rights activists around the world.

Notes

1. Wiseberg ("Protecting Human Rights Activists"), in one of the earliest references in the human rights literature, describes accompaniment as a potentially effective but "costly" protection.
2. Peace Brigades International founding statement, issued at Grindstone Island consultation, Ontario, Canada, September 1981.
3. Peace Brigades International, meeting minutes, Bergen, Netherlands, August 28, 1982.
4. The Witness for Peace model developed in quite a different direction from PBI and is not the focus of this study. For a dramatic and perceptive analysis of Witness's growth and work in Nicaragua, see Griffin-Nolan, *Witness for Peace*.
5. For a brief survey and categorization of related efforts prior to 1995, see Schirch, *Keeping the Peace*.
6. Galtung, "Three Approaches to Peace."
7. Schirch, *Keeping the Peace*.

PART I

1

Descent into Terror

THE GUATEMALA THAT Peace Brigades International entered in 1983 was a land of great beauty and great suffering—lush rain forests and towering volcanoes, scattered with the bodies of 100,000 victims of state violence. It is a land of rich Mayan culture, ancient ruins, and an export-based plantation economy that has long kept the majority of the population on the verge of starvation.

For Guatemalan Mayans, the violence of the 1980s continued a long history of attacks and humiliations begun by the Spanish conquistadors in the sixteenth century. Enslaved and Christianized, the majority Mayan population was impoverished and steadily robbed of its land. Even after Spain lost colonial control in 1821, Spanish descendants and mixed-blood ladinos retained all political and economic power. By the 1980s, Guatemala had the most skewed land distribution in Latin America. Three percent of the population owned 70 percent of the arable land, some of the most productive land in Central America. This powerful minority controlled both political and economic power and is still referred to in Guatemala as the oligarchy.

Nearly all Guatemalans are of mixed Mayan and European origin, and the distinctions between Mayan and ladino are largely cultural and linguistic. Over the centuries, many Mayans have migrated to the cities, intermarried, and accepted the dominant ladino culture. But in the rural areas, the diverse Mayan culture varies from region to region and includes more than twenty distinct languages. Spanish, for the rural Mayans, is the language of interregional commerce and government, and many never learn it. The Mayan culture stresses the importance of the community, and land and corn are invested with powerful spiritual significance.

Despite pressures toward assimilation and a gradual loss of many Mayans to the dominant ladino society, the Mayan culture and community remain distinct. With rare exceptions, ladinos do not speak Mayan languages, nor do they understand Mayan culture. It is not uncommon to hear present-day wealthy Guatemalans referring to Mayans as "children," "savages" or "animals." That these "savages" are the majority threatens the elite, who have consistently relied on the military to quash periodic revolts. This polarization and lack of communication have given Mayan communities a greater cohesion and resistance to cultural and political manipulation or infiltration than most other poor communities in Latin America.

Guatemala was run by repressive military dictatorships for most of its postcolonial history. But in 1944, a general strike forced dictator Jorge Ubico to abdicate and ushered in ten years of democracy. When the ambitious social reforms of Presidents Arévalo and Arbenz decreased the profits of the oligarchy and U.S. corporations, however, this "democratic spring" was ended. In 1954, a CIA-supported coup, prompted by pressure from the United Fruit Company, placed military dictator Castillo Armas in power. Guatemala's short-lived democracy, and its untimely demise, had a profound impact on all future political developments.[1]

Attempts to organize opposition were vigorously suppressed. In the first week after the coup, 250 activists were executed, 17,000 were imprisoned, and thousands went into exile. Eight thousand campesinos were killed. Their land was returned to the oligarchy, from whom it had been bought in President Arbenz's 1952 agrarian reform.

After the Cuban revolution in 1958 and the birth of a Marxist armed revolutionary movement in the early 1960s (hereafter referred to as the guerrilla movement), the United States and its allies increased economic and military assistance. The CIA and U.S. military advisers became a fixture in the planning and implementing of Guatemalan counterinsurgency campaigns. Repression came in cycles: rising drastically whenever civilian movements or guerrilla resistance gained strength, then dropping off once the army considered the situation under control.

In the late 1960s, under General Arana Osorio, the army annihilated a rural guerrilla movement a few hundred strong and, in the process, murdered between 8,000 and 10,000 noncombatant campesinos. With the assistance of the first self-labeled "death squads," the labor and student movements and opposition parties were decapitated.* In the early 1970s, the repression relented somewhat. Union and peasant organizing increased. The guerrilla movement regrouped and set its sights on organizing Mayans in the highlands.

The Catholic Church had been labeled subversive by the military ever since the 1960s, when priests and catechists (lay religious workers) began working to apply the Bible's teaching directly to alleviate the suffering of the poor, empowering them to take responsibility for social change. This movement, globally known as "liberation theology," was represented in Guatemala by a new organization called Catholic Action, which became a major force among the Mayan population.

---

*According to General Mejía Victores, death squads were started at the suggestion of the CIA. (See Nairn, "CIA Death Squad.")

The 1976 earthquake, which killed tens of thousands in a few minutes, further polarized the situation. International disaster relief flowed into Guatemala, only to be siphoned off by corrupt officials. The government failed to respond to immediate medical needs and was not up to the challenge of reconstruction. The Mayan communities organized self-help efforts, and Catholic Action and other NGOs came to people's aid. Disillusionment with the government increased.

By the time General Lucas García came to power in 1978, the guerrillas were a significant force in the highlands. Strong peasant and labor movements were insisting on political change. Guatemala's elite were further alarmed by the successful revolution in 1979 in neighboring Nicaragua. The Guatemalan army escalated the repression. On June 21, 1980, after a series of massive and disruptive strikes, twenty-seven labor leaders were abducted from a single meeting and were never seen again. On January 31,

1981, the major Mayan peasant league, known as the Committee for Campesino Unity (CUC), held a sit-in at the Spanish embassy to publicize the repression. Police stormed and firebombed the embassy, killing thirty-nine people, including government and embassy personnel. The only Guatemalan survivor was abducted from his hospital bed the next day. Spain severed diplomatic relations with Guatemala.

From 1981 to 1983, the military relentlessly swept the highlands in a scorched-earth strategy, massacring unarmed civilians and burning hundreds of villages. In Guatemala City, the army used exhaustive intelligence gathering and analysis to locate every urban guerrilla safe house and then wiped them out in a single sweep.[2] High-profile moderate opposition politicians were machine-gunned on busy streets. Catholic bishops were forced into exile. Priests, catechists, union activists, student leaders, and their professors were killed by the hundreds; Mayan campesinos by the thousands. By the mid-1980s, out of a population of 9 million, an estimated 40,000 were disappeared, 100,000 assassinated, and 1.5 million forced to flee their homes.

The military restored control and then maintained consistently high levels of repression, initiating surveillance and reindoctrination campaigns in the rural highlands, while at the same time launching a political strategy to reverse Guatemala's notorious international reputation as a human rights pariah. After the coup of March 1982, President Rios Montt announced a "democratic opening," promising that in March 1983 the state of siege would be lifted. The plan was that an elected constituent assembly would write a new constitution, after which elections would be held. Rios Montt invited political parties to operate publicly and urged international organizations that had fled to return.

Peace Brigades International took advantage of Rios Montt's public declaration to deploy a team of nonpartisan observers for the democratic opening. Between January and March 1983, PBI's international secretary, Dan Clark, a Quaker lawyer from Walla Walla, Washington, and Hazel Tulecke, a fifty-eight-year-old Quaker and retired French teacher from Yellow Springs, Ohio (U.S.), traveled through Mexico, El Salvador, Panama, and Costa Rica, making contact with Guatemalans in exile. In Guatemala, they met various activists working clandestinely. Meanwhile, PBI began looking for the right volunteers and enough money to get a team in place by March 23, the day the state of siege was to be lifted.

Hazel Tulecke arrived in Guatemala on March 21, 1983, to meet her two teammates. She didn't know that one of them had changed his mind at the last minute and the other had been denied a visa. For a brief interval, Hazel *was* the first PBI team. As she swept out the empty house that had been rented from an exiled Guatemalan professor, she wondered what she had gotten herself into:

> I had doubts . . . and some fears. Would the government lift the state of siege? Would any parties come forth to challenge the government? What could we really do as such a small group anyway? How would "international presence" be important as so many people said it might? Could we be effective in any way without seriously risking getting kidnapped or killed, or endangering the very lives of those we hoped to help?[3]

With two team members no longer available, Dan Clark, back in the United States, scrambled to keep the project alive. He called Alain Richard, a French Franciscan priest whom he had met in January. Alain, a worker priest who had survived the Nazi occupation, was in Panama doing a fast for peace. He made a quick decision and went to Guatemala.

Next Dan called Pablo Stanfield, a nonviolence activist from Seattle (U.S.), and convinced him to leave for Guatemala inside of a week. A three-person team was in place, almost on schedule. But this sort of ad hoc, last-minute scramble for volunteers was a weakness that PBI would not overcome for several years.

The team of three set to work. The meetings and impressions of that first month were a preview of things to come. Rodíl Peralta, head of the Bar Association, urged them to do everything possible to document the human rights situation. (Years later, as interior minister, Rodíl would threaten to expel PBI and block its request for legal status.) Religious workers in CONFREGUA, the Conference of Religious of Guatemala, introduced PBI to many contacts. CONFREGUA would be an encouraging ally throughout PBI's tenure in Guatemala. A high official in the Rios Montt government, Jorge Serrano, spoke of the need to educate the army, defended the sincerity of the "political opening," and urged PBI not to be like Amnesty International, "spreading bad stories about Guatemala." (Eight years later, President Serrano would expel half the PBI team after police fired on a group of campesinos that PBI was accompanying.)

By the end of that first month, Alain, Pablo, and Hazel hashed out a plan that would define PBI's presence in the coming years: PBI would *not* do political organizing or form groups, would *not* initiate activities that Guatemalans themselves could initiate, would *not* attempt to cover the entire national territory, and would at all costs *avoid* any indiscretion or disclosure of information that might put others in jeopardy. What PBI *would* do was a little more vague. The team's plan included such phrases as "serving continually as an international presence . . . giving moral support to those who really want a democratic opening"; "witnessing"; "[providing] technical support in nonviolent methods, . . . [establishing an] organizing skills clearinghouse"; and above all, "taking the lead from local groups." More ambitiously, they also proposed "direct action with regard to disappearances" and "creative nonviolent action in a crisis period." Their prognosis, though, was cautious:

> It is clear that the government puts obstacles in the way of those who threaten in any way the status quo. One experienced person even said very clearly that he thought the project was unlikely to succeed at this time; in his judgment it is "not the time to speak truth to power."[4]

During their first year, PBI team members traveled throughout the highlands, visiting rural farmers, clandestine contacts, and government and military officials, introducing themselves and feeling things out. When necessary, they helped people flee the country. In one case, PBI learned of a man who was about to be sentenced to death by Rios Montt's Special Tribunals. PBI and other groups outside the country put together an overnight campaign, using confidential diplomatic channels of pressure, and got a stay of sentencing and execution. PBI later helped hustle the man out of the country.

By the end of the first year, the team had made many contacts and tested several program ideas, but none of them had developed into a clear mission. The terror continued; popular organizing was still stifled. PBI was still waiting for an opening.

Notes

1. For a detailed exposé of the 1954 CIA coup, see Kinzer and Schlesinger, *Bitter Fruit*.
2. Payeras, *El Trueno*.
3. Hazel Tulecke, personal notes, April 1983.
4. Pablo Stanfield, Alain Richard, and Hazel Tulecke, *Report to PBI on the First Month in Guatemala, April 23, 1983* (internal PBI document).

2

Out of the Ashes: The Mutual Support Group

I N EARLY 1984, a young schoolteacher lost her husband. As far as she knew, he didn't die. He simply disappeared, and she was left alone with their one-year-old daughter. She checked the hospitals. She checked the morgues. Nothing. Eyewitnesses had seen him taken by police, so she inquired at Guatemala's numerous security agencies. She got a judge to issue a writ of habeas corpus. Still nothing. No husband, no father, no body. And no one to help her.

One day she heard about a group of foreigners who had recently opened an office in Guatemala City to work for peace. With little left to lose, Nineth Montenegro de García contacted Peace Brigades International.

In Guatemala, investigating disappearances, or any other human rights abuse, was a deadly pursuit. When the Association of University Students (AEU) began filing habeas corpus petitions in the 1960s, there was a rash of assassinations of law students. In the early 1970s, the AEU tried again, forming the Committee of Relatives of the Disappeared. On March 10, 1974, men in plain clothes walked into the San Carlos University legal aid center in broad daylight and gunned down the committee's principal organizer, Edmundo Theilheimer. The committee disbanded. In the late 1970s, Irma Flaquer created the National Commission for Human Rights. On October 16, 1980, her son was shot, and Flaquer herself was disappeared. The commission dissolved. Flaquer had actually resigned from the commission a few weeks before her disappearance, stating, "No one wants to join it, because it is useless and suicidal."[1]

On March 11, 1984, Nineth de García wrote to PBI:

Dear Friends in Peace Brigades,
I am pleading for your aid in my anguish. My husband, Edgar Fernando García was kidnapped, or more accurately, illegally captured on Saturday, February 18 this year. Eyewitnesses of the event say that at 10 A.M. on the corner of 3rd avenue and 7th street in zone 11 there was a roadblock of BROE, the Police Special Operations Brigade, at which place they put my husband in the back of a bus. It's now been 23 days without a trace of his whereabouts. . . .

I am deeply tormented by not knowing what has become of Fernando García—a young man who is needed in his home, and who still has much to offer to his country.

A thousand thanks in advance.

Nineth Montenegro de García, wife

Fernando García was twenty-five years old. After studying at the University of San Carlos, he went to work for the Central American Glass Company (CAVISA) and became a leader of the CAVISA labor union. He was one of hundreds of union activists to disappear in the early 1980s.

PBI's initial response was not very promising. PBI volunteer Pablo Stanfield talked to Nineth:

I remember her reciting everything she had tried. I think she was expecting us to provide a lawyer and private detectives and go out and start doing something. So I explained what our work and limits were. . . . She asked, "What should we do?" I responded, "It seems to me that you have done everything possible, legally, in this situation. You have to understand that we're guests in this country, and we can't organize Guatemalans. But it was our hope that if any group organized, we might be able to help them. Don't you know other people in this same situation?"[2]

It was not much to go on, but it was a start. Nineth remembers the process of gathering people together and the start of her relationship with PBI:

The truth is, it wasn't that difficult to bring people together or organize them, because every time we went to the body dumps, the morgues, or the hospitals to identify bodies, there were always other mothers, women, everyone looking for their loved ones. So we would talk there.

Peace Brigades gave us some talks as well, from their pacifist perspective and nonviolent vision. We decided we could move forward, especially because of the support of a few foreigners. I say a few, because at that point they were only three! One of them, Edith, was a very dynamic woman, very humane and warm, and she supported us a great deal.[3]

Edith Cole was a bilingual psychologist in the California public schools, active with the Central America solidarity movement. A fifty-seven-year-old mother of six grown children, she'd first read an article on PBI by Dan Clark in a Quaker newsletter. PBI's principles echoed her Quaker belief in "seeing that of God in every person." Now she was in Guatemala, answering the door to many women who had lost family members:

They would go to the police station and be mocked, and be told, "Oh, your husband is missing? Well, he probably got a lover somewhere else!" Just agonizing situations. Their friends and families and neighbors were afraid and didn't want to associate with them anymore. Some of them had tried to push their cases, but then other family members disappeared. Or somebody called them and said, "If you pay us 10,000 pesos we can get a letter to him."[4]

One of these women was Blanca de Hernandez, who recalls:

> In 1982 and 1983 there were ten or fifteen people disappearing every day! But I didn't know what a disappearance was, much less how to denounce it. When they kidnapped my son, my friends told me to find a lawyer to file a habeas corpus. But the lawyer said if I did that the G-2 [military intelligence agency] would kill me. So I didn't.[5]

The Tape Recording

After about a month in Guatemala, Edith took a trip to El Salvador in April 1984. She met with the Committee of Mothers of the Disappeared and Assassinated (COMADRES), a group of women who had organized with the support of Archbishop Oscar Romero in the late 1970s. Impressed by their work, Edith asked the Salvadorans to record a message for women in Guatemala.

> I took the tape back, not quite knowing how the opportunity would arise to play it. Miraculously, a few days later, a couple of the families set up an audience with the Guatemalan archbishop to bring their individual petitions and ask for the mass for the disappeared. They asked me to come along. I took my little tape recorder and the tape, just in case.
>
> There we were, maybe about twenty people, in the waiting room. Time dragged on, and they were told that the archbishop would see them, but much later. Finally I said, "Well, while we're waiting, some of you know I've been to El Salvador and I have a message for you. Maybe you could listen to it."[6]

The message of the COMADRES could hardly have been more timely. They had gone through the uncertainty of starting their organization seven years earlier. The anonymous voice on the tape spoke with hope and confidence:

> As a young mother myself, I send a greeting to the mothers in Guatemala who are concerned for their people and their children. I believe that pain is what makes us struggle. Our committee is based on pain and suffering. Mothers feel the pain of their children, the loss of a child, whether it's because of an assassination, a disappearance, or if they're in some jail in Guatemala. We hope that you can unite yourselves to demand liberty for your children.
>
> You can start, as we started, by making a definitive decision to *do* something. Don't just think about it: try to make it happen. This drive that you feel to struggle for your children: put it in practice! Try to move forward. . . .
>
> One of the first things you should do is visit the government and try to establish yourselves as a legal committee, so your work is not clandestine. That's how we earned our credibility, visiting the Legislative Assembly, the Supreme Court, the Ministry of Justice, even the directors of the National Police and the wardens of the prisons. You visit them so they know that someone is watching, someone is looking out for these disappeared.

There are so many things you can do! Our committee has taken over the Red Cross, the public parks, churches, embassies, even the Ministry of Justice. . . . In 1980 we won the release of eleven political prisoners. We also forced improvements in the conditions and feeding of political prisoners in jail. . . . We hold press conferences for both the national and international media. . . . We've gotten support from the churches, and from international groups. . . .

There have also been losses. The death squads keep on killing people. We've been threatened for the ads we've published. One of us was killed in March 1982, and another disappeared in August 1982. But we keep on going. . . . If the mothers don't struggle our whole lives, this voice will be not be heard. It will be lost.[7]

The COMADRES' message struck an emotional chord. It also emphasized the importance of direct action and outlined a list of organizing tactics. Finally, it suggested that the effort was survivable—but not without losses, and not without external support. The COMADRES had sought allies in two of the only spheres relatively independent of state control: the church and the international community.

Edith continues:

The Guatemalan women were tremendously moved after hearing the tape. They were weeping . . . right there in Archbishop Penados's waiting room. . . . At the end of the tape, somebody was saying, "Yes, that's right. And if it can be done in El Salvador, it can be done here, and we must do it. We're going to do it."

They went in to see the archbishop, and they told him about how the COMADRES had had the support of Bishop Romero and maybe the same thing would be very helpful here. They wanted Penados to allow them to hold their meetings somewhere in the archbishop's place, as Romero had done.

Archbishop Penados was very hesitant, saying things like, "This situation is very different from El Salvador," and "Many people thought that Romero was a Communist."[8]

What the Guatemalan archbishop did not need to point out was that Salvadoran Archbishop Romero was dead—murdered in 1980 for being too politically outspoken. With the Guatemalan church under attack as well, Archbishop Penados was cautious. He agreed to allow a mass for the disappeared in the cathedral but would not risk more active support. As the women left the building, Edith offered them the use of the PBI house. "We can't offer you the protection of the church, but at least it's something."

The women placed ads in the Guatemala City daily papers inviting the public to a special mass sponsored by the archbishop and the rector of the national university. With just three days' notice, a large crowd turned out for the event. The same day, the women came over to the PBI house to establish a new organization: the Grupo de Apoyo Mutuo, or GAM (Mutual Support

Group). Their founding statement carefully avoided any hint of political affiliation or even protest:

> We are not in opposition to anyone, nor are we accusing anyone in particular. What brings us together is our profound love for our lost ones and our need to give each other moral and spiritual support.
> We are asking all mothers, wives and family members in general who have suffered the same situation to join us. Together we will succeed in bringing our loved ones home. They are the center of our lives.[9]

Every Saturday they met at the PBI house. In no time, hundreds of people were showing up, overflowing the house and patio. Not surprisingly, though, many viewed PBI with suspicion. Ester de Herrarte recalls, "At first I was frightened to come. It might be a trap. I didn't know who these 'Brigades' were."[10] Some feared that they might be the CIA, but the family members kept coming. There was nowhere else to go. Mixed in with the mistrust was a feeling of safety. Ester de Herrarte continues:

> All of us have fond memories of how PBI opened their arms to us. The simple fact of being located in a house with foreigners committed to nonviolence was a big support in the beginning. It's thanks to that support that we were able to organize ourselves, because those were really difficult times.[11]

Hundreds of Guatemalans had lost their loved ones and had met in the morgues before, without forming an organization. What was different in the spring of 1984? In fact, there were twice as many disappearances in the first half of 1984 than in the latter half of 1983.[12] But the women were not analyzing these statistics: their need was too immediate. The GAM's founders had all lost loved ones in 1984. In fact, due to a rash of kidnappings at the University of San Carlos, more than half had lost someone in the two weeks prior to the founding. They may have been desperate, but they had not yet given up. They were still looking. Most of all, they were looking for hope.

Hope was not enough, however. They needed a plan. The social function of terror is not simply to destroy hope. It also serves to isolate people and convince them that there is nothing that *can* be done, even if they have the motivation to try something. Confusion, inaction, and frustration can quickly snuff out a spontaneous flame of hope.[13] The COMADRES' tape moved these frightened family members from confusion to decisiveness. It demanded concrete action and provided a list of suggestions. The GAM added to this list through discussions with PBI volunteers, who shared information about other countries' experiences.

But they still needed security. They had families, other loved ones who were vulnerable to disappearance. They had to have some minimal assurance that their struggle to find their loved ones would not simply compound the tragedy. The COMADRES had formed in 1977 with the powerful figure of Archbishop Romero to protect them; the Salvadoran Catholic Church was still a credible deterrent. It was only after the archbishop's assassination that COMADRES activists were targeted.

The GAM women also wanted church protection. When Penados denied their request, they turned to PBI, an unknown international NGO. It was a desperate move to keep the momentum going.

From Impotence to Action

The hundreds who showed up every Saturday were mostly Mayan, and mostly women. Women's groups have pioneered the formation of such organizations of victims' families in many countries. In Guatemala, most of the disappeared were men, leaving women alone to deal with the loss. Though they faced a reduced probability of lethal attack, women risked rape or sexual mutilation, among other tortures.* Official denials of the existence of disappearances exacerbated the trauma, utterly negating these women's pain, and even their widowhood or motherhood.

The GAM was the only place where women could commiserate with others in the same situation. The shared trauma of the disappearance forged bonds of loyalty and drove them forward, no matter the fear. In fact, the psychological demands of this trauma help explain why families like those in the GAM were the first to break the silence in Guatemala, as well as in other countries facing state terror. Their own recovery process required a search for truth and the building of a community of support.† The GAM responded to both needs. Its meetings were occasions of great sadness and great hope.

The GAM organized more memorial masses and published advertisements regularly in the newspapers, listing disappearances and asking for

---

*Aron et al., in "The Gender-Specific Terror," argue that in Guatemala and El Salvador, the overt political sanction of rape transforms it from an isolated criminal act into a normative act of social control executed in behalf of a collective goal. Residents of El Quiche province, Guatemala, for instance, testified in 1988 that "the army's pattern of raping young women has made it difficult in some communities to find women between the ages of 11 and 15 who have not been sexually abused by the army." See also Agosin, *Surviving Beyond Fear.*

†Like the COMADRES or the Mothers of the Plaza de Mayo in Argentina, the drive behind the GAM's risk taking came from a deep sense of loss. Dealing with loss requires a grieving process. Psychologists affirm two critical conditions for this to occur: (1) direct information about what happened and why, and (2) the existence of certain symbolic and cathartic practices or rituals, such as a funeral or community event. Disappearance denies both conditions. The organization fulfills them, and thus has a transforming therapeutic—and political—effect. (See Pelento and de Dunayevich, "La Desaparicion"; Farina, "El Terror"; and Suarez-Orozco, "Grammar of Terror.")

Photo by Edith Cole

GAM demonstration with PBI volunteer observing at top left.

public support and official investigation. The media and general public expressed sympathy for the members' losses and even praised their courage. By August, only two months after its founding meeting, the GAM was granted an audience with the president, General Mejía Victores. Mejía also expressed sympathy, but he professed to believe that most of the disappeared had left the country or joined the guerrillas.[14] He promised to look into the matter.

The GAM had no long-term strategy. These women had one clear and immediate goal: to find their loved ones. Feeling that they had exhausted every other available option with no visible results, members organized the GAM's first direct protest. On October 12, 1984, hundreds of Guatemalans walked from San Lucas to Guatemala City in a silent march for peace, the first mass protest in years. The twenty-mile march was accompanied by a team of peacekeepers trained by, and including, Peace Brigades volunteers. The police, who had promised to provide security, were nowhere to be seen. PBI volunteers found themselves directing traffic around the marchers. The day passed without incident, but within a week, several students at the University of San Carlos who had attended the march were abducted, and more family members flocked to the GAM.

A month later, the GAM boldly announced its intention to charge elements of the security forces of the government with the disappearance of their family members. On November 14, 248 GAM members held a sit-in at the congress building. On November 29, they met again with President Mejía, who agreed to establish a tripartite committee to investigate disappearances, made up of the vice-minister of defense, the minister of the interior, and the attorney general. In the following week, the mutilated bodies of two students who had vanished after the October peace march were found.[15]

Upping the ante further, the GAM began calling on the international community to cut off aid to Guatemala. Two British parliamentarians took the GAM's testimony at the PBI house in October 1984 and subsequently released a report condemning Guatemala and questioning economic aid from the European community. Foreign affairs minister Fernando Andrade Diaz accused the politicians of having both imperialist tendencies and links to the guerrillas.

In January 1985, the GAM publicly urged Harry Schlaudemann, President Reagan's special ambassador to Central America, to link further economic aid to Guatemala with demonstrable improvement of the human rights situation. Later that month, the GAM urged the Organization of American States (OAS) and Lord Colville de Culross, the United Nations special rapporteur,* to condemn the Guatemalan human rights situation.

International aid was a sensitive point. As early as 1978, the Carter administration had begun attaching human rights conditions to U.S. military aid. In typical nationalistic fervor, General Lucas García had responded by renouncing such aid as an infringement on sovereignty and turning to Israel for support. By 1984, especially since the burning of the Spanish embassy, the "human rights pariah" image was affecting other countries' foreign policy decisions toward Guatemala. Even though the Reagan administration had renewed aid, significant elements in both the military and the economic elites in Guatemala were feeling the international pressure. Tourism, a major income producer, had been completely disrupted by the violence. Guatemala faced a foreign debt for the first time in its history.

Hector and Rosario

General Mejía had legitimized the GAM's existence with two presidential meetings and a high-level commission. But now the GAM was threatening international aid and ridiculing the "democratic opening," which was fundamental to the international image his government was trying to create. As a result, according to Nineth:

> In December [1984] we began to receive the first threats. We didn't want to take them seriously at first, so we wouldn't lose our morale—they want to break one's morale. In January we all started getting anonymous threats. In February, Hector Gómez, our public relations secretary, told us he was being

*A rapporteur is a special emissary named by the United Nations Human Rights Commission in Geneva to monitor the human rights abuses of an accused nation, as a sign of international concern and rebuke.

followed and closely watched. He had even discovered that his identity papers had been removed from the local municipal offices. We were very worried.[16]

The GAM was beginning to feel besieged. On March 14, 1985, General Mejía publicly accused the GAM of being manipulated by the "forces of subversion."[17] On March 15, police searched the home of GAM member Angel Reyes. PBI and other human rights organizations in the United States, Canada, and Europe began an international pressure campaign to safeguard the GAM. Various GAM members reported that their houses were being watched and that they were receiving telephone threats. Father Alain Richard, now on his second tour of service with PBI, remembers the tension:

> It seemed clear that something was going to happen. I visited many of the embassies, telling them that this Holy Week, with the increase of threats against the GAM, there would be some killing. I told even the U.S. embassy, saying, "you have to take some urgent measures if you don't want someone to get killed."[18]

On Saturday, March 30, Hector Gómez left a GAM meeting at the PBI house. He was found dead the next day with his hands tied behind his back, no tongue, and signs of beating and burns.[19] At Gómez's funeral on Monday, unknown men in civilian dress took photos of the mourners. Alain visited the U.S. embassy again to urge a response.

On Wednesday, April 3, Hector Gómez's grave was vandalized and burned. Guatemalan Interior Minister López Sandoval announced that "negative elements have infiltrated the so-called Mutual Support Group [GAM], who keep making problems."[20] Alain describes an emergency GAM meeting at the PBI house that same day:

> The GAM members were completely discouraged. There were only a few people—I shouldn't say only a few—there were sixty to eighty people, but compared to having hundreds and hundreds at previous meetings. During that meeting, they had a phone call announcing that some U.S. Congresspeople would come for the GAM demonstration scheduled for April 13. At that moment the group got more courage.
>
> After that meeting, I took Nineth and Isabel and María Rosario aside and told them, "You know, they will do everything to kill you this weekend. Please promise me not to leave your home this weekend for any reason."[21]

GAM member Blanca de Hernandez recalls leaving that meeting:

> On all the streets leading to the house there were cars, with armed men standing outside them, watching everyone who passed by. . . . I was scared, but right up beside that fear was a sense of indignation and rage: they had killed my friend and comrade, a humane and good man. This indignation just propelled me onward, as if it had charged my batteries. "I have to go on. In spite of the fear, I have to go on." I was carrying my one-and-a-half-year-old

grandson—left with me after they had kidnapped my son. I passed the first car and looked at the men, and then another car at each block, and all I could think about was what else might happen to my family. I couldn't think of anything else then, just this little child, and if they took me what would happen to the child.[22]

It was the last GAM meeting for María Rosario Godoy de Cuevas, a founder and secretary of the group. The next morning, she drove to the pharmacy with her brother and two-year-old son, who was ill. Their bodies were found that evening in their car in a ravine. The police report declared it an automobile accident, but Western diplomats said that all three had been slain before the car plunged into the ravine. Archbishop Penados angrily told the press that he had information that the cause of death was strangulation. Mourners at the funeral noted that the baby's fingernails were missing.[23]

"Remember Hector and Rosario" would become the rallying cry of the GAM. At the time, though, both the GAM and PBI were stunned by the assassinations. Nineth recalls:

> It was a terrible time for us. There was a recomposition of the GAM at that moment. A lot of people fled into exile, and others left the GAM for good. The rest of us decided that we had a historical responsibility, from that moment until the last day of our lives. We were weak—just human beings—but we knew we had a great love for Guatemala. . . . We decided, "OK. Fine. We're brave, we're strong, and we're decided, but if we don't have the support of foreigners here we will not survive." After that we were accompanied for twenty-four hours a day by Peace Brigade members.[24]

PBI was very shorthanded. In fact, when Hector Gomez was killed, Alain Richard was alone in Guatemala and had to leave the country soon to renew his visa. Just before María Rosario's death, two more volunteers arrived. But according to Alain, the idea of personal accompaniment did not arise until after her death:

> The night before I had to leave, a close diplomatic contact visited me, along with Jean-Marie Simon of Americas Watch, and they told me, "Listen, you've started to be with these women. That has to continue. How can you make sure you have enough people to do that?" I got on the phone right away, and I kept calling even from Mexico while renewing my visa, to round up more people.[25]

This was the beginning of PBI "escorting": providing the surviving GAM leadership with around-the-clock unarmed bodyguards. At the time, such a commitment was utterly beyond PBI's capacity. Yet this service would come to define its role in Guatemala. Protection by proximity to foreigners was, of course, implicit from the moment PBI had offered the GAM its house. Before the assassinations, PBI had sometimes accompanied people home who were afraid to be seen leaving the PBI house after GAM meetings. At times, GAM activists had asked PBI to visit their families so that "whoever was watching" would know of the international concern. But this unstructured and intermittent protection had not stopped the assassinations. The volunteer demand—and the risks—were now vastly greater.

Peace Brigades recognized that this service was something new in the field of human rights protection, but no one knew if it would work. Why would a death squad, which had pulled out the fingernails of an infant, restrain itself in the presence of an unarmed foreigner?

Soon after escorting began, Alain Richard learned from a confidential diplomatic source that the entire GAM directorate was on a death list:

> I had to report that to the team. It was quite scary for one guy who was escorting. He broke down, and we had to try to encourage him during the night. I said to him, "We can discontinue your escort. One of us can do it. If you think it is not fair to your wife, we understand that you might not want to." I had to be pretty calm, even cold. This was not a time to give someone a false sense of security. He said, "So do I understand that the person I am to escort might be killed?" I said, "That is correct." "And does it mean that I might also be killed?" "That is correct." And I added, "Isn't this why you came?" "Well, yes, I wrote my will before I came, but now that it's closer . . ." I said, "I think they will try to avoid killing you. But you never know if someone who is not experienced might hurt you by mistake."
>
> The following morning I asked him if someone should go in his place. He said "No, I'll go." In fact he stayed with us for quite a time.[26]

The GAM held a memorial event the following week. Carrying banners with huge photos of Hector Gómez and Rosario de Cuevas, they marched silently to the National Palace. The press reported that foreigners were prohibited from participating in the march, although PBI attended. U.S. Congressmen Theodore Weiss and Bob Edgar canceled their plans to attend after the U.S. embassy received threats against them.[27]

The pressure on the Guatemalan state after the two killings was immediate. PBI made sure that high-level authorities knew about the escorting and the political costs that further attacks would carry. Alain explains:

> After several days of pressure, the State Department made a little communiqué, saying that the United States would be upset if there were more killings in this group of families of the disappeared. That communiqué made Mejía furious, and the army published a communiqué saying that the United States was interfering with their internal problems. The State Department partially ate its words, but the communiqué still had its effect. PBI had been very active in Washington. . . . Eventually each embassy expressed its concern in some way. I think all that played a role [in protecting the GAM].[28]

In Washington, the House Foreign Affairs Committee subsequently voted to cut all but $300,000 in direct military aid to Guatemala and imposed human rights conditions on economic aid. If the GAM assassinations were intended to squelch efforts at building international pressure against Guatemala, they had clearly backfired.

No other GAM leaders were killed. The following year, U.S. journalists Allan Nairn and Jean-Marie Simon, citing military sources, reported that Jaime Martínez Jiménez had carried out the two killings. Martínez, chief of the homicide division of the Department of Technical Investigation, was operating under orders of a G-2 military intelligence commander named Colonel Carlos Dorantes Marroquín. No one, however, was ever prosecuted for the killings.*

Some GAM members were still certain that they were going to die. First they had lost family members. Then in the previous year, they had built an organization for mutual support and grown to depend on one another like family. They were living through the trauma of loss all over again. For many, it was too much, and they fled into exile or just stopped coming to the meetings. The *New York Times* reported:

> The two remaining directors, Nineth de García and Isabel de Castañon, said this week they hope to keep the group alive. But the two young women are clearly terrified. . . . After months of emotional agony in their search for their husbands who have disappeared, they now confront a barrage of death threats that diplomats say are chillingly credible. . . . At least three nations have quietly offered asylum.[29]

But the GAM's leaders stayed and fought, risking all. Nineth credits PBI for her survival: "Thanks to their presence, I am alive. That is an indisputable truth. If it had not been for them, I would not be here telling you this today."[30]

Notes

1. Americas Watch, *Group for Mutual Support.*
2. Pablo Stanfield, tape-recorded telephone interview by author, June 29, 1994.
3. Nineth Montenegro de García, tape-recorded interview by authors, Guatemala, July 8, 1994.
4. Edith Cole, tape-recorded interview by authors, Seattle, WA, June 15, 1992.
5. Blanca de Hernandez, tape-recorded interview by authors, Guatemala, July 13, 1994.
6. Cole interview.

*The G-2 is the bureaucratic label, and the popular name, of the most notorious of the army's agencies. With as many as 2,000 employees collecting and computerizing information on "subversives," the G-2 directed official death squads to carry out assassinations and disappearances. General Benedicto Lucas Garcia explained, "If the G-2 wants to kill you, they kill you. They send out a squad and that's the end of it" (Nairn and Simon, "Bureaucracy of Death").

7. COMADRES (names withheld), interview recorded by Edith Cole in San Salvador, May 25, 1984.
8. Cole interview.
9. GAM founding statement, June 1, 1984.
10. Ester de Herrarte, tape-recorded interview by authors, Guatemala, July 13, 1994.
11. Herrarte interview.
12. *PBI Guatemala Team Bulletin,* August 1984. Statistics cited are from an unnamed embassy source: 103 disappearances from July–December 1983; 232 disappearances from January–June 1984.
13. See Lawrence Goodwyn's classic study *The Populist Moment* for a more detailed argument on the concept of prerequisites or thresholds for the appearance and growth of popular organizations and resistance.
14. Agosin, *Surviving Beyond Fear.*
15. Americas Watch, *Group for Mutual Support.*
16. Montenegro interview.
17. "Mejía Victores: Apoyo Mutuo Está Ligado a la Subversión," transcript from *Teleprensa,* March 14, 1985; also *La Palabra,* March 15, 1985.
18. Alain Richard, taped telephone interview by author, January 17, 1995.
19. Americas Watch, *Group for Mutual Support.*
20. *Prensa Libre,* April 3, 1985.
21. Richard interview.
22. Hernandez interview.
23. Kinzer, "1000 Marchers"; Preston, "Dwindling Protest Group"; and interviews with GAM members.
24. Montenegro interview.
25. Richard interview.
26. Richard interview.
27. Kinzer, "1000 Marchers."
28. Richard interview.
29. Kinzer, "Killings Chill Rights Group."
30. Montenegro interview.

3

Honor and Duty

ACCORDING TO A Guatemalan news report:

> With respect to any allegations of connection between members of the Army
> and various massacres that have been reported, the chief of state [General
> Mejía Victores] asserted that the army had only limited itself to fulfilling its
> mission to protect the country from terrorist groups who were trying to dom-
> inate it. "Keep in mind," he stressed, "that we are the only state which has
> succeeded in emerging victorious against terrorism all by ourselves, without
> any external help. As for accusations against the army, if the army had not
> acted, we would today be living under a Communist totalitarian government.
> Therefore, each of you can judge for yourselves what happened."[1]

The reputation of accompaniment as a successful tool in Guatemala was
founded above all on the GAM's survival. The women's decision to keep
going after the assassinations of 1985 was a historic moment for Guatemalan
human rights. But were they actually safer because of the accompaniment?
The security forces had carried out the killings, and the rest of the GAM
leadership was also on a government death list. Given all the international
support the GAM had earned, why was the decision made to assassinate
Hector Gómez and Rosario de Cuevas? And why did the killings stop with
just those two?

For the answers, we must look to President Mejía Victores. There is no
direct evidence to prove that GAM family members were abducted or killed
by General Mejía himself, nor is there any proof that he ordered the killings
of Hector Gómez and Rosario de Cuevas. Most human rights investigators
concur, however, that the violence of the early 1980s in Guatemala was
centrally directed and controlled by the army. Many of the disappeared,
like Nineth's husband, Fernando García, were taken in broad daylight by
uniformed security forces.

General Mejía, the supreme commander, prides himself on having restored
order and discipline to those security forces. If he didn't order the assassinations, then he would have been responsible for punishing those who did,
if not for moral or legal reasons, then for reasons of discipline. And if the
security forces had a work order targeting the remaining GAM leaders,
someone had to give the order *not* to carry it out.

To the GAM and to the international solidarity and human rights communities, General Mejía is a mass murderer. As minister of defense for Rios

Montt and then as president, he supervised the scorched-earth campaigns in the highlands, resulting in tens of thousands of deaths and over a million campesinos driven from their homes. The family members of the GAM's founders were all disappeared under the Mejía dictatorship. He controlled one of the most vicious and effective state terror systems in Latin American history.

But Mejía's defenders see a different man: a patriot defending the honor and Christian values of his country. To them, he was a general fighting a war, making all the terrible decisions of life and death that face generals doing their duty. He had to live with the political and moral consequences of those actions and defend them both to himself and to the world. The decisions affecting the GAM or PBI were made by a professional soldier with a lifetime of ideological and institutional training for the decision making of a head of state.

Interview with an Ex-Dictator

Ten years after these events, the authors found the general's number in the telephone book. Considering that he was in the midst of a campaign for Congress, arranging the meeting was surprisingly simple—Mejía himself answered the phone and penciled the interview in on his calendar.

A security guard let us through the gate of a well-protected compound of modest apartments in Guatemala's Zone 10, a wealthy neighborhood of embassies and five-star tourist hotels. The general met us in his shirtsleeves and politely invited us into the living room. He listened carefully to the description of our project. Then he took a breath, fixed his gaze on us, and launched into a commanding twenty-minute monologue on the military perspective of the Guatemalan situation in the early 1980s:

> We were facing a very difficult situation. First of all, the subversives had slowly been working their way into all different sectors of society. They were running the unions and had control of the university. They had infiltrated the church. For instance, we had our daughters in a Catholic school, as did most of our friends. And the priest and nuns there began taking them out to visit poor people, to give them food or make them clothes or other acts of charity. Slowly but surely, they were putting Communist ideas in our children's heads. We eventually had to pull our children out of these schools. The priests were a real problem, especially the Spanish priests. A point came where we discovered that all the Spanish priests in some regions were gun-carrying members of the subversion. The Communists had managed to take over three entire departments. Huehuetenango, El Quiché, and Chimaltenango. Chimaltenango! That's very close to the capital.
>
> We had to look seriously at how we had let this happen. And we didn't have to look far. Officers were in charge of every aspect of civilian government, and our military sense of unity and discipline were suffering. This problem had been developing for years. In the '70s we had reached a point where every political party would be naming a general or a colonel as their presidential

candidate. The petty conflicts between the political parties were being reflected inside the military, with different factions forming, and individuals all having the ambition of becoming president. Why, the training school for the high command even had the nickname of "The School for Presidents." The military institution was suffering. We were divided and overextended.

Really, the military is not made for taking care of civilian government. I've always said that—even earlier when it was not very popular. I even lost some promotions because of this stance. But by 1983 I had served in many different capacities, and I had earned a lot of respect in the institution. When I received the government, thanks to God, it was clear that we needed to make some changes.

By that time we were totally isolated, as far as any international aid. We couldn't even get military aid. In a way this was a good thing, because it stimulated our creativity as Guatemalans. We had to do things for ourselves. We started producing our own munitions. We produced our own armored vehicle, the "armadillo." I traveled internationally and visited weapons factories. We produced our own spare parts for the Israeli Galils [rifles] we had bought. We bought weapons on the black market. We even bought weapons from behind the Iron Curtain, for instance from Yugoslavia.

We worked like crazy. It built self-respect. We saw that we could work and develop ourselves without help from the outside. We didn't need international help. The poor indigenous people, who have always suffered the most, they were supporting the subversives. The subversives themselves weren't indigenous. They were all university-bred ladinos, and they knew how to manipulate the population. The indigenous are simple people, really. Their main interest is just survival. It's a curious thing, but sometimes the population supports the guerrilla more than they support their own army. I don't know why. We were just doing our duty. We didn't *start* the war.

But the population was the water and the guerrillas were the fish. We realized that to kill the fish we had to drain out the water. We had to pull the indigenous population over to our side, and this is why we created the civil patrol system.* We knew this would work. You can see how much they like to show off their badges and their guns. It gives them a sense of power. It's very effective. Thanks to the civil patrols, we won the war.

With a wave of his hand, Mejía dismissed the GAM and PBI as just two more bothersome organizations manipulated by subversives.

We didn't really pay much attention to the international organizations. The human rights organizations that would visit the country—they're just coming to justify their existence. They can't raise funds for themselves in their own country unless they go back from Guatemala with a report saying how bad things are. I talked to Amnesty International and Americas Watch. I said, "Go ahead. Investigate wherever you want. We have nothing to hide." But they never did any real investigation. They just wrote whatever they wanted to in their reports. I think sometimes they had the reports written before they got here.

We had studied the topic of human rights. In fact, we watched closely what happened in El Salvador. Human rights policies had softened their army and its resolve. We decided we would not repeat that mistake. We couldn't

*The civil patrols are a forced militia system whereby nearly all adult men in the highlands were placed under military direction. Their function and the ensuing resistance to them are outlined in chapter 6.

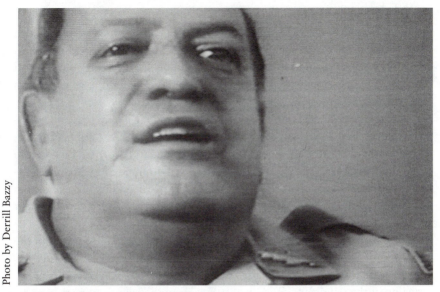

Photo by Derrill Bazzy

General Oscar Humberto Mejía Victores

allow human rights to get in the way of our essential military strategy. There was really nothing to gain from it.

Most of these foreigners come from countries with their own human rights problems. Who are they to point fingers at us? I remember once in a press conference, some German fellow was hassling me about what we were going to do about human rights violations. I told him, "What did you do to your Jews?" Really! Who does he think he is, coming here to criticize?

As I said, international pressure was not a big concern for us. We had a war on our hands. I couldn't be bothered. Mine was a government of transition. We had a commitment to get the subversion under control and to hand over the government to civilian leadership. The International Red Cross was interested in coming in, but I decided it would be better if they waited until the next government. We really didn't need more outside hands in here. We didn't need the complications. We had a calendar for this transition process and as long as we kept to it, other governments were happy.

Cerezo took over the presidency right on schedule [in 1986]. But he was nothing but a cheeky opportunist. He could use his smile to convince anyone of anything, and everyone would give him money. But he didn't *do* anything during his government. Nothing tangible. He didn't build anything! In my government, just to name a few, we finished a new port, a major new highway and a dam project. Cerezo didn't get anything done at all![2]

General Mejía communicates like a tank: blunt and direct. He is not someone who carefully considers the diplomatic consequences of what he says. This does not mean that everything he says is true, of course, but his lack of subtlety and the absolute certainty of his beliefs would make it difficult to consistently maintain a facade. He didn't seem to be trying to fool us with propaganda; he wished to convince us of what he believed.

The interview demonstrates some of Mejía's attitudes: his loyalty to the military establishment, his distaste for ineffectual politicians; his lack of respect for and comprehension of indigenous Mayans, his rigid nationalism and visceral dislike of meddlesome foreigners, and his need to defend or "correct" the reputation that history and public opinion have given him *and his institution.*

In part, the political confrontation between soldiers like Mejía and groups like the GAM was a clash of two different visions and experiences of the same national history. Mejía's attitudes and beliefs were formed long before the military crisis of the early 1980s. Although dominated by the anticommunist national security ideology of the postwar period, his biases are also consistent with tendencies that appear throughout the historic development of the "professional soldier" in Latin America.

Latin American military ideology draws from the *caudillo* traditions of the postcolonial nineteenth century. Strong, repressive military leadership was defended as the only way to forge a nation, control chaos, and confront the venality of the politicians. With professional training from European experts, the military in Latin America became the dominant political force.[3]

In Guatemala, the development of a professional and corporate military institution is closely linked to the *Escuela Politécnica,* the officers' training school established in 1873 by dictator Rufino Barrios. The *Politécnica* was run by Spanish soldiers, emphasizing the classic values of "honor, valor, loyalty, unity, strength, patriotism, virtue, knowledge, responsibility, discipline, abnegation, and sacrifice."[4] Entrance by exam made a military career a path of social advancement for young middle-class men. High attrition, competition, and discipline built a powerful sense of institutional loyalty, conformity, and esprit de corps.

Since 1908, when a *Politécnica* cadet tried to assassinate dictator Estrada Cabrera, the school and the military have claimed to protect the country from corrupt politicians. The officer corps, however, has consistently been divided against itself. Estrada, and later, in the 1930s, Jorge Ubico, promoted officers for their personal loyalty to the dictator rather than to the military as an institution. The division was further exacerbated by differing attitudes toward the influence of U.S. training, which was started by Ubico. Some in the military complained of "Yankee condescension."

During the 1944 revolution, military "institutionalists," led by Colonel Jacobo Arbenz, sided against Ubico and protected the transition to democracy. But in the next ten years, the social policies of Presidents Arévalo (1944–49) and Arbenz (1949–54) were too "radical" for other officers. Most officers came from rural areas, and throughout its history the army had helped plantation owners control the Mayan labor force. Arbenz's new rural land policies and support for rural cooperatives threatened this control.

Arbenz had to put down officer revolts in 1949 and again in 1950. When the United States sponsored the 1954 mutiny, Arbenz found himself without military support.

Despite the 1954 mutiny, ten years of democracy had inspired some young officers with progressive ideas, and the conflicts within the army continued after the coup. Two such officers, Yon Sosa and Turcos Lima, formed the first guerrilla army in 1963. Ironically, both guerrilla leaders were graduates of the *Politécnica* and had received U.S. training at Fort Benning before their defection. Their model for Guatemala's future, though, was progressive and socialist.

The guerrilla rebellion gave the military a source of unity—a common mission. After 1963, the army consolidated control over the government. As one officer observed: "We are needed to fight the subversives. In the old days, we did not have a real enemy. Now the army is essential, and the people know it."[5] The oligarchy felt threatened, U.S. military aid increased, and almost any violence was justified as "fighting communism." Defense Minister Colonel Arana Osorio, who had vowed, "if it is necessary to turn this country into a cemetery in order to pacify it, I will not hesitate to do so,"[6] commanded Guatemala's first scorched-earth campaign (1966–68), with U.S. military advice and support, earning the nickname "the Butcher of Zacapa." The most ominous lesson the army learned from Arana's victory was that terror was an effective strategy.[7]

The anticommunist national security doctrine had a firm grip on the army by the 1960s. The United States promoted an ideology in which all opposition, both internal and external, was perceived through the lens of communism. The doctrine demonized all presumed enemies, either military or civilian, thus psychologically and politically justifying increased repression. National security doctrine answered the military's need for a legitimate mission and vindicated military uneasiness about the chaos it associated with the concept of democracy.[8]

By the 1970s, the desire for power and wealth got the best of military discipline and institutional unity. Dictators Arana Osorio, Kjell Laugerud, and Lucas García each finished his presidency a phenomenally wealthy man. Corruption was rampant. The military controlled the entire government bureaucracy, as well as an airline, TV station, bank, electric company, munitions factories, and organized crime. Colonels and generals carved out huge tracts of land, using army labor to build private plantations. Elections were unabashedly fraudulent.[9]

Under President Lucas García (1978–82), death squads roamed the capital, and rural massacres multiplied. The international recession and the collapse of the tourist economy due to excessive violence were making the elite uneasy. The guerrilla rebellion commanded massive popular support. Soldiers on the front lines began to protest the corruption of the higher echelons of command. As Mejía said, things were out of control.

The 1982 coup put a younger generation of officers in charge. The army launched a political-military strategy, calling for a rapid escalation of the counterinsurgency war in the short run, but a gradual devolution of formal control over the government to civilians. Systematic massacres began immediately in rural areas. Thousands of displaced and fleeing peasants were corralled into "model villages," where they could be closely watched and indoctrinated through the army's new civilian affairs education programs. Hundreds of thousands were forced to serve in the civil patrols. Mejía, the last remaining general of the older generation, took over in another coup in August 1983, but he stuck with the new strategy, which, in military terms, was proving dramatically successful. By 1984, the guerrillas were on the run.

This, then, is the background of General Mejía and the military institution that the GAM and PBI encountered in 1984. It is an army with a century of conflicting traditions of nationalism and corruption. Despite recurring political rifts in the officer corps, the army maintains a distinct corporate identity. Even though its interests frequently coincide with those of the economic elite or the politicians from the capital, the Guatemalan army is above all else loyal to itself. General Mejía spoke with great pride of his success in restoring unity and discipline to the institution he loved, and he was proud of standing up to the economic elite in his attempts to institute new economic policies.

There was, by 1984, a decades-long tradition of military and paramilitary action against "civilian arms of the subversion." Soldiers like Mejía considered their opponent to be dangerous and insidious ("putting Communist ideas in our children's heads"). They saw repression as a legitimate military action, even if, for the sake of public image, it was frequently carried out at night and out of uniform—and the International Committee of the Red Cross could not be allowed in to see it.

The moral impact of these repressive actions further strengthened the military's belief systems. If soldiers, death squad members, and dictators believe themselves to be moral human beings, then the commission of war crimes and human rights abuses requires a justification to counterbalance a potentially overwhelming guilt.

The theory of *cognitive dissonance* suggests that people change their beliefs to be consistent with their behavior when the two are in conflict. The act of killing provokes a powerful dissonance with most moral frameworks. The necessity of confronting this dissonance cannot be underestimated, especially in a military institution that cannot tolerate disobedience or hesitation. National security doctrine partially resolved the dissonance, arguing that killing "communists" was essential to protect self, family, nation, society, and even Christianity.

Cognitive dissonance is particularly illustrated by the relationship between the Central American militaries and the Catholic Church. Church workers are not only very active in community organizing and political resistance. They are also the recognized voice of moral authority in Latin America. Military officers and soldiers, themselves Catholic, were ordered to kill priests and catechists—a potentially paralyzing moral dilemma. When Salvadoran Archbishop Oscar Romero publicly demanded that soldiers disobey orders and stop the repression "in the name of God," he was an extreme threat. Within days, he was assassinated.

Defining Catholic activists as the enemy, as communists and subversives, had the effect of legitimizing the repression of church workers. But equally important was the objective of delegitimizing the moral voice of those in the church who might condemn the military's actions and thus reinforce the dissonance and weaken morale.

This partial resolution provokes a new dilemma: these soldiers are still Catholic, so who is now their moral authority? The growing availability of Protestant fundamentalist sects provided one answer: conversion. Many Guatemalan officers, General Rios Montt among them, left the Catholic Church. With their new religious identity, they could demonize the Catholic Church with less confusion. Others, like Mejía, remain Catholic and defend their role as one of cleansing their church of evil "external" forces, such as communism or "Spanish priests."

Thus, as military violence against civilians continued, the commitment to the ideology behind it hardened. Such rigidity of belief systems often yields an inability to understand other views. Political and military leaders have particular difficulty empathizing with opponents or even imagining how others see them. Their own beliefs about themselves are too powerful to allow for contradiction. The isolation of the military institution from civilian society exacerbates this tendency. Military thinking also tends to divide the world into allies and enemies—Mejía obviously did not perceive the GAM and PBI as allies. The inherent moral message of the GAM's search for the disappeared threatened the very identity and existence of the military.

Even though a leader may overcome the tendency toward ideological rigidity, he or she does not usually have the time or capacity to analyze all the rational possibilities or to profoundly understand the other actors on the scene. The seemingly overwhelming amount of demands for prompt decisions leads to a process of shortcuts, also known as heuristic thinking.[10]

One such shortcut is the "availability heuristic": the first or most easily available explanation or judgment is chosen without further analysis, in order to move on quickly to other decisions. Mejía's dismissal of the GAM and PBI as part of the international communist conspiracy was an extremely available choice, encouraged by U.S. policy and decades of habit.

A second common shortcut is the "representative heuristic": an actor categorized as a member of a class is assumed to have all the characteristics that one associates with that class. In the case of the GAM and PBI, once the label "subversive" is applied, the human rights activist is no different from the guerrilla in the mountains with a gun. All are enemies.

A third heuristic is the tendency to attribute greater coherence and control to one's adversary than evidence warrants. Throughout Latin America, military establishments tended to assume that anyone who opposed them, or anyone who voiced notions of social change, must be directly controlled by the insurgents. Since it was in the guerrillas' interest for the GAM to protest disappearances, the army assumed that it was all part of the insurgents' grand plan.

When the GAM surfaced in June 1984, the government reaction was at first polite, even "sympathetic." The group was not really causing Mejía a problem. It may have even fit his worldview to take some pity on "these poor women." It was his first year in charge and he was still consolidating control. He did not want any trouble. He agreed to meet with them. He made public statements about how tragic the problem of disappearance was, but he went on to say of the disappeared: "They like to travel, and then sometimes they come back to Guatemala, sometimes with different names."[11] He did not take the problem seriously, though he recognized that he had to say something. He may have assumed that eventually they would give up.

At first, GAM members were also polite and diplomatic. When a month passed after their first meeting with no action, they published a letter that attempted to play on Mejía's military sense of honor:

> On August 1 we had the high honor of being received by you in a private audience, and we left that meeting quite optimistic. We were hopeful because we know that when you promise something you can be counted on to fulfill it, based on the high moral values inherent in your person. 28 days have now passed.[12]

Later, responding to both internal and external pressure, Mejía met the GAM again and set up a special commission. But when the GAM began to challenge international aid, Mejía was simultaneously facing serious resistance from the economic elite to his proposed economic policies, and there were rumors of another coup.[13] In this context, he publicly labeled the GAM part of the "forces of subversion."[14] Two weeks later, the two GAM leaders were assassinated.

The decision to kill the GAM leaders may have been made at a lower level in the government hierarchy, or it may have been made without any expectation of an international outcry. Perhaps an outcry was expected but considered manageable. A state that burns embassies to the ground might have a different perspective than most as to what is "manageable." A third possibility is that Mejía, faced with policy resistance from the elite and threats of a coup, moved decisively to eliminate a lesser opponent. In any case, global human rights attention had not been sufficient to protect the GAM. Responding to the international outcry after the death of Rosario de Cuevas, Mejía said, "When a soldier has a car crash, nobody notices. But if it's someone who thinks like a Communist, that life is much more valuable."[15] It was not a denial.

The killings garnered more international support for the GAM. The diplomatic community protested, hinting at the military aid cutoffs that Mejía feared. Meanwhile, PBI's escorting was reported to the government by diplomatic contacts, noted by the press, and obviously noticeable to all the government agents doing surveillance of the GAM. A decision to continue the attacks or to leave the GAM alone would be made only at the highest level and would carefully consider the implications of the PBI presence.

Thus, one can infer, but not prove, that PBI accompaniment played a role in preventing further GAM killings, affecting even a hard-line military man like Mejía, who claimed to be indifferent to international pressure. Direct evidence that PBI was on Mejía's mind, however, would have to wait until later in the year.

Notes

1. "El ejercito acatará las órdenes del presidente," *La Hora*, November 5, 1985.
2. General Oscar Humberto Mejía Victores, interview by authors, Guatemala, July 12, 1984.
3. See Loveman and Davies, *The Politics of Antipolitics*, for a general analysis of the development of Latin American military ideology. For analysis specific to Guatemala, see Handy, "Resurgent Democracy," and Patterson, "Guatemalan Military."
4. Patterson, "Guatemalan Military," p. 364.
5. Patterson, "Guatemalan Military," p. 374.
6. Sloan, "Political Terrorism," p. 309.
7. For a more thorough analysis of the development of state terror in Guatemala, see Figueroa Ibarra, *El recurso del miedo*.
8. Aguilera Peralta, *Seguridad*.
9. Painter, *Guatemala: False Hopes*, p. 49.
10. For a summary of the common heuristics and processes of perception and cognition in political psychology, see Milburn, *Persuasion and Politics*. Vertzberger, *World in Their Minds*, provides more detailed psychological analysis of decisions of political and military leaders.
11. Kinzer, "Guatemalans Organize."
12. GAM, advertisement in *El Grafico* (Guatemala), September 4, 1984.
13. Kinzer, "1000 Marchers."
14. *La Palabra*, March 15, 1985.
15. Preston, "Dwindling Protest Group."

4

The Comeback

A foreigner accompanies me always as a means of protection. The mentality of those who repress us is that a "gringo"* is very valuable. According to them, my own life, as a Guatemalan woman, is worth less than nothing.[1]

THE ASSASSINATIONS OF Hector Gómez and Rosario de Cuevas earned the GAM sympathy in Guatemala and around the world. But they also signaled to Guatemalans the danger of having anything to do with the organization. The GAM's numbers, and hopes, were shrinking.

Shortly after the killings, President Mejía's tripartite commission released its findings on the problem of disappearances in Guatemala: it consisted of three pages, with no detail, concluding simply that "not a single one reappeared." Incensed and depressed, GAM members met again with Mejía on June 21. It was a tense meeting, with the GAM members frequently in tears. Mejía scolded them for being disruptive and told them to "calm down." One GAM member boldly responded, "You would not calm down if it were your family!"[2] The GAM left feeling patronized, insulted, and frightened.

After four months of around-the-clock accompaniment, PBI received its first direct physical threat. French volunteer Didier Platon was crossing the street not far from the PBI house when a car pulled up alongside him. The door opened, revealing four men inside. One of them pointed a gun at him, saying, "Get in! Get in!" Didier froze, but then yelled to another volunteer down the street. Canadian Mary Morgan screamed and came running toward them, and the car sped off. Didier wrote home, "Now I understand a little better what people like Nineth are going through."[3]

PBI discreetly voiced concern to its embassy contacts but made no public protest. Shortly afterward, Guatemalan embassy officials in Washington accused PBI of illegal participation in GAM activities. In September, PBI formally wrote to the ambassador, denying outright participation and identifying PBI volunteers as "international observers."

* "Gringo," a pejorative Latin American reference to U.S. citizens, is frequently used in Guatemala to refer to all whites, North Americans, or Europeans.

Stealing the Show

In 1985, the "democratic transition" was the major news in Guatemala. The constituent assembly had finished a new constitution, with military oversight and approval. Political parties were campaigning for the November elections. Favored to win was Christian Democrat Vinicio Cerezo. As the elections approached, Mejía assured an apprehensive public that the army would accept the results. Guatemala seemed to be on the road to democracy.

The GAM was still gaining international support. In October 1985, it was awarded the Letelier-Moffitt Human Rights Award in Washington, and Canadian parliamentarian Jim Manley came to Guatemala to show support. Nevertheless, in Guatemala, human rights concerns were being pushed offstage. For the women of the GAM, it was frustrating and painful to hear all the propaganda about "democracy" while they knew that nothing was being done about their lost loved ones. Repression and disappearances continued.

On the morning of October 31, 1985, three days before the preliminary elections, 113 GAM members entered the national cathedral on the main plaza and locked the doors behind them. Peace Brigades volunteers observed from outside. By 11:00 A.M., the journalists hovering around Mejía's National Palace on the adjacent side of the plaza came over to see what was up. The door opened a crack and someone handed out a press release clarifying the demands of the occupation: the GAM wanted a special independent commission to investigate the disappearances of 775 family members and produce a report before the de facto government handed over power in January.

They stayed in the cathedral for five days. PBI stood by outside, day and night. The local press noted that "in two hundred years the Cathedral had never been taken over for the purpose of political or humanitarian pressure."[4] Archbishop Penados quickly rejected an offer from General Mejía to remove the occupiers by force. Each day of the occupation, the GAM gave two press conferences to an eager audience of national and international journalists who had come to Guatemala to report on the elections— the end of military dictatorship in Guatemala. None of the demands were met, but the GAM succeeded in calling into question the "democracy" heralded by the elections. They also made General Mejía very angry.

The Expulsion

Between the first election in November and the runoff a month later, the Guatemalan government orchestrated a sequence of events culminating in the expulsion of most of the Peace Brigades' volunteers from Guatemala.

The carefully executed expulsion was a far cry from the blunt attacks against the GAM the previous spring, and they demonstrated the weight that the government was now giving to PBI's role with the GAM.

The first hint of trouble came the day after the cathedral occupation ended: General Mejía published a detailed advertisement alleging that the occupation had been planned in Washington by foreigners allied with the subversives. He noted in a press conference the suspicious presence of foreigners at all GAM events.[5]

The next day, November 7, a carload of men in plain clothes stopped PBI volunteers Alain Richard and Gilbert Nicolas a block from their house and demanded to see their passports. The PBI volunteers insisted on seeing police identification, and when this was not produced, they refused to show their passports and just walked away. Later, a jeep containing six men sat in front of the PBI house for an hour. That afternoon, Alain went to the immigration office to pick up his visa renewal, only to discover that he had been granted two days instead of the customary two months.

On November 8, uniformed police were stationed outside the PBI house, registering the passport numbers of everyone going in or out, giving no reason. The same day, Alain was warned by a close diplomatic contact that he had been targeted and should be careful.

In a letter dated November 12, the Guatemalan embassy in the United States sent a carefully outlined legal argument to PBI's international secretary in the United States It detailed why the government would not consider PBI volunteers international observers:

> The only subjects of International Law are the governments of countries and the international organizations formed by those governments. Thus it is impossible for individual persons to attribute to themselves the quality of International Observers. To obtain the quality of International Observer it is necessary to have been named by a competent government authority. . . . Your organization involves a group formed by individual persons. . . . Their participation, actively or passively, in political activities in any country of the world is regulated by the local laws of public order.[6]

On November 18, immigration police came to PBI's house to inform Alain Richard and Didier Platon that they had to leave the country the same day. The French embassy immediately came to their aid and negotiated an extension with Dimas Rangel, the head of the immigration department and a relative of General Mejía. In the process, PBI learned that eight volunteers were on the expulsion list and that the orders came directly from General Mejía, who was furious with both the GAM and PBI.

Immigration chief Rangel claimed that there was photographic proof that PBI was manipulating the GAM to disrupt the elections. But then he privately offered to delay the expulsion if the GAM would promise that there would be no disruptive actions during the coming runoff.[7] PBI and the GAM both rejected this option.

PBI had been applying for formal legal status in Guatemala since the previous March, meeting consistent delays.* In the meantime, PBI volunteers could enter the country only on tourist visas. PBI knew that to make a public issue of the expulsion would make it even more vulnerable legally: some of the volunteers were going to have to leave. The negotiated delay gave them time to scramble for replacement volunteers. Alain Richard met with president-to-be Vinicio Cerezo before leaving the country and urged him to look out for the GAM's safety, which Cerezo promised to do.[8] The PBI volunteers left quietly after their replacements arrived. Some had been scheduled to leave anyway. Several others returned the day after the elections. The GAM was never without accompaniment.

After an uneventful runoff election, General Mejía admitted to the press that the "foreigners" had been expelled for being involved with the GAM. He claimed that they were violating immigration laws concerning foreign meddling in internal political matters. His spokesman, Zelada, referred to them as "wolves in sheep's clothing."

The argument that PBI was "manipulating" the GAM to disrupt the elections was insulting to Nineth:

> It was this attitude that people cannot think for themselves . . . this paternalistic notion that we needed orientation and advice. Of course we needed advice—it was very necessary, but we also worked on our own initiatives. They believed in some international plot. They wanted to deny the pain and suffering which really brought us together.[9]

The military may have believed that both PBI and the guerrillas were manipulating the GAM. Machismo would make it hard for them to credit women for the successful pressure campaign the GAM was waging. In addition, the army saw the guerrilla movement speaking out on human rights in international forums and doing everything possible to convince national and international organizations to take stands against the Guatemalan government. Given the army's biases, this circumstantial coincidence was enough to condemn the GAM.

What stands out in this episode is how the government covered itself. First, it prepared a justification with propaganda alleging foreign manipulation of the GAM. Then the Guatemalan embassy in Washington warned PBI of the legal precariousness of its presence. Finally, the police collected

---

*PBI was not confirmed as a legal organization in Guatemala until May 1995.

passport numbers on the street and passed them on to immigration officials for expulsion. This last step would have been legally sufficient in and of itself: a sovereign government needs no justification to expel "tourists." The preparatory steps suggest preemptive damage control to limit the potential political repercussions of the expulsion.

The previous spring, death squads had simply murdered GAM leaders. Now, after seven months of accompaniment and increased international pressure, the strategy completely changed. By dangling legal arguments and visas over PBI's head, Mejía tried to use PBI to control the GAM. Through Rangel, Mejía offered to delay the expulsion *if PBI would stop the GAM from being disruptive*. Despite all the propaganda about manipulative foreigners, Mejía was willing to let them stay if they could help *him* manipulate the GAM. He did not expect the GAM to cause another disruption without a PBI presence.

When PBI would not help Mejía control the GAM, he wanted the foreign volunteers out with no fuss and no bad press before the runoff election. This was achieved. But as long as tourist status was the only one PBI volunteers were allowed, there was nothing to stop PBI from finding half a dozen new "tourists" on short notice. GAM leaders believed that PBI should have gone public, denouncing and resisting the expulsion, so that it would not happen again. Since Mejía would soon be leaving office, PBI chose to quietly acquiesce and make sure that the GAM would not be left alone.

Independence Day

The GAM did not disrupt the runoff election, and Vinicio Cerezo was elected by a large majority. Before his inauguration in January 1986, the Constituent Assembly, under pressure from the military, passed an amnesty law preventing prosecution for any prior human rights violations. Disappearances and assassinations continued unabated under Cerezo's leadership. In fact, human rights statistics in 1986 were slightly worse than in 1985. The military was still in charge.

Day after day, PBI volunteers accompanied GAM leaders wherever they went. For many Guatemalans, these women were the country's sole symbol of courage and resistance, the only ones who refused to forget the past or deny the truth of the present. By late 1986, the GAM was renowned in the international human rights community. Its leaders began traveling around the world, speaking out against Guatemala's human rights record. Holding weekly or biweekly demonstrations in front of the National Palace, the GAM criticized the amnesty law and pressured Cerezo for a commission to investigate disappearances.

Despite the GAM's protests, Cerezo was popular both nationally and internationally: this was his honeymoon year. People were relieved to have a civilian government and had high hopes for change. But Cerezo did nothing about disappearances, and GAM members felt that he was shielding the army. It would take a dramatic action to force the public focus back on the army. The GAM chose the army's Independence Day parade on September 15, 1986.

PBI volunteer Paul Weaver had only recently arrived in Guatemala, and he was escorting Nineth de García that day. He recalls:

The women, mostly women, all were dressed in black. They were carrying around their necks posters that were blown up pictures of their disappeared relative with the name and the date of the person that disappeared. What was the most striking was a large banner on two sticks with just a picture of two people: a soldier in camouflage fatigues carrying a rifle with a bayonet on the end with blood dripping off of it; and in front of him an indigenous person with wounds all over his body, bleeding and falling over.

They just stood there silently, about two hundred of them, with this banner. The parade bands went by. Then the cadets. Finally the real soldiers with their machine guns, dressed exactly like in the banner, in camouflage fatigues. As one group of soldiers passed, the GAM members quickly got into the march behind them and held this banner right over the soldiers' heads.

As the bystanders noticed, there was this murmuring throughout the crowd on both sides of us: "Son las Madres! Son las Madres!" [Those are the mothers.] Then I heard a clap and then another clap, and it started building, and more and more people started clapping. . . . The soldiers were being ridiculed and indicted. I could feel tension rising, but the parade kept moving.

At the end of the march, after there were no more spectators, the soldiers closest to us did an about-face, just a few feet from us. Then they were ordered to present their arms. They all cocked their rifles and aimed them straight at the GAM members. Then they started yelling slogans, "Death to the communists! The army is the defender of the people!"

I was off to one side, but I decided to jump in close enough for the soldiers to see me and see my camera. There were guns pointing at me, and I was taking pictures. A foreign photojournalist did the same thing on the other side.

These [soldiers] were young kids, seventeen and eighteen year olds, maybe even younger. I got the impression that they were somewhat scared. But they were disciplined: I imagine they would have shot if they were told to. I don't ever recall thinking they would actually shoot, though. . . . I basically felt, "Well, they can't do this. And I'm taking their picture to let them know."

A few seconds later—though it seemed longer to me—the commander issued another order. The soldiers lowered their guns, broke ranks, turned around, and started running. The GAM members started running after them, which to me seemed a little foolish at that point. I felt like they had made their statement. But of course I ran with them.[10]

Nineth remembers staring at those gun barrels:

Frankly, it was a terrifying moment. We said, "Well, gentlemen, kill us." To all of Guatemala, we demonstrated that as women we have courage and power. I'll tell you, when we look back now, almost ten years later, we think that maybe that was an error. In those years we were an open wound. We were filled with such a sense of impotence. Impotence can impel you to actions that perhaps put your own life in danger. We felt powerless, and we chose actions which would have a more direct impact on them, and delegitimize them, because we knew it was the army who was committing these crimes. We thought, "What independence do we have, if they're kidnapping our loved ones?"[11]

Paul Weaver continues:

I stayed close to Nineth. Later I saw a plain clothes man taking pictures of all of us. So I took a close-up picture of him. I felt more intimidated by seeing him taking those pictures than I had felt having the guns aimed at me. I knew that this was where the real threat was: where the intelligence services kept track of who was doing what, and would take care of things later, somehow. I resented that, and I wanted to let him know that in some way they, too, would be held accountable for their actions.

The next day, Paul was at a bus stop after leaving Nineth's home, and a man brushed up against him, whispering, "Communist!" Meanwhile, the photojournalist who had been up front with Paul found a note in his hotel room, telling him to destroy the pictures if he valued his life.

Two days later, the GAM had an audience with Vinicio Cerezo, accompanied by several PBI volunteers. Cerezo listened but would not promise to create a commission to investigate disappearances. The GAM held a brief sit-in in the palace before leaving. At this point, the PBI volunteers faced a dilemma: if they stayed when everyone was ordered to leave, they could reasonably be accused of sitting in with the GAM. They took the risk. The next day's newspapers cited "official sources" who said that foreigners had entered the palace with the GAM and had counseled them not to leave.

Peace Brigades' concern about its nonpartisan image was pushed to the side by the army's furious public declaration in the same newspapers. Claiming a "right to self-defense," the army decried a "perverse campaign of harassment and persecution by the so-called 'GAM' . . . in open hostility to the dignity and prestige of the armed forces." It accused Nineth de García of "reckless provocation" and of violently forcing her way into the parade, and it praised the calm response of the soldiers of the honor guard. It continued: "[The GAM's] false accusations transcend the limits of mere exercise of liberty and tolerance for public expression, falling in the realm of the criminal. . . . They are losing their public image, so they resort to spectacle." The army repeated the allegation that the GAM was being manipulated by foreigners who wanted to damage Guatemala's good name and accused Nineth of trying to make a martyr of herself:

Nineth Montenegro de García in 1989.

> If any accident should befall the President of the GAM or any of its members, this was clearly planned by their puppeteers who conceived this whole Machiavellian plan. . . . The army holds Nineth Montenegro responsible for any eventuality that her intransigence might provoke.[12]

Even the timid Guatemalan press interpreted this as a public threat. The GAM and PBI began alerting all their international contacts to put pressure on the Guatemalan government to protect Nineth. Nineth began receiving more threatening telephone calls at her home.

Guatemalan columnists openly debated whether the GAM's actions were ill-considered, given the vulnerability of the democratic transition and the risk

Photo by Joe Gorin

that the military could always change its mind. Some counseled GAM members to restrain themselves for the sake of Guatemalan democracy, but others criticized Cerezo for his lack of courage in confronting disappearances.[13]

With the "democratic transition" and the government's concern over international image, it would have been self-defeating for the army to kill Nineth de García—it was self-defeating even to attack her in print. But the GAM had destroyed the fantasy image of the Independence Day parade, violating the very core of military ideology. The response was more vehement than anything the army had publicized in years. A "revenge" attack was not inconceivable, regardless of whether it was politically advisable.

The feared attack did not occur, and the GAM stayed in the headlines for the rest of the year. In early November 1986, the GAM held a major demonstration during a meeting of the Organization of American States (OAS) in Guatemala. The next week, it occupied the front steps of the National Palace. Interior minister Rodíl Peralta—who, as head of the Bar Association, had encouraged PBI in 1983—sent in the riot police. GAM members were beaten, and the PBI team briefly formed a human chain between them and the police. As a result, Rodíl threatened to expel Peace Brigades International. PBI scrambled again for international support and published a public statement clarifying its nonparticipatory role with respect to the GAM.[14] Americas Watch came to PBI's defense, stating publicly, "In our view, it would set a bad precedent for the Guatemalan government to take such a drastic measure."[15] The expulsion threat was not carried out.

In the years that followed, Nineth de García was one of the most frequently quoted political figures in the country. For the government and the army, she and the GAM were an incessant annoyance, but for many others, they personified resistance and courage. Few Guatemalans dared to state publicly the types of accusations and analysis for which the GAM was becoming famous. The GAM women could not stop the army from intimidating most of the Guatemalan population, but they could at least show people that resistance was possible. They shouted a persistent and visceral "No!" from the palace steps to the morgues.

The GAM's continued existence was a source of hope and inspiration. In 1987, the group received the Carter-Menil human rights award and used the proceeds to buy its own house, which became an important center of popular movement activity.* In 1988, it began organizing demonstrations in highly militarized rural areas and initiated the first public exhumations

---

*Popular movement is a particularly Latin American term for an array of nongovernmental civilian organizations, including unions, peasant groups, human rights organizations, church groups, and others. The phrase usually, but not always, implies a leftist political analysis and a certain degree of unity.

of clandestine cemeteries, uncovering and identifying victims of earlier massacres. In subsequent years, its offices were bombed several times, and many members were killed, but the GAM never gave up. In 1996, Nineth Montenegro (de García) took her seat in the Guatemalan Congress, continuing the struggle for human rights in a different arena.

The GAM opened a door. True to its slogan "Sí se puede!" (Yes we can!), it redefined what was possible in Guatemala. Other organizations were now stepping into the new political space to push the door open wider. The initiative in the budding civilian democratic movement in Guatemala was shifting now, from the GAM to the labor movement, as it would later shift again to a new and historic rural movement for Mayan rights and self-determination. With each passing of the torch came new demands for accompaniment.

Notes

1. Nineth Montenegro de García, interview by Julio Lemus, "Pedimos justicia . . . ," *La Revista* section in *El Gráfico*, June 1, 1986.
2. Meeting transcript of the GAM's meeting with General Mejía (tape-recorded by the GAM, June 21, 1985), from PBI files.
3. Didier Platon, letter home, August 3, 1985.
4. *La Hora*, October 31, 1985.
5. "Jefe de Estado critica al GAM," *El Grafico*, November 6, 1985.
6. Sr. José Antonio Montes, Ministro Consejero, Guatemalan embassy, Washington, DC, letter to PBI International Secretary, November 12, 1985.
7. PBI internal documents, citing confidential diplomatic sources (names withheld).
8. Alain Richard's personal notes from the meeting, December 1985.
9. Montenegro interview.
10. Paul Weaver, tape-recorded telephone interview by author, October 20, 1993. Subsequent quotes from Weaver are from this interview.
11. Montenegro interview.
12. Guatemalan Army, "Campo Pagado" (paid ad), *Prensa Libre*, September 18, 1986.
13. Mario Antonio Sandoval, "Cataleo," *Prensa Libre*, September 19, 1985; Jorge Palmieri, "Buenos Días," *El Gráfico*, September 19, 1985; and Carlos Rafael Soto, "A la zaga de la noticia," *El Gráfico*, September 19, 1985.
14. Karen Brandow, taped telephone interview by author, June 25, 1994.
15. Americas Watch, *Human Rights in Guatemala During Cerezo's First Year*, p. 69.

5

The Accompaniment Relationship

The Volunteers

U PON HIS RETURN FROM GUATEMALA, Canadian PBI volunteer Sel Burroughs wrote:

> Escorting Nineth de García for five days was one of the most dynamic experiences of my life. Nothing happened. But I had time while I followed and waited, to observe and support a brave, dedicated, caring and vulnerable woman. The fact that the GAM has survived and developed to the extent that it has is largely a result of the single-mindedness of this remarkable person. Escorting is difficult. It involves being ready to move at someone else's schedule, hours of waiting and intermittent exclusion and inclusion in the lives of the person you are responsible for.[1]

To meet the accompaniment needs of the GAM and, later, of other organizations, PBI set up a two-tiered system of long-term team members and short-term escorts. Long-term team members maintained political contacts, analyzed the political situation, and determined the team's work priorities. They provided orientation and support for hundreds of two-week or one-month escorts.

The volunteers were women and men of all ages from dozens of different countries and from different religious, professional, and educational backgrounds. In a questionnaire-based study of the earliest accompaniment volunteers with PBI in Guatemala, Professor Donald Irish found a broad variety of occupations prior to service, ranging from teachers and doctors to a boatbuilder and a credit manager. Most frequent were human service professions: education, medicine, and clergy. With an average age of forty years, most had some level of college education. Most common religious backgrounds were agnostic/humanist, Catholic, and "peace churches" (for example, Quaker, Mennonite, Brethren). More than three-quarters of the sample had prior experience in Central America and prior experience with nonviolent peace actions. Most had a firm commitment to nonviolence "as a way of life."[2]

What they had in common was a commitment to doing the right thing, based on religious or humanitarian motivations and a willingness to take risks to be of service. Although their motivations ranged widely, there were also certain recurring themes: a basic belief in moral humanitarianism, a personal connection to the region, and a background of previous political activism in nonviolence or solidarity networks.

Eva Fogelman, in her studies of rescuers of Jews during the Holocaust, developed a classification system for the motivations for risk-taking altruistic acts.[3] Fogelman identifies five categories of rescuers: (1) moral: general humanitarian; (2) Judeophiles: moved to act through personal connections with Jews; (3) professionals: social workers, doctors, teachers whose professions brought them into contact with Jews and predisposed them to be helpers; (4) network/ideological (anti-Nazi) activists; and (5) children: brought into rescue work by their parents.

Fogelman's categories can be applied with some modifications to accompaniment volunteers as well. The fifth category, children, is not applicable, since accompaniment is a thoroughly voluntary decision. Analogous with Judeophiles are volunteers with prior personal connections to the regions where they go to accompany. Our own research suggests that accompaniment volunteers, both in PBI and in other accompaniment projects, are heavily weighted toward two categories: those with moral, religious, or humanitarian motivations (category 1) and those who are political activists (category 4). The "helping" professions (category 3) are common in accompaniment work, and it is likely, as Fogelman suggests, that these people are predisposed to service. However, with the notable exception of some teachers and therapists who worked with refugees, their professions were not usually what brought them into contact with accompaniment, and they tend to cite their commitment to political activism as a primary motivation.

Frequently, volunteers from wealthier nations see accompaniment as a way to offset their own society's contribution to economic injustices and human rights abuses in the third world. "I thought, *finally*, [an alternative to] being in a country and feeling guilty about being from the developed 'first world.' I liked the idea of using that status in a positive way."[4]

Doing Accompaniment

Each volunteer went through a short orientation session upon arrival and then began accompaniment. One day, a volunteer might be tagging along with Nineth wherever she went, and the next day she or he might travel up into the countryside with another GAM member. Other days were spent accompanying Nineth's young daughter Alejandra, who was also threatened. A volunteer would take her to school, sit outside her school all day, and then take her home and stay with her until Nineth came home. On Saturdays, as hundreds of GAM families arrived at the PBI house for meetings, PBI volunteers would stay out of the way, make coffee, and watch the street for suspicious vehicles.

A great deal was happening, from continued violence in the highlands to the steady and heroic growth of a civilian popular movement. But it wasn't happening in any easily visible way to a volunteer who came for only a few weeks. Volunteers who had gone through a soul-searching decision to come to Guatemala often found the experience anticlimactic. As the organization itself learned what accompaniment was all about, it prepared a letter to help those who were getting ready to come:

Dear Friend,

If you are considering accompaniment, please reflect on the following points. . . . We have seen many people suffer a lot of emotional turmoil because they were not adequately prepared for the difficult situation they had to face here. . . .

We cannot guarantee our presence will prevent acts of violence, rather we hope it will lower the probability of such acts. The possibility of violence against the people we are with and against ourselves remains very real and we need to be able to accept that. Do not think, as many do, that you are safe because you are an international. You may be safer than the Guatemalan you are with, but unfortunately in this country that is not saying much. Your ability to respond to a violent or tense situation could well depend on how honestly you have accepted the danger and prepared yourself.

To do accompaniment you need to be able to understand what is going on around you, in spite of the tension, and you may need to be able to communicate it, by telephone, in Spanish. . . . We simply have no right to send someone into a situation for which they are not equipped linguistically.

Volunteers often find themselves with a great curiosity and desire to understand the situation better through active investigation. This is sometimes encouraged by a desire to serve the solidarity movement at home, with contacts and "inside" information. But asking questions in this country can be dangerous: for you and for the Guatemalans you talk to. Balancing curiosity with discretion is an art which many of us who come from countries where there are more freedoms and less risk simply do not have. We often have to satisfy our curiosity through passive observation while keeping our mouths shut. But this does not mean that accompaniment is a job that won't satisfy your curiosity. On the contrary, we don't know of any volunteers who left unsatisfied with how much they learned here.

Do not come to "do someone a favor." Come if you feel a genuine concern for justice and humanity and wish to share the responsibility of fighting against serious denial of human rights. Do not expect special appreciation or thanks. Be prepared to accept the groups we work with, their leadership and functioning, as they exist. These are Guatemalan groups working out their own modes of operation. We come as outsiders, strangers, and stay for only a relatively short time. It is not up to us to define either the struggle or the means of struggle. We are trying to help protect the space that the Guatemalan people have opened up to work for freedom; we are not here to tell them how to do it.

Some volunteers develop close and warm relationships with those they accompany; others do not. While the Guatemalans we accompany recognize and appreciate the service we offer, it is difficult for them to constantly share their lives, even some of their most intimate moments, with a relative stranger. For you, this is an interesting and novel experience. For those you accompany, you will be another in a series of persons who pass through their lives.

For some you represent a painful contradiction. The very protection you offer as an international observer is in itself a constant reminder of the danger they face and the oppression that makes you safer than they. The response to this contradiction varies, but it can express itself in outright anger and mistreatment. Dealing with this requires patience and tolerance, and a belief that people who fight for human rights have a right to live, and an accompaniment service cannot be contingent on their personality or their emotional response to an intensely stressful situation. We must all keep in mind that it is not their responsibility to please us, to meet our needs, or even to pay attention to us. We are there to serve.

The idea of accompaniment may sound glamorous or romantic from a distance, but in fact it is hard work, and very demanding. It should not be looked on as an adventure. In fact, one of the most difficult problems volunteers face is boredom. The work is not for everyone, and we'd like you to think seriously in advance about whether it is the right work for you.[5]

The relationship became particularly difficult for Nineth. She lived with accompaniment constantly for over four years, all the while receiving threats against both herself and her daughter.

I have to tell you that I am very grateful for it, but it was also very hard. I felt I had no space. I don't know how to explain. I was watched in the streets, the press always wanted to know what I thought and did, my life was hanging from a thread, and I needed these foreign volunteers. But they are from different cultures and different ways of thinking, and in one's home things are totally different. There were moments of happiness, but also difficulties, like in any human relationship. First of all, it's pretty hard for a foreigner to understand all the pain that you are carrying around with you—I've seen many friends fall. Sometimes you feel so hopeless and desperate, and all you want is a space where you can yell and scream. And you get home, and there's still this foreigner with you, and there's nothing you can do. You're stuck.[6]

Spending so much time in close contact with GAM members led to endless and fascinating discussions. The Guatemalans' situations and culture were completely different from those of the volunteers, most of whom came from North America and Europe. One volunteer remembers how strange her vegetarianism seemed to the Mayan GAM leader she was accompanying: "I assured her I was none the weaker for it. 'We'll see how strong you are when they kidnap me!' she laughed."[7]

Such macabre humor was not uncommon. The situation was, after all, somewhat surreal for both the volunteers and the GAM. But the joke points out a real problem that provoked endless discussions: what *was* an escort supposed to do when "they" showed up to kidnap an accompanied Guatemalan? On the one hand, if the volunteer tried to intervene, she might be kidnapped or killed. On the other hand, it might be more important to get to a telephone and initiate a campaign of high-level pressure, which might save the person's life.

There were no simple formulas or easy answers to all the what ifs. But in the course of day-in, day-out accompaniment and endless discussion, PBI was developing a new protective tool. Formal orientation manuals were created for short-term escorts. Regular discussions among volunteers analyzed the political situation and potential risks. Logs were kept, noting any threats, surveillance, or suspicious coincidences, to maintain continuity and organizational memory amidst rapid volunteer turnover. These logs helped volunteers recognize the risks around them, even if their own brief visits were uneventful.

Outside Guatemala, PBI built links with human rights and Central American solidarity organizations and developed an extensive rapid-response network to mobilize international pressure in response to emergencies. This emergency response network became a major feature of PBI's operations. Over the years, the organization built up a telephone tree of thousands of people around the world. If a GAM member were attacked or threatened, the team would contact the project staff in Canada, who would quickly alert key callers around the world, who would in turn activate their branches of the telephone tree. Within a few hours, network members would send hundreds of telexes protesting the attack. Usually the target would be the Guatemalan government or military. Later, however, the network sometimes targeted members of congress or parliament in the callers' own countries, urging these politicians to put pressure on Guatemala. The goal of the response network was to multiply the protective power of the accompaniment, while giving thousands of citizens around the world a way to learn about Guatemala and take effective action.

Shifting Relationships

PBI was more than protection for the GAM. For three years, the GAM depended on the PBI house, telephone, and office for all its work. According to Nineth:

> We needed the PBI house both for security and for lack of another location. But we—really I'm embarrassed to remember it today—we just took over their house. We just went in and practically never left. It's incredible, the sorts of attitudes and decisions that impotence can force you into. We just stayed there.[8]

PBI debated internally whether the relationship contradicted PBI's non-partisan stance. But the team argued that such support was consistent with

Photo by Didier Varrin

PBI volunteer accompanying the GAM office in 1993.

PBI's mission, since the GAM could not risk meeting anywhere else. In fact, the two organizations were extremely interdependent. The GAM gave PBI its raison d'être, a clear mission.

At first, PBI put the GAM in touch with various contacts in the diplomatic community and frequently offered advice on organizing and nonviolent tactics. In the beginning, GAM members were grateful for any counsel and support they could get. Later, as the GAM developed its own strategies as an organization, such advice became unwanted, and both organizations agreed that PBI would stop attending the GAM's meetings.

Operating Guatemala's most vibrant popular organization out of PBI's living room was never easy. The space was limited and lacked privacy. Frictions between the two organizations accumulated over time. PBI found itself caught up in the GAM's internal tensions and transitions and was not always happy with the GAM decisions about accompaniment. PBI also wanted to expand and work with other organizations in Guatemala. When in June 1987 the GAM moved into its own building about a mile from the PBI house, it was a relief for both organizations.

PBI continued to escort GAM leaders and events and maintained a constant presence at the new GAM building for years to come. But the physical separation enabled PBI to begin to define itself more clearly as an independent organization. That same month, volunteers made contact with striking workers occupying the Lunafil thread factory outside the capital.

The subsequent thirteen-month presence on the sidewalk outside the factory firmly established PBI as a source of protection for the rapidly expanding Guatemalan labor movement. In later years, PBI accompanied threatened labor organizers, as well as maintaining a regular presence in the offices of key union federations and at dozens of strikes.

With the labor movement, and with most subsequent groups that PBI accompanied, the relationship was different from that with the GAM. These later groups tended to see accompaniment as a tool to be used sparingly, at specific moments of noticeably increased danger. For instance, according to labor organizer Sergio Guzman:

> It's not that the threats necessarily stop when you have accompaniment. Accompaniment *questions* the threat. It confronts it. . . . I once got a threat on the telephone and the voice said: "Even while you have accompaniment you're going to be the victim!" That says a lot in itself: that they're paying attention to the accompaniment. For them it is something that matters.
>
> During the times when we've had accompaniment personally it has helped to have more freedom in our activities. It's enabled us *not* to leave off of those activities which we're committed to.
>
> When we decide for the accompaniment to stop—it's a situation where the threat lasts some time. We figure the average threat might last fifteen days or a month. You can't really have accompaniment on a permanent basis, just because the violence is permanent. Rather the use of accompaniment is determined by an analysis of the specific moment and situation, in political terms. . . .
>
> You call off the accompaniment when you feel you've reached a politically different situation. It doesn't mean the systematic violence is over, because that's a question of roots. It's more subjective—when the accompaniment has fulfilled its task of calling the violence into question.[9]

Eventually PBI decided that the continual stream of short-term volunteers was too problematic. In 1989, the minimum length of stay was increased to six months, and the two-level team structure was eliminated. This shift curtailed one of the key sources of institutional growth: the publicity and support work of volunteers returning home, since the flow of over a hundred volunteers a year was reduced to a trickle. But PBI was more concerned about maintaining trusting relationships in the field, a high level of discretion and analysis, and a strong sense of team continuity and affinity, all of which were suffering from the rapid turnover.

The accompaniment relationship thus changed over time. PBI began to take on many more short-term missions: perhaps maintaining a presence at an organization's office or with an activist for a few weeks after threats were received, but then gradually reducing the level of accompaniment. By the late 1980s and early 1990s, PBI was accompanying dozens of different Guatemalan organizations. As Guatemalans kept pushing the envelope and testing the limits of political action, human rights work expanded outside of Guatemala City. PBI, with more volunteers and more flexibility, extended its accompaniment to new groups operating in the previously paralyzed Guatemalan highlands.

Notes

1. Sel Burroughs, letter to friends, November 30, 1985.
2. Donald Irish, *Reflections of the Volunteers: Peace Brigades International, 1983–1987*, unpublished manuscript. Results were based on fifty-seven respondents, or 38 percent of the total population of returned PBI volunteers between 1983 and 1987. Respondents came from eleven different countries, although 64 percent were from the United States.
3. Fogelman, *Conscience and Courage.*
4. Anne Marie Richards (PBI volunteer), tape-recorded interview by authors, Guatemala, July 1994.
5. PBI Guatemala team, letter to prospective volunteers, undated, PBI files.
6. Nineth Montenegro de Garcia, tape-recorded interview by authors, Guatemala, July 8, 1994.
7. Chris Corry, personal letter to friends, January 15, 1986.
8. Montenegro interview.
9. Sergio Guzman, Union of Guatemalan Workers (UNSITRAGUA), author interview, Guatemala, July 18, 1994.

6

Fear in the Highlands

*I*N LATE 1988, a new human rights organization surfaced in the highlands of El Quiché, challenging the army's control over rural Guatemala.
The Council of Ethnic Communities "Runujél Junám" ("everyone equal"
in the Maya Quiché language), or CERJ, united the efforts of thousands of
men in dozens of villages who were refusing to serve in the civil patrols.
The army viewed these *Patrullas de Auto-defensa Civil* (PACs) as the cor-
nerstone of their counterinsurgency victory over the guerrillas. The CERJ not
only coordinated mass refusal to serve in the patrols but also quickly placed
the civil patrol debate squarely at the top of the nation's agenda, and on the
agenda of the international human rights community.

By the mid-1980s, El Quiché had an almost mythic reputation in the
Guatemalan psyche. In El Quiché, the Guerrilla Army of the Poor had first
surfaced in the 1970s. By 1981, it nearly controlled the whole department.
It was the birthplace of Rigoberta Menchú, Guatemala's most famous
human rights activist-in-exile, who in 1992 won the Nobel Peace Prize. In
the late 1970s, the Committee for Campesino Unity (CUC) formed in El
Quiché. Its founders, including Menchú's father, were later burned to death
in the Spanish embassy in 1981. The worst of the scorched-earth campaigns
occurred in El Quiché and neighboring Huehuetenango. Thousands of
Quiché Mayans were still in refugee camps in Mexico; thousands more had
fled to other parts of the country. Thousands of others, calling themselves
the Communities of Population in Resistance, were still eluding the army
in the rugged El Quiché jungles.

The civil patrols, started in 1981 under the presidency of Lucas García,
were a fundamental counterinsurgency tool for keeping the population from
supporting the guerrillas. Patrol service consisted of a twelve- to twenty-
four-hour shift without pay each week. Poor campesinos were forced to do
road construction, spy on neighbors, and accompany army soldiers searching for guerrillas. A force of 25,000 civil patrollers in 1982 grew to 900,000
by 1984—more than three-quarters of the adult male population of the
northwest highlands.[1]

According to General Hector Gramajo, the patrols were started to
co-opt the guerrillas' irregular forces and civilian support. "Today's Civil
Patrollers used to be guerrillas. Now we control them. The fact is, in the

Photo by Derrill Bazzy

Amilcar Mendez Urizar

rural areas, there are two governments: the military government and the elected civilian government."[2]

The military sometimes forced patrollers to commit grotesque murders and dismemberments of people from their own communities, with powerful psychological effect. Archbishop Penados decried the "moral damage affecting our brothers' conscience when they are obligated to act against innocent people." Americas Watch claims that the patrols increased suspicion and aggression, dividing communities and making them easier to dominate.[3]

Amilcar Mendez and the CERJ

Amilcar Mendez is an activist to the core of his being. With a glint in his eye and a lively smile, he will tell you five fascinating stories before you've finished introducing yourself. The stories always have a point: to recruit you to the cause of human rights for indigenous Guatemalans. On a given day, he might take testimony from the poorest victimized campesino or publicly condemn the president. In his rapid ladino style, which could not pose a starker contrast to the soft-spokenness of the Mayans around him, he was an outspoken voice for human rights in El Quiché long before the CERJ was even an idea.

Born to a large family in the Quiché village of San Andrés Sacjabajá, Mendez grew up in the departmental capital, Santa Cruz del Quiché, during the dictatorships of the 1950s and 1960s. In the 1970s, he worked with a center-left political party and was elected president of his student association. He went on to do social work in rural El Quiché, first with a Catholic youth organization and later as a grammar school teacher. In 1980, as the worst of the violence descended on El Quiché, Mendez was targeted, along with most other activists. After surviving an attempt on his life, he fled El Quiché to the capital.

Mendez is one of the few educated ladinos in Guatemala who speak the Maya Quiché language. He returned to El Quiché in early 1983, regained his teaching job in the village of Paquinác, and began working to help some of the local women who had been widowed by the violence. In August, armed men whisked him out of his classroom. He was freed after twelve hours of interrogation, due to the intercession of a family contact in the army. Mendez chose to stay in El Quiché and keep working with the widows.

> But I was afraid. It was a few months later that I met Peace Brigades. We could speak honestly about the situation in Guatemala and what the violence had been like. . . . It's a very subjective thing that's hard to explain. You just feel it—the words and the presence of these foreigners in my house was a stimulus and a strength that made me feel safer.[4]

The GAM did not exist yet, nor the accompaniment idea. PBI was still exploring. Mendez enlisted PBI's support for the widows' projects. His activism got him threatened and fired from his job. In 1985 and 1986, he was back in El Quiche, this time trying to organize the national teachers' union. Throughout these years, his efforts seemed futile. The Quiché population was too frightened to resist openly. Mendez was alone and isolated.

The new 1985 constitution contained an element of hope: Article 34 declared that no Guatemalan could be forced into servitude. With civilian President Cerezo in office, Mayan campesinos began to ask whether they had to continue in the civil patrols. In several instances, Mendez put them in touch with PBI. The men wrote letters to President Cerezo and sometimes met with the governor. But in every case, with or without PBI, they were eventually called in to meet with the local military intelligence department and intimidated into giving up the attempt.

> In October 1986 I went to the north, to Chajúl, to spread the word about the teachers' union. When I came back, we found the words painted on my house: "Amilcar = Communist. He will Die!" About two weeks later I got a call on the telephone—the guy told me everything I had done that day. That I had gone to such-and-such an office at this hour, and over there at a different hour. And I said to myself, "Not just anyone could do this." They even told me what I had been wearing! We were pretty worried. What were we to do? In January I got another telephone threat, and we started talking to PBI about how to get out of the country.[5]

PBI helped put Mendez in touch with the refugee program of the Canadian embassy, and within a few months, he and his family were safely, but unhappily, in Toronto:

> Once there, we felt an even stronger commitment to the people here. We felt like a cloud hung over us. Each day we felt a stronger yearning to be back in Guatemala. Each day we got more worried. I was only there about fifty days. We finally decided to return, but this time in a much more public way. I talked to some friends in New York and Washington, and they sent letters to President Cerezo to tell him that we were coming back. And when we did return, we already had the idea of forming an organization.[6]

Amilcar Mendez's exile in Canada was a turning point. He decided to return to Guatemala and keep organizing. He had a deliberate plan to use international connections and pressure as his primary means of protection. Once back in Guatemala, he wrote to a friend in Canada:

> It's hard to explain my motives. In spite of all the risks, I *had* to come back. I couldn't stop thinking that outside my country there was little I could do, but here inside there are many things I can do. I won't be surprised if soon they start to threaten me again. But international solidarity has really helped me. . . . From Germany they sent a telex to President Cerezo asking for security for my life. I will stay in close touch with PBI.[7]

This time, Mendez was not alone; others in El Quiché were ready to organize.* In March 1988, residents of various villages in the township of Zacualpa delivered a letter to President Cerezo demanding that Article 34—the constitutional prohibition against forced servitude—be enforced, and listing acts of intimidation by local civil patrol leaders. At the labor demonstration in the capital on May 1, 1988, Mendez marched with about forty Quiché campesinos under banners reading, "We demand enforcement of Article 34" and "We the people of Quiché refuse to serve in the patrols. We want the army OUT of our communities." Later that month, the governmental human rights ombudsman† received formal letters from campesinos in the townships of San Andrés Sacjabajá and Laguna Seca announcing their refusal to serve.

These were the first signs of organized resistance to the patrol system. The response was immediate. Before May was over, the Zacualpa civil patrol leaders captured Marcos Canil Saquic, one of the signers of the March letter.

---

*We distinguish here between "resistance" and "organization." Mayans exercised a constant cultural, even subconscious, resistance throughout 500 years of repression but only rarely organized into "protest" movements or rebellion. See Scott, *Weapons of the Weak*, a classic study demonstrating this dynamic in Malaysian peasant society.

†The Guatemalan human rights ombudsman was a supposedly independent office established by the 1985 constitution to respond to citizen complaints. The first ombudsman was named in 1987, but the office was dysfunctional until Ramiro De Leon Carpio took over in 1990.

He was taken to El Quiché army headquarters and interrogated until he divulged the names of others in the resistance movement. In early May, a friend of Mendez's overheard an army captain and a right-wing politician talking in a bar about how they were going to kill Mendez. PBI volunteers were followed in the streets of Santa Cruz del Quiché. On May 28, Amilcar Mendez received the following letter under his door:

> The Secret Anti-Communist Army is watching you closely, little Professor Amilcar Mendez, and we know the path you are walking and we can see that you are following the objectives of international communism. Truly. We see the daily visits you get from campesinos, and from your Communist gringo friends. . . . But bear in mind that we have defeated communism and we will continue to defeat it. The best thing you can do for yourself is abandon the country, or else completely renounce your loathsome objectives, little teacher, little Communist agitator. If you don't you will be executed together with your family. . . . From this day forward you have 60 days to make a decision. . . .
>   Long live the Secret Anti-Communist Army! Long live The White Hand! Long live Anti-Communism![8]

PBI activated its emergency response network. Alerts also went out from Amnesty International, the World Organization Against Torture, Americas Watch, and Central American solidarity organizations. These resulted in telegrams and letters to President Cerezo demanding that Mendez be protected. Mendez had no intention of leaving. Though the threat specifically mentioned his "Communist gringo friends," he asked PBI for constant accompaniment. In late June, Pedro Pablo Ramos, another anti-patrol activist, was killed in his home by military commissioners.* All during June and July, Mendez traveled through the highlands. In each village, the meeting was larger than the last. PBI rented a house in Santa Cruz del Quiché, just down the street from Mendez's home, to be more readily available to accompany this new movement.

The sixty-day deadline for the death threat passed quietly. Three days later, on July 31, hundreds of Quiché campesinos met at Mendez's home and founded the Council of Ethnic Communities "Runujél Junám" (CERJ). The CERJ's goals went far beyond resistance to patrol service and included providing human rights education, investigating government behavior, and organizing to struggle against all cultural and ethnic discrimination.[9]

The movement was spreading like wildfire. Men from isolated, remote villages traveled for days on foot to get to the meetings. They began to show up from other parts of the country as well. After three months, the CERJ boasted a membership of 6,000 people. Seventy-eight villages were resisting patrol service. In half of these, the resistance was unanimous.

---

*The military named a civilian representative in each community, whose role was that of informant and enforcer. These military commissioners were often, but not always, the local patrol leaders as well.

Within a few weeks after the founding, two CERJ activists, Valerio Chijal and Pedro Cumes Pérez, were killed. Military commissioners in the town of San Andrés told villagers that if Mendez showed up there, he would be killed. That same week, Minister of Defense Hector Gramajo told Guatemalan congressmen that the guerrillas had adopted a new strategy of using political front organizations to press for the dissolution of the civil patrols. In November, two more CERJ activists were disappeared. Each attack proved the CERJ's allegation that the patrols violated human rights, and Mendez publicized them nationally and internationally.

The CERJ put new tools in the hands of these Mayan campesinos: the constitution and the law. Although it cost the equivalent of a day's wages for a poor campesino, hundreds were buying copies of the 1985 constitution and struggling through the Spanish to understand it. No CERJ press event went by without constitutional argument. Article 34 of the constitution became a powerful symbol and a topic of national debate. Mendez constantly pointed out other constitutional articles and international human rights covenants that were routinely ignored by the military. CERJ members gave formal testimony to representatives of the Guatemalan Congress and international organizations on human rights abuses by the civil patrols. This constant legal emphasis made it difficult for the Guatemalan government to justify any action against the CERJ. It also made the CERJ very popular within the international human rights community, which always needed legal "angles" to buttress its denunciations.

PBI stationed two volunteers in Santa Cruz del Quiché for most of the next four years. At first, only Mendez was accompanied constantly. Mayan activists were more hesitant at first, but later, as others began to take leadership roles, they too asked for protection, especially when they visited communities where patrollers and resisters were in conflict.

PBI met with local military and civilian authorities and informed them of its presence in El Quiché. The meetings called attention to the protection, and international interest focused on the CERJ and opened lines of communication that could prove useful later on. The results of these meetings were mixed. Local mayors were generally polite; some were even quite supportive. The governor, however, on at least one occasion threatened to have volunteers thrown out of the country if they got involved in internal politics by attending CERJ events.[10]

Rural realities posed new challenges to accompaniment work. No PBI volunteer spoke a Mayan language. PBI had no car and thus depended on the public bus system. Telephone service was erratic. In El Quiché, someone could easily vanish on a deserted rural road; it might take hours, or even days, to find a telephone to report an incident. PBI's "deterrence" depended on its capacity to set the wheels in motion for a rapid international response.

Transportation and communication difficulties could transform this threat into little more than a bluff.

Mendez was so driven by the momentum of the movement he had launched that he seemed at times to throw caution to the winds. After a long day's and night's work, with little sleep, he might rise at 3 A.M. and head off with a PBI volunteer on the back of his motorcycle, trying to get to a local CERJ meeting in a small village six hours away. PBI cautioned him, reminding him how easy it would be for someone to run him off the road in the dark and call it an accident. If Mendez himself did not always appreciate these admonitions, his wife and family did. The threats kept coming. Volunteer Jeff Smith wrote of one of them in his journal:

> Last night while I was with Amilcar in Santa Cruz del Quiché, the phone rang. While reaching for another tortilla I noticed an uneasy expression come across his face. It was a short call, lasting only a few seconds, but one that changed the mood of the evening quickly. Amilcar informed us that it was an anonymous death threat, something that he had begun to get accustomed to. This phone call, however, was different. They told him that if he left the next day at 6:00 A.M. that he would be killed. This scared Amilcar a bit because he could not figure out how they knew he was leaving the next day. He had not discussed the trip with anyone on the phone, which led him to suspect there were infiltrators in the organization.
>
> After discussing the implications of the call, Amilcar decided he would go anyway, after all, I would be with him, he said. Needless to say I was not thrilled with the prospect of driving to the Capital at dawn, especially through the winding mountains in Quiché. The thought of an ambush seemed to weigh heavily on my heart, but I guess this was exactly why I was there. . . . I didn't sleep much.[11]

Taking on the Local Thugs

The heart and soul of the CERJ were the hundreds of local activists who refused patrol service. These Mayan campesinos in isolated rural villages suffered most of the violent consequences of the CERJ's challenge to the patrol system. Most highland campesinos hated patrol service, but the army had no trouble finding a few men in each village who were eager to take advantage of the power and control that civil patrol leadership gave them. With the blessing of the military, these patrol leaders had replaced civilian or traditional community leadership by force of arms. As the years passed, with no civilian authority over them, their power and despotic tendencies increased. Mendez, with constitution in hand and PBI at his side, tried to put international pressure to work against the system. But CERJ members out in isolated villages were facing local thugs who seemed impervious to pressure.

On March 2, 1990, the GAM organized a caravan, including 140 GAM members, journalists, and PBI volunteers, from the capital up through El Quiché to protest the harassment of GAM and CERJ members by local civil patrols. At a rest stop on the Pan-American Highway near the village of Chupól, they were met by a large number of civil patrollers armed with guns and machetes. Paying no heed whatsoever to the presence of accompaniment and the press, the patrollers attacked the GAM members with a rain of rocks and insults, provoking a panic and leaving several people injured, including GAM president Nineth de García.

Two weeks later, in the village of Parraxtut, further north in El Quiché, two local military commissioners shot and killed CERJ member María Mejía and wounded her husband. Mejía's two sons were refusing patrol service. The CERJ publicized the attack, and the government's human rights ombudsman promised that the men would be arrested. Nineteen members of the Mejía family fled Parraxtut to take refuge in the CERJ office in Santa Cruz.

On March 27, a caravan including two policemen with arrest warrants, a representative of the human rights ombudsman, Amilcar Mendez, two PBI volunteers, and the nineteen "exiled" members of the Mejía family cautiously made its way back to Parraxtut to arrest the two killers and return the family to their home. Louise Palmer, a PBI volunteer from the United States, reported:

> After nearly three hours of being jostled up and down, we passed the final turn and could see the entrance of the village of Parraxtut. A barricade made of poles had been placed across the street behind which were five or six men pointing guns at us.
>
> The women and children became very silent. Amilcar Mendez grabbed his video camera and began to film the scene. As we approached the barricade one armed man after another began to appear in front of us and on the mountain directly to the side of us.
>
> As soon as the human rights ombudsman presented his official card, the patrolmen began to shout that we were guerrillas and Communists and that they didn't want to have such people in their village. Amilcar identified himself, which provoked even greater indignation.
>
> The atmosphere was tense and worsened with every moment. Since the patrolmen seemed to have no respect for the authorities, Amilcar decided it was best to withdraw. . . . Together with the rest of the family members we fled from the scene. This created further tension, and while some of the patrollers kept the ombudsman's car surrounded, others began firing shots and throwing stones at our fleeing vehicles.[12]

The human rights ombudsman reported later that his delegation had been forced into the town square and threatened with rifles and machetes before being released unharmed.

The attacks in Chupól and Parraxtut raised serious question about the effectiveness of accompaniment against the civil patrols. These patrollers were attacking unarmed GAM members in front of the press and blatantly threatening even police and government representatives. In neither case did a foreign presence seem to have any impact on their behavior.

The army encouraged this behavior and put out the message across El Quiché that working with the CERJ was equivalent to joining the guerrillas and that such subversion would not be tolerated. Army public-relations staff even produced a cartoon video comparing the CERJ to a fox in a chicken coop. They traveled around the countryside with it, complete with portable generator to power the video-player and television.

Chunimá

Twenty-seven active CERJ members were killed or disappeared from 1988 to 1991—five of them from the small Mayan village of Chunimá, in southern El Quiché, a few miles off the Pan-American Highway. Manuel Perebal Ajtzalam III considered the village of Chunimá his private reserve. As the local civil patrol leader, he had the power to extort money, threaten, or kill, knowing that he would be protected by his close connections with the army. Though illiterate, he claimed that he read the Bible, and he unabashedly absolved himself of his crimes, saying that he killed only when the Lord told him to do so. Except for God and the army, he was contemptuous of other authorities. He threatened the local mayor for not actively supporting the patrols. To the national police he was known to snarl, "I wipe my ass with arrest warrants!"[13]

In May 1988, twenty-five Chunimá men took the bold step of refusing to patrol. They were led by Sebastian Velásquez Mejía, who a few months later became the Chunimá delegate to the CERJ. Chunimá CERJ members filed formal complaints in September 1988, accusing soldiers of beatings, threats, and house searches. Velásquez Mejía sent letters to the Congressional Human Rights Commission, President Cerezo, and the Supreme Court, demanding an investigation of the army's behavior.

On May 17, 1989, one of Perebal Ajtzalam's patrollers told Velásquez Mejía in a public meeting that he would cut off Velásquez's head with a machete if he kept on encouraging people to stop patrolling. In February, the commander of the El Quiché military zone wrote a letter to the human rights ombudsman accusing Velásquez Mejía and seven other CERJ members of harassing the patrollers, throwing rocks at them, and filing false complaints.[14]

On Saturday morning, October 6, 1990, Velásquez Mejía was waiting for a bus at the busy market of Chupól, where the dirt road from Chunimá reaches the Pan-American Highway. He was on his way to the capital to

PBI archive photo

*PBI volunteer Diane St. Antoine (Quebec) with a
family fleeing the village of Parraxtut after Civil
Patrol harassment (January 1991).*

buy medicines for his children. Eyewitnesses saw Manuel Perebal Ajtzalam
amiably greet five men near a covered blue pickup truck and motion
toward Velásquez. Moments later, two of these men grabbed Velásquez,
pointed a gun at him, quickly threw him in the truck, and drove away.

The family and the entire pro-CERJ faction of Chunimá were so frightened that they fled the next day, taking refuge in the CERJ office in Santa
Cruz and in the GAM office in the capital, where PBI volunteers accompanied them. Police found Velásquez's body in Guatemala City two days later
and buried it without notifying the family.

A week later, under pressure, the governmental human rights ombudsman sent his assistant to accompany the CERJ families home to Chunimá. Despite the presence of an army escort, Perebal Ajtzalam and his patrollers fired on the group. No one was injured, but the Chunimá CERJ members fled back into refuge. The CERJ used its international connections to put more heat on the government: former U.S. president Jimmy Carter made a personal protest on October 21. Velásquez's wife filed criminal charges against Perebal Ajtzalam.

On November 16, Peace Brigades volunteers accompanied the human rights ombudsman in a second attempt to return the Chunimá refugees to their homes. Among them were two witnesses to the Velásquez killing, Diego Perebal Leon and his brother Manuel Perebal Morales (not to be confused with patrol leader Perebal Ajtzalam). PBI volunteer Winnie Romeril remembers:

> It was a muddy rainy day, and we had to leave the cars in one place and then walk about twenty minutes to get to Chunimá. We got to Chunimá, and they had a town meeting with everybody. I remember the men coming up to us later, to say good-bye. They were crying and giving us hugs. They were really scared. They were going to stay, and they said, "Everything right now looks fine. It looks OK, like nobody is going to hurt us. But in three months time, that's when they're going to attack us again, when everyone has forgotten about us, and nobody cares anymore, and they think that there is no attention. So please come back and visit."[15]

The three-month estimate was eerily precise. On February 17, at 5:30 A.M., Manuel Perebal Morales and Diego Perebal Leon were walking toward Chupól with their father, Juan Perebal Xirum, when they were ambushed by six men. Manuel and Juan were both shot to death. The younger brother, Diego, survived the attack and was taken to the nearest hospital, in Sololá. He had three bullets in his intestines and a shattered vertebra and was paralyzed from the waist down.

Besides Diego, there were two other eyewitnesses to the attack. All three identified two of the killers as Manuel Perebal Ajtzalam and another patrol leader, Manuel Leon Lares. New arrest warrants were issued the next day against both men. Fearing for Diego Perebal's life, the CERJ asked Peace Brigades to accompany him around-the-clock in the Sololá hospital.

PBI had visited Chunimá only once between November and February. In the meantime, another Chunimá CERJ activist, Diego Ic Suy, had been killed in Guatemala City while working with the GAM. A judge who had issued arrest warrants for Perebal Ajtzalam and Leon Lares in January was receiving death threats. The quandary for PBI, in this context, was not knowing whether international accompaniment would influence a patrol leader like Perebal Ajtzalam. It might just make him madder. In other

Quiché villages, rural members of the CERJ and CONAVIGUA (the national widows' organization) had explicitly told PBI *not* to visit them, because they didn't want to call undue attention to themselves. They feared that the civil patrols would equate foreigners with guerrillas and harass them even more after PBI left.

So the Sololá hospital was a frightening accompaniment assignment. Perebal Ajtzalam had fired on the governmental human rights ombudsman, shot at soldiers, insulted police, and carried out assassinations in broad daylight. Now he was killing the witnesses. Diego had witnessed two of Ajtzalam's crimes and now lay paralyzed in a rural hospital bed. The hospital had no security—it barely had any doors. PBI volunteer Heike Kammer, from Germany, was with Diego:

> Passing the night in the hospital . . . it was really incredible. We were sitting on one bed, Diego in another. We listened for every little noise. Every few minutes we were checking to see if he was still alive, and if his intravenous tube was still OK. Then we'd go check the doorways to make sure no one was coming in to mess with him. All the doors were just wide open. It would not have been very difficult for someone to come in. And in the shape he was in, it wouldn't have taken much to kill him.
>
> His family told us that back in Chunimá the patrols were still boasting that they were going to kill him. They said they were going to poison him and boasted other ways they would kill him. But no one came to the hospital.[16]

PBI volunteer Cristina Banzato, a social worker recently arrived from Italy, described the experience as almost surreal:

> I felt really bad there. Diego is a good person, very calm and friendly. During the night we were really afraid. Things would happen that would wake you up at night. We were sleeping in the room next to his, and one night I woke to find a man urinating in the corner of our room. Another time we found ourselves giving blood for another man in the hospital who needed a prostate operation. It was really a crazy situation.
>
> On a psychological level I'm sure we were helping him, but I think it was obvious that if anyone wanted to do anything to him in the night . . . well, we could be witnesses, but we certainly couldn't stop them. But he felt it was really important to have us nearby. There were also police around, but he was afraid of them. He thought *they* might be the ones to hurt him.[17]

PBI stayed with Diego when he was moved to a bigger hospital in Guatemala City. Perebal Ajtzalam kept boasting that he was going to kill Diego. Dozens of other CERJ members fled Chunimá. When he was released from the hospital, Diego took refuge in the GAM office in the capital. Months later, the CERJ helped him and his family find a home near its office in Santa Cruz. PBI volunteers accompanied him for the rest of the year.

Meanwhile, the international human rights community mobilized around the case. On February 21, 32 U.S. senators and 143 House members sent a letter to President Serrano demanding an investigation. Americas Watch and the Center for Justice and International Law began a formal process to bring the Guatemalan government before the Inter-American Court of the Organization of American States (OAS).

In early May 1991, forty policemen and Assistant Human Rights Ombudsman Oscar Cifuentes went to Chunimá to detain the patrol chiefs. As they entered the village, someone blew a warning horn, and a crowd appeared armed with guns, machetes, and rocks. The police left.[18] They made another halfhearted attempt on June 13, with some help from the treasury police and the aid of an informant to locate Perebal Ajtzalam's house. Perebal Ajtzalam rounded up his patrollers and surrounded the police. He then fired over their heads, called them "Women!" and accused them of being guerrillas in stolen police uniforms. The informant was beaten and threatened right in front of the police. Again the police left without arresting anyone. Perebal Ajtzalam and Leon Lares went directly to the home of a Chunimá member of the GAM and beat him up for good measure.

Each of these incidents was duly reported to the Inter-American Court of the OAS. On July 15, 1991, the court asked the Guatemalan government to take steps to protect the Chunimá CERJ members and witnesses, as well as the judge. Judge Lemus, who had been harassed and threatened ever since he had filed the original arrest warrant, fled the country the same month.* The Inter-American Court called on the Guatemalan government to testify on July 30 in order to formally respond to the charges and present the protective measures it would implement.

A day before this scheduled hearing, police captured Manuel Perebal Ajtzalam and Manuel Leon Lares in Santa Cruz del Quiché and charged them with five murders. The convenient timing of the arrest called into question the seriousness of the previous attempts. President Serrano's office distributed letters to the various human rights groups and members of the U.S. Congress to inform them of the happy event, emphasizing that it represented a positive step for Guatemala's struggle toward democracy and an end to impunity.

Unfortunately, the Guatemalan judicial system was not up to the task. During the ensuing trial, the judge was threatened, key witnesses never received their subpoenas, and vital video evidence showing the defendants threatening their victims was disallowed. On July 15, 1992, almost a year after their arrests, Perebal Ajtzalam and Leon Lares were acquitted on all counts.

Americas Watch, the Center for Justice and International Law (CEJIL), and the CERJ pressed for appeal. Another year dragged by. President Serrano was ousted for suspending the constitution and was replaced by

---

*Judge Lemus had also angered the army and the patrols by issuing court orders to allow some of the first exhumations of clandestine cemeteries containing victims of massacres in El Quiché.

human rights ombudsman Ramiro De Leon Carpio in June 1993. Finally, on July 6, 1993, Manuel Perebal Ajtzalam and Manuel Leon Lares were sentenced to thirty years in prison and 10,000 quetzales (about US$2,000) in damages. The CERJ subsequently rebuilt an active chapter in Chunimá.

The persistence of the CERJ, Americas Watch, and the CEJIL achieved an important legal precedent. Meanwhile, PBI received more and more requests for accompaniment in rural areas where people were threatened by the civil patrols—from the widows' group CONAVIGUA, the Committee for Campesino Unity (CUC), the Council of Displaced Guatemalans (CONDEG), and other groups that sprang up in the early 1990s. A circular process was at work: Accompaniment helped protect witnesses and provided evidence for international pressure. The growth of international pressure, in turn, encouraged Guatemalans in the belief that accompaniment might really protect them against these thugs, a hypothesis that they had sorely doubted in earlier years. The Chunimá case signaled to other civil patrol leaders that international pressure could not be completely ignored.

Between 1988 and 1991, the CERJ did for the civil patrol issue what the GAM had done for disappearances. Through sheer courage and perseverance, it took a taboo subject and put it on the national agenda. The government insisted that the patrols were necessary and voluntary. In 1985, a U.S. embassy human rights attaché, Lynn Shively, had supported the civil patrols, saying, "The patrollers like being in the countryside, out in the fresh air, It's a good life!"[19] But by 1991, the press, the Guatemalan Congress, the OAS, and the United Nations were questioning the patrol system, largely due to the work of the CERJ. The U.S. State Department finally reversed its position in 1992, stating in a Country Group Report to the Foreign Affairs Committee:

> In 1991, the military, civil patrols, and police continued to commit the majority of human rights abuses, including extra-judicial killings, torture, and disappearance of, among others, human rights activists, unionists, indigenous people, and street children.[20]

Amilcar Mendez declares unequivocally that he would not be alive were it not for international accompaniment. Even President Cerezo agrees with him:

> This foreign presence diminished the possibility of threats and human rights violations. Take Amilcar Mendez as an example. Now of course we never thought to do anything against him. But there were definitely people and groups who were out to get him. The fact that he had these international connections, right up to the U.S. Congress, protected him—even from attacks that might have come without high-level authorization.[21]

Mendez's protection was much broader than just a PBI presence. He gathered together a complex web of support, including Americas Watch, Amnesty International, the R. F. Kennedy and Carter Foundations, congressmen, parliamentarians, and many more. Mendez eventually invited other North American organizations to send volunteers and researchers to live and work with the CERJ. By the early 1990s, the CERJ had more independent accompaniment than most of the rest of the burgeoning popular movement. Reasoning that the latter were facing serious threats with considerably less protection, Peace Brigades shifted its accompaniment focus, ultimately closing its El Quiché office in 1994.

In December 1995, Amilcar Mendez was elected to the Guatemalan Congress. Diego Perebal regained his ability to walk and continues to be active with the CERJ. He and his family never returned to Chunimá. In 1996, after eight years of CERJ pressure and a series of negotiations with the National Revolutionary Unity of Guatemala (URNG), the Guatemalan government began to dismantle the civil patrols.

Notes

1. Documentation on the civil patrols can be found in Americas Watch, *Civil Patrols*, and Americas Watch, *Persecuting Human Rights Monitors*.
2. General Hector Alejandro Gramajo Morales, tape-recorded interview by authors, Guatemala City, July 1994.
3. Americas Watch, *Civil Patrols*.
4. Amilcar Mendez, tape-recorded interview by authors, CERJ office, Guatemala City, July 8, 1994.
5. Mendez interview.
6. Mendez interview.
7. Amilcar Mendez, letter to Alaine Hawkins, August 15, 1987.
8. Photocopy of original typed threat, from CERJ archives.
9. CERJ press release, August 17, 1988.
10. PBI internal report, August 24, 1988.
11. Jeff Smith, personal journal, October 21, 1988.
12. Louise Palmer, *PBI Project Bulletin*, May 1990.
13. Sources for the Chunimá case study include the archives of Americas Watch, the Center for Justice and International Law, affidavits filed with the Guatemalan human rights ombudsman, newspaper reports, PBI monthly bulletins and internal reports, and Jay, *Persecution by Proxy*.
14. Colonel Julio Fidencio Otzoy Colaj, letter to Guatemalan human rights ombudsman, February 1990.
15. Winifred Romeril, tape-recorded telephone interview by author, July 1, 1994.
16. Heike Kammer, tape-recorded interview by authors, Guatemala, August 5, 1994.
17. Cristina Banzato, tape-recorded interview by authors, Guatemala, July 11, 1994.
18. Christian, "Guatemala Defense Patrol."
19. Americas Watch, *Civil Patrols*.
20. U.S. Department of State CG Reports on Human Rights Practices for 1991, submitted to Foreign Affairs Committee (USDOS 1991 Report), cited in Jay, *Persecution by Proxy*.
21. President Vinicio Cerezo Arevalo, author interview, Guatemala, August 1994.

7

The "Democratic" Strategists

DURING THE LATE 1980s, while the GAM and CERJ struggled for survival, President Vinicio Cerezo and Defense Minister Hector Gramajo struggled for a "clean" international image. They were acutely aware of the damage that could be done by international witnesses or, worse yet, international victims. According to Cerezo and most other Guatemala analysts, political violence was still centrally controlled by the army. In theory at least, with internationally conscious leadership in charge of state violence, accompaniment should have been effective.

When we asked him whether international accompaniment successfully protected people during his presidency, Cerezo responded, "Definitely!" citing Amilcar Mendez as an example. Likewise, Gramajo is quick to explain how carefully they tried to analyze the international consequences of each decision, taking into account the political costs of upsetting the international human rights community.

Nevertheless, the Cerezo-Gramajo regime faced a series of human rights embarrassments: highly publicized massacres in El Aguacate (1988) and Santiago Atitlán (1990), the death squad elimination of the leadership of the student movement in August 1989, and bombings against the GAM, PBI, and even the International Committee of the Red Cross. Government "damage-control" skills were sorely tested by the international reaction to the torture of a U.S. nun, Sister Dianna Ortiz, in late 1989 and the early 1990 murder of Michael Devine, another U.S. citizen. The logic of accompaniment was also tested, as PBI found itself more dangerously threatened under the new "democratic" government than under the Mejía dictatorship. To better understand this apparent contradiction, we must look more closely at Cerezo and Gramajo.

The Man in the Middle of the Sandwich

In the 1980s, Vinicio Cerezo was one of the most charismatic and controversial figures in Guatemala. Elected president in 1985 at age forty-four, he boasted a progressive background that included having been a student leader at the University of San Carlos. He had followed this with a career of unflinching devotion to and promotion of the Christian Democratic Party, a political party viciously attacked by military death squads in the late 1970s and early 1980s. Cerezo himself survived three assassination attempts. He explained to journalists that a progressive politician must protect himself in Guatemala: he had a black belt in judo, always carried a sidearm, and subscribed to *Soldier of Fortune*.[1]

Describing himself as a realist, presidential candidate Cerezo admitted that the army would hold most of the power in the new "democracy" and that he could not attempt radical measures such as agrarian reform or prosecution of military human rights abusers. As president, he tried to facilitate a consensus among mainstream political parties, the army, and the economic elite in order to implement timid incremental changes in economic and political policy. He said: "In many areas I moved things forward in my government from negative ten degrees to zero degrees. The situation was so bad, that I could only leave it a little less bad."[2]

Cerezo worked with President Oscar Arias of Costa Rica to achieve the Esquipulas II regional peace accords, and he firmly resisted Reagan administration pressure to oppose the Sandinista government in Nicaragua. True to his word as a candidate, he never criticized the human rights record of his own army. To some international progressive activists, he seemed to be a well-meaning politician stuck in a powerless situation—almost a tragic figure. To many human rights activists, however, his silence was a sign of criminal collaboration, and he became the target of widespread criticism. Cerezo now claims to have appreciated this criticism:

> Human rights pressure actually enabled me to put more pressure on the security forces. The army was committing human rights abuses because they believed this was part of their job, and they thought the human rights groups were aligned with the guerrillas. You have to realize that the civilian government is always between two fires: the conservative sectors on one side and the human rights groups on the other. I was sort of in the middle of the sandwich.[3]

Finding himself in that sandwich was no surprise. In 1977, Cerezo had written a document for the Christian Democratic Party entitled "The Army: An Alternative," proposing a strategic alliance between the army and the Christian Democratic Party.[4] The party built close ties with the more moderate and development-oriented officers in the army, as well with the younger generation of businessmen-entrepreneurs who were competing with the traditional agricultural oligarchy for control over economic policies. In rural areas, Christian Democratic activists began moving into leadership positions in the civil patrols. According to Cerezo, "It was the only way to stop the killing of our people—to make them heads of the civil patrols."[5] By the 1985 elections, Cerezo had the blessing of both the army and the U.S. embassy.

He did not, however, have the blessing of the traditional oligarchy, which proceeded to block most of his proposed policy changes, while threatening his presidency with coups. The landowners were far more concerned with economic policy than with human rights, and they exasperated Cerezo.

> The economy improved during my presidency, and with all the problems of unequal distribution in this country, they all got richer. So why do they hate me so much? Because I passed a tax reform law, that's all! No matter how backward the tax system was, they had been free from taxation and wanted no changes.* They cannot widen their vision.[6]

Cerezo never won the support of the oligarchy, and he steadily lost the faith of those who had elected him. He invariably backed down on promises in areas of social reform, minimum wage, and other issues that affected the poor. By the end of his presidency, he and other Christian Democratic leaders were widely accused of corruption. He never criticized the civil patrol system and never named the independent commission he had promised to investigate disappearances. The popular movement and human rights groups concluded that Cerezo was a facade. The army was still in charge.

The "Enlightened" General

General Hector Alejandro Gramajo Morales, minister of defense for most of the Cerezo presidency, is credited by many—including himself—with having dragged the army kicking and screaming through Guatemala's democratic transition. As one officer put it, "While Gramajo is thinking about the army of the 90s, most of his officers are still anchored in the 50s."[7] The U.S. State Department saw him as a staunch defender of democracy and claimed that his leadership saved the Cerezo presidency from two serious right-wing coup attempts.

Gramajo can also be credited to a large degree with the planning and implementation of the entire counterinsurgency war in the highlands after 1982. While directing the Military Studies Center in 1980, he oversaw the development of a document called "A Strategic Appraisal," which outlined perceived weaknesses in military and political strategy and the steps needed to overcome them. In particular, this document called for the scorched-earth campaigns, the removal of military officers from civilian responsibilities, and the election of a civilian president. After the 1982 coup that

---

*Tax reform was indeed one of the most explosive issues in Guatemala. Even General Mejía had been threatened with a coup when he tried to raise taxes in 1985 to pay for the army's transition plan.

Photo by Derrill Bazzy

President Vinicio Cerezo (hand on heart) and General Hector Gramajo (left).

placed General Rios Montt in power, Gramajo was promoted to the position of vice-chief of staff in the high command and given command over the implementation of the war in the highlands as well as the powerful G-2 military intelligence department. He looks back on this "soldiering" time with great pride.[8]

Gramajo was both a soldier and a political strategist. With previous experience in Washington, he understood international diplomacy better than his predecessors in the military. He recalls his early contacts with nongovernmental organizations (NGOs) working in Guatemala:

After the coup of March 23, 1982, I suddenly found myself in the high command in the job of coordinating planning and analysis. We had a tremendous crisis in the army, because of the previous government. One day a friend of mine came to me and said, "I need your help. All the nongovernmental organizations are getting ready to leave Guatemala—*all* of them!"

I said, "What are you talking about?" and he continued, "Look, there are a lot of foundations who invest a lot in Guatemala, in social and economic projects. The army is suspicious and doesn't always know exactly what they're up to. So they've been bothering them, interfering with their work. So the NGOs are all going to leave, because it's too dangerous to stay."

So all of a sudden I found myself in an emergency meeting of these NGOs. All these NGOs, and little me stuck in the middle of them. It was a bit of a shock: all these men with beards, long hair, sandals, women without makeup and wearing jeans, and even with their hair cut short like men. You could tell that the world of NGOs had a certain common identity, and to me it seemed . . . well, at first it seemed pretty militant and aggressive. Secondly, I characterized it as a sort of subculture—a rejection of comfort, sort of a mystique of service which compels them to reject luxury, not wear makeup, not comb their hair . . . sort of Beatnik. So there I am stuck in the middle of them! Really, it was terrible. I could understand the suspicions of my comrades. But I also understood that it was in the interest of our government that these people did not leave Guatemala. They were making a tremendous contribution, [but their] work of reconstruction was running into problems with the military hierarchy.

The problem is, military men always view with suspicion anything that looks like social organization, especially when they are facing subversives. It's a logical suspicion. What are we going to do? So the effort of trying to reconcile the needs of security and development, through the process of reconstruction, was really forcing the army to come to grips with a new concept: *internationalism*.[9]

Gramajo is of a younger generation of officers than Mejía. He attended the *Escuela Politécnica* in the late 1950s and was the classmate of many of the rebel officers who later formed the first guerrilla movement. He boasts of studying Mao, Ho Chi Minh, and General Giap and applying their lessons to defeat the insurgents. In 1960, Gramajo took the "Ranger" course at the U.S. Infantry School at Fort Benning, Georgia; received training from U.S. special forces advisers in 1965–70; and attended the Command and General Staff College at Fort Leavenworth, Kansas, in 1971. In the 1980s, he was a paid asset of the U.S. Central Intelligence Agency.[10]

During the bloody counterinsurgency campaign of 1965–66, Gramajo led a special forces company called the *Flechas* (arrows). The key officers of the *Flechas* advanced through the ranks together, forming a tight and loyal clique. "Gramajo's Boys," as they were nicknamed by the U.S. Defense Intelligence Agency, became a major force in the army, controlling the high command well into the 1990s.*

Gramajo claims to have changed military codes of conduct, especially with regard to armed action against civilians. He tried to shift military ideology to escape the confines of national security doctrine and understand the appropriate role of a professional military in a democracy. Under his leadership, the epithet "communist" disappeared from military rhetoric, replaced by "subversive" or "insurgent."

Inside the armed forces, we began a long process of discussion about doctrine. The question was, "Are we an anticommunist army or a pro-democratic army?" Another question was, "Are we warriors or soldiers?" Anyone can be a warrior, but a soldier needs to have values, character, and principles.

*These officers included, besides Gramajo, General Mario Enriquez, minister of defense under President Ramiro De Leon Carpio, 1993–95; General Kilo, chief of the national defense staff (1994); General Mata Galvez, former chief of the *Estado Mayor Presidencial*; Colonel Terraza-Pinot; General García Catalan; and General Valconi, named minister of defense by President Arzú in 1996. Blake, *Guarding the Guards*.

Gramajo's strategic plan, initiated in 1982, encompassed not only the problems of military conduct, discipline, and unity but also a more coordinated and deadly assault on the highlands and, paradoxically, a conscious attempt to win back international support. Gramajo recognized that the government was losing the international propaganda battle.

> We had the tremendous case of the Spanish embassy, and the world opinion that that event created and the new organizations it generated. Solidarity organizations, protest organizations, all sorts of groups, and all the slogans started surfacing: "Struggle against Repression," "Political Assassinations." . . . These themes started to be discussed at the UN, the OAS, and even the World Bank and the International Monetary Fund.
>
> The subversives had managed to convert the UN and OAS into our enemies. So, we invited the OAS and the UN to visit and see the real situation in Guatemala. We explained that we had a legitimate responsibility to defend the state, and that unfortunately we had to use weapons. And yes, we had to admit that sometimes there were excesses.

When Gramajo and Cerezo were in power in the late 1980s, the two leaders were constantly besieged by international human rights campaigns. But Gramajo took it in stride.

> Really, there were literally volcanoes of letters of protest. But if you look into it you find they're really just chain letters. The signers don't even know what they're signing. Or maybe they're from student associations or something. So you have to figure out how to measure the difference between an unimportant chain letter and a real clamor that's going to affect the international conscience. And that's very difficult to distinguish.
>
> You have to figure out how to evaluate it. You have to watch for when it reaches the level of an intergovernmental problem—when it moves from the opinion of an organization to the opinion of a state. If Amnesty International puts out a report, well, that's just Amnesty International. But if the Organization of American States, informed by Amnesty International, puts out a report against us, then we're fucked! If they can penetrate the OAS we're screwed, because we're signers of all these covenants and treaties.
>
> So, when we get a letter from Congressman Obie, or Senator Helms, or a letter from Mr. Giovanni Versiani of the European Parliament—shit! Something's happening, because these folks are not just protesting for its own sake. They represent a lot of people. But if we get a letter from Philip Hyman, of the Harvard Human Rights Program—well, he's an important person, but he's still just Philip Hyman. Jimmy Carter is an important person, but he's just one person. But then when you hear from Emory University and the Carter Center, you can tell that things are starting to move.

Credibility is a major power factor in the field of human rights. Like Mejía before him, Gramajo accused international groups of a bias against Guatemala and questioned their professionalism.

There have to be some sort of credentials to give these organizations credibility. Some proof of scientific credentials, or at least good intentions. But then, it doesn't matter how good—or bad—intentioned, or whether they are objective or completely biased, if the Foreign Relations Committee of the U.S. Congress latches onto their results, we're screwed anyway!

Gramajo also applied the same sort of analysis to the presence of foreign activists on Guatemalan soil. He questioned their legitimacy and did his best to undermine their credibility, as well as that of the groups they accompanied. But he clearly understood their function.

This is something which flourished in Nicaragua and earlier in Cuba. A lot of people went from California, to help cut sugar cane, to write, to "cooperate with the oppressed and persecuted people." The collaborators come in all shapes and sizes, and they bring their "internationalism" with them. They might be advisers to Rigoberta Menchú, or Señora Tuyúc.* But they're mostly just summer projects. They come here and end up accompanying some leader, as an international presence, in order that no one touches or attacks or something. This sort of collaboration is always shielded behind the name of some NGO. They might call it "Doctors for Peace," or "Solidarity." They're just words, but formally, they're NGOs.

Jimmy Carter once wanted to come down and work directly with CONAVIGUA, and CERJ, and CUC. I told his assistant, Robert Pastor, "Look, you'd better think it over carefully, because these people don't have a genuine agenda. It's been distorted. They're not really organizations which are 'pro-human rights.' All they do is denounce and protest. You want to keep the Carter Center's image above that sort of stuff."

In our interview with him in 1994, General Gramajo explained some of the difficulties of trying to educate his fellow officers about these new international realities.

But this shift, well, inside the army it was dreadful! And it continues to be to this day. Let me explain. [He begins drawing a diagram.] It's hard for them to distinguish the different levels—here you have international organizations, regional organizations, intergovernmental organizations. They have to understand where each one is situated. And they have to know the difference between a nonstate organization like Amnesty International, which is global, for instance, and one like Americas Watch or the Washington Office on Latin America, which is regional in scope. They have to see how internationalism builds connections between all these organizations and the international solidarity movements, and how these in turn connect to each national group here in Guatemala, such as, for example, the CUC. [He continues fitting each group into a schematic diagram.] Then they have to look at how this "solidarity" functions here in the country. Then there are the Guatemalan organizations in exile, including Rigoberta Menchú. Then you have groups like the Robert F. Kennedy Foundation, etc., etc. You see?

*Rosalina Tuyúc was president of the National Council of Guatemalan Widows (CONAVIGUA).

Apparently, not all his colleagues did see.

> We had a big problem at one point with this one private development foun-
> dation, which is funded by the U.S. government sometimes. They do little
> agricultural projects and direct aid, but they had connections in the field with
> the guerrillas. So many in the institution [army] jumped to the conclusion that
> they were all the same: the U.S. government was supporting the guerrillas!
>
> Then let's look at the Spanish priests in Guatemala. They could not resist
> the trauma—the culture clash of coming face-to-face with the extreme poverty
> of the highlands. I admit some prejudice here, but maybe they are still suf-
> fering some psychological baggage from the conquest. Anyway, all the
> Spanish priests in the highlands took up arms. There were also other priests
> who were honestly concerned about their parishioners. How were we sup-
> posed to be able to distinguish between those that were working with the
> subversives and the others? It was terrible!
>
> It takes a monumental effort for the uncultivated mind to make all these
> distinctions, but this is the key. You must see with clarity that there are some
> who really are concerned with the people in a disinterested fashion. Our task
> at the highest level was to convince the officers that it was actually convenient
> for there to be an opposition which was not using weapons. We had to give
> these new organizations the benefit of the doubt, and not jump to the con-
> clusion that everything that coincided with certain concepts of the insurgency
> was necessarily subversive itself.

It is possible that Gramajo was able to draw these distinctions more
clearly when interviewed after several years of retirement. Unfortunately,
as defense minister, he did not always set a very good example of giving the
benefit of the doubt. He frequently proclaimed that the GAM, the CERJ,
and other popular movement organizations were guerrilla front organizations. Such accusations were interpreted as direct threats by the international human rights movement and undermined any hope of an image of a
democratic and professional army.

In Gramajo, local activists and the international human rights movement
faced a shrewd strategist who had designed a long-term strategy of mass
atrocity followed by "pro-democracy" rhetoric. Unlike Mejía, Gramajo
went out of his way to understand his international critics, in order to delegitimize them. But he was still a career soldier, with a commitment to the
war he had "won," and he shared many of the same biases and ideological
blinders of his predecessors.

General Gramajo enjoys interviews and debate. He is not known for
understatement. But when asked about human rights atrocities under his
command, about all he's got to say is, "There were excesses." When pressed,
he carefully explains that each of the more publicized massacres was the
result of deliberate provocation. Rather than admit to the ever-mounting and
incontrovertible evidence of abuses, he tells romantically detailed stories of
guerrilla intrigue to back up the inevitable conclusion in every case: the subversives were responsible.

General Mejía was frank enough to say, "We did what we had to do." President Cerezo's defense is generally, "The army did it, not me." But Gramajo denies army abuse almost entirely. Under the Lucas García regime (1978–82), he admits that "an atrocious campaign of political persecution was carried out, principally by the political parties, who had access or control over security forces."[11] In the case of the killing of American journalist Michael Blake in 1985, Gramajo acknowledges that it was done by the civil patrols, but he romanticizes, suggesting that it was a poor Mayan who, after 500 years of oppression, could not resist the temptation to shoot "two gringos with long uncombed hair, adventurers looking for the enemy."

Gramajo does not blame his predecessors; he even justifies abuses that occurred before he took over. The 1981 Spanish embassy firebombing was the most damning massacre in Guatemala's diplomatic history. But according to Gramajo, "They [the CUC] took over the embassy and then immolated themselves as a protest. They made their point, the same as the Buddhists had done in Vietnam."

Stories like this are repeated by other Guatemalan military officers of the period—and by Gramajo's successors well into the 1990s. They have an almost mythic quality—one hears the same words and phrases over and over. And some of the stories may contain elements of truth. (The guerrilla forces *did* commit some human rights abuses, although the evidence of army abuse is several orders of magnitude greater.) More often than not, the stories are incontrovertible for lack of survivors or evidence. "In the mountains, you can't see anything," says Gramajo.

Even while Gramajo was in charge in Guatemala, military officers were being indicted for human rights abuse in Argentina, and similar anti-impunity campaigns were under way in Uruguay and Chile. The function of Gramajo's stories is obvious: faced with allegations of war crimes from the international community (and, in the 1990s, from U.S. courts and the United Nations), the army was creating a defense—a simultaneous denial of and justification for its actions. That the army would engage in such mythmaking is psychologically and politically comprehensible. What is more curious, though, is that a politician of Gramajo's caliber could not come up with more sophisticated arguments. In the eyes of the international human rights community, these blatant and implausible denials negated all Gramajo's other attempts to create an image of a new and democratic army. His loyalty, like Mejía's before him, was still first and foremost to the army.

In general, Gramajo and Cerezo were probably much less likely to blunder into international scandal than their predecessors. They wouldn't order assassinations in front of international witnesses. In fact, under their regime, death squads consistently targeted unknown rank-and-file members of popular organizations, avoiding the more high-profile leaders whose deaths would create scandals. But Gramajo was committed heart and soul to the defense of "his" counterinsurgency strategies—strategies whose heavy human rights toll increased steadily throughout his regime. And Cerezo, unwilling or unable to protest, was above all committed to staying in the presidency. These two leaders walked the tightrope of creating a new "democratic" image for Guatemala while denying human rights abuses.

This contradiction has long-term implications for human rights workers and their international accompaniment in Guatemala. In the mid-1990s, thousands of bodies were being exhumed from clandestine cemeteries, and demands mounted for justice and an end to impunity. In cases of U.S. victims, even the U.S. embassy began to demand prosecutions. The army and the government, still controlled by "Gramajo's Boys," consistently refused to cooperate. Accompanied activists pressing for "truth with justice" are not only questioning the army's entrenched myths about its past but also demanding individual prosecutions. As the government, under increasing domestic and international pressure, begins to allow prosecutions, activists face a new threat. Like patrol leader Perebal Ajtzalam in Chunimá, accused officers may take independent action in "self-defense" against activists, judges, or witnesses.

Looking even further ahead, given the fixed promotion schedule of the Guatemalan army, officers involved in the atrocities of the 1980s will be in charge for another twenty years. Cadets in today's *Escuela Politécnica* are being trained in this same denial of history by Gramajo's protégés.

Cerezo and Gramajo endeavored to undermine the credibility of both domestic and international human rights organizations. They won broad support in the diplomatic corps, garnering increased aid from the United States and Europe. Meanwhile, however, Cerezo's minimal efforts at reform alienated and angered the extreme right. When right-wing attacks increased against the popular movement and human rights groups, the government's rhetoric deflected the resulting human rights pressure. Groups like the GAM, CERJ, and PBI were thus more vulnerable to attack. While human rights groups worked to strengthen their international "shield," Cerezo and Gramajo worked to weaken it.

Notes

1. Painter, *Guatemala: False Hopes*, p. 74.
2. President Vinicio Cerezo Arevalo, author interview, Guatemala, August 1994.
3. Cerezo interview.
4. Painter, *Guatemala: False Hopes*.
5. Americas Watch, *Civil Patrols*.
6. Cerezo interview.

7. Gramajo, *De la Guerra*.
8. Blake, *Guarding the Guards*.
9. General Hector Gramajo, tape-recorded interview by authors, Guatemala, July 7, 1994. Subsequent quotes are from the same interview, unless noted.
10. Nairn, "The Country Team."
11. Gramajo, *De la Guerra*, p. 32.

8

Deterrence, Encouragement, and Political Space

Accompaniment as Deterrence

THE ROOT OF THE WORD "deterrence" is the Latin *ter*, or fear. In a human rights context, it means threatening sufficient negative consequences to frighten the aggressor into not committing the human rights violation. Deterrence, one of the most prominent justifications for taking the risk of accompaniment, deserves a closer theoretical examination.*

Deterrence is always difficult to prove. The rational argument seems straightforward enough: A state concerned with its political and economic relationships with other more powerful nations presumably wants to minimize the political cost of its human rights practices. Embarrassing actions witnessed by foreigners can result in economic and political pressure. So those who are accompanied by foreigners are less likely to be attacked.

It's not hard to undermine this argument. One cannot necessarily treat a government-military complex as a rational decision maker. These are situations in which complexity and uncertainty are the prevailing forces. Decisions are affected by subjective factors such as ideology, personal biases, and prejudices or by past errors. Bureaucratic inertia, internal power struggles, internal inefficiency, and poor communication further distort decisions. As we saw with General Mejía, decision makers are not always astute enough to understand the international ramifications of their actions. Training, information processing, cognition, perceptions, and misperceptions are all critical factors in the decision-making processes of the aggressors, the victims, and the international observers who purport to protect one from the other.

One of the first complications we confront when applying classical theories of deterrence to human rights protection is the multitude of variables

---

*A more inclusive concept would be dissuasion, defined by nonviolence analyst Gene Sharp as "the result of acts or processes which induce an opponent not to carry out a contemplated hostile action. Rational argument, moral appeal, increased cooperation, improved human understanding, distraction, adoption of non-offensive policy and deterrence may all be used to achieve dissuasion." Each of these other tactics is used at different times by the accompaniment organization or by the international human rights community that the volunteer indirectly represents. Sharp, *Making Europe Unconquerable*, p. 33.

and actors. Accompaniment, for instance, is only one of several tactics an activist uses for protection. The concept of "international pressure" comprises a dizzying number of different nongovernmental and governmental institutions, each making independent decisions. As we saw with the civil patrols in Chunimá, the aggressor may also comprise a complex array of loosely knit governmental and paramilitary factions, each with some independence in their decisions and strategies.

Hence, accompaniment cannot directly threaten very much. Its presence is more of a hint—a suggestion that a series of consequences may occur, depending on decisions by other players. Meanwhile, an accused government frequently claims that it has no control over the specific aggressor—a claim that can be difficult to disprove. The analyst is left to draw conclusions from circumstantial and coincidental information. The links between cause and effect are fuzzy.

Deterrence analysts distinguish between "general deterrence" and "immediate deterrence."[1] In the case of human rights protection, general deterrence consists of the combined effect over time of the different international and local efforts at protecting human rights: the moral condemnation and protests, the historic examples of other violators who have been punished in any way, the diplomatic hints, the potential lobbying against aid—everything done by the international community to create a generalized understanding that human rights violations will result in negative consequences. Immediate deterrence, as represented by accompaniment, sends a specific message, at a given time, to a specific aggressor, to forestall attacks against a specific target: "Don't touch this one while we're here!"

If the general deterrence attempt of the international community could ensure respect for human rights, there would be no need for accompaniment. When Mejía underestimated or ignored the international community's concerns about the GAM, and Hector and Rosario were killed, PBI accompaniment was the next line of defense. Immediate deterrence becomes necessary when general deterrence fails.

Accompaniment does not replace the general deterrence attempts of the international human rights community: the two complement each other, as demonstrated in Chunimá (see chapter 6). Accompaniment without international support is a facade with no real protective value. The stronger the international interest in a particular region, country, organization, or individual, the more likely it is that accompaniment can deter an attack.

To demonstrate that accompaniment deters aggression, a series of conditions must be met. First of all, the accompaniment and the activist have to clearly communicate to the aggressor what types of actions are unacceptable. This may seem unnecessary, especially if the message is as simple as "don't kill me." If, however, the message is more complex, such as "honor the UN Declaration of Human Rights and humanitarian law," one must assume that the aggressor understands the content of these documents (or else teach the aggressor the content—the characteristic tactic of the International Committee of the Red Cross). If the goal is to prevent more subtle forms of repression, such as discriminatory economic practices or defamation of character through propaganda, this must be articulated. Deterrence cannot work if the aggressor does not know which actions will provoke a response.

Second, the deterrence commitment must be articulated: the aggressor must know in advance that the activist is accompanied and that there will be consequences to an attack. Again, this is not as obvious as it seems. A death squad that carries out an order may well see that there is accompaniment, but whether those who gave the original order know of the presence in advance is another matter, especially if the targeted victim is relatively unknown.

Third, as General Gramajo explained, the aggressor must believe that the organization is capable of carrying out its resolution. If the threat of an international reaction is not credible, there is no reason to expect it to have a protective effect. The chain of communication from accompaniment to the international community to governmental pressure must be clear and effective. In practice, each link is uncertain, and results cannot be guaranteed.

Fourth, deterrence has occurred only if the aggressor seriously considered an attack and then decided not to carry it out because its perceived costs (due to the accompaniment) were higher than its benefits. It is usually impossible to find evidence of this. If no attack takes place, the aggressors will seldom admit that they ever had any intention of doing any harm. More often, we are limited to circumstantial evidence: an activist may have already suffered an attack, an organization may have been bombed or have had some members killed, or the aggressor may actually be making public threatening statements. None of these facts proves intent to attack in the future, but they are useful signals.

One additional condition must be added to this list: the accompaniment must know who the aggressor is. Death threats are often anonymous. Death squads usually work in the dark of the night, and no one claims responsibility. The identity of the attacker must be deduced from little evidence. It often comes down to an analysis of motive: who might benefit from stopping this activist's work? A union activist may assume that the threatening telephone calls are coming from the factory owner's thugs; the peasant activist blames the landowners. Frequently, where repression is national policy, victims assume that "the state" is the culprit by default when there is no evidence to the contrary. This lack of evidence can severely constrain the deterrence attempt. The international reaction may be mistargeted. And even if the assumption of state responsibility is correct, one must know which part of the state apparatus is responsible to effectively target an international response.

Some aggressors, though, may not care about international pressure. This might happen when the government can be punished by the international community, but the government cannot, in turn, punish the actual culprit, which might be a private force with no shared interests with the government. In some cases, a faction within the state apparatus politically opposes the ruling party and may even attack human rights activists or international observers to discredit the government.

The accompaniment never knows in advance if its presence will be enough to deter an attack. International teams are constantly guessing, reassessing, and planning fallbacks, responding to the unexpected at all times.

There are different kinds of deterrence failures, some of which are more difficult to avert than others. First, the aggressor may be unaware of the presence or may not understand how the organization will react. Second, recognizing both these factors, the aggressor may simply underestimate the accompaniment organization's capacity to inflict punishment. These failures fall into the category of "political blunder." Since the accompaniment also wishes to avert such blunders, it pays to communicate clearly and diplomatically with the aggressor, so that misperceptions damaging to both can be avoided.

Deterrence also fails when the aggressor decides that the attack is worth it, because other benefits outweigh the political costs. The accompaniment cannot control this cost-benefit calculation. The threat of an international reaction is simply not enough to deter in these cases. All that is left is to apply the threatened consequences as firmly as possible after the attack, in the hope of changing the calculation next time around.

Terror as Policy

Guatemala, El Salvador, and Sri Lanka were each implementing planned policies of state terror in the 1980s and early 1990s. Activists were not asking for accompaniment merely to confront a personal fear or an immediate threat. They were confronting systemic policies of violence that had frightened most of the population into political paralysis. How and why were such policies implemented? What was their psychological impact? How could an individual accompaniment volunteer help the activists face such a staggering fear?

The U.S. State Department definition of terrorism is as follows: "The use or threatened use of violence for political purposes to create a state of fear that will aid in extorting, coercing, intimidating or otherwise causing individuals or groups to alter their behavior."[2]

Deliberate political use of terror is as old as war itself. In the twentieth century, however, advances in the sciences of weaponry, information control, mass media, and psychology have facilitated the exercise of mass-scale terror with a previously inconceivable efficiency. Social control is achieved by efficiently manipulating varied individual responses to danger and fear.

The potential threat perceived by the state comes from social movements, armed or unarmed, that attempt to change the status quo. These movements may be urging redistribution of societal resources, resisting infringements of civil liberties, expressing frustration about the limited options for social or economic advancement, or perhaps questioning a state's chauvinistic policies of ethnic discrimination.

In cases of armed insurgency, the state contends that it is "protecting" the population and the country. The international community often accepts this defense, despite the fact that the victims are usually civilians. But non-violent democratic movements pushing for structural or economic changes also face terror as a state response. The terror bureaucracies in the Soviet Union, China, Argentina, and Chile, among others, could not be justified on the grounds of self-defense against armed rebellion. Even in Guatemala and El Salvador, state terror policies predate the rise of armed insurgencies.

In every case, though, some sort of "enemy" is needed to excuse or explain mass violence against civilians. That enemy may be ideological rather than military. The perceived "threat" may be projected from the past or from events outside the nation's border. The military or oligarchic leaders of other Latin American nations perceived the Cuban and Nicaraguan revolutions as palpable threats—not external military threats, but internal threats-by-example. In Sri Lanka, politicians provoked fear among the Sinhalese population of the "Tamil hordes" in nearby India and accused enemies of attacking the national Buddhist faith.

How does state terror function to control movements for change? In his study of state terror, political scientist David Pion-Berlin wrote about its centralized, methodical, yet unpredictable deployment in Argentina in the mid-1970s:

> The generals' capacity for method in terror should impress all social scientists. As General Iberico Saint-Jean, governor of Buenos Aires during the first junta regime, put it, "first we will kill all the subversives, then we will kill their collaborators, then . . . their sympathizers, then . . . those who remain indifferent; and finally we will kill the timid."[3]

The general was exaggerating; the timid are a terror state's favorite citizens. His statement nevertheless demonstrates a deliberate and overarching strategy. Terror, however, is more efficient: you don't need to kill everyone if you can paralyze the majority by directly attacking only a minority. It is the audience that counts, with each victim advertising the state's power to others. Torture, short of death, is especially effective.

Guatemalan military historian Gabriel Aguilera Peralta argues that the goal of state terror is to keep people isolated from one another. In this context, civilian organizations are a threat to overcoming that isolation: any organizing is empowering and, as such, confronts and questions the terror system.[4]

The policy of terror has been used on relatively nonresistant populations, such as the Germans under the Nazis or in Argentina in the 1970s. It has also been used against well-organized resistance movements such as in Nicaragua or El Salvador. Terror has been carried out with the finesse of high technology and psychiatry in the Soviet Union and with the bluntness of machetes and rape in Haiti. In every case, the common strand is the conscious strategy to manipulate fear to control the population.

Extreme examples, such as Idi Amin, Adolf Hitler, or Joseph Stalin, often lead people to dismiss terror as a policy of psychopaths. The extreme insurgent terror of the Shining Path in Peru or the suicide squads of the Tamil Tigers in Sri Lanka often prompt the same reaction. This reaction may, however, be a deliberate goal of the terror: people are more frightened of confronting the unpredictable and irrational randomness of the deranged mind than a tormentor who seems like someone who can be reasoned with. The epithet "insane" carries an aura of invincibility.*

Terror is, in fact, a rational choice made by strategic thinkers. The techniques have been developed through a long history of military psychological operations. To policy makers, terror may seem no more immoral than other strategic choices in a war against an enemy. And, as with other military or strategic policies, states study the successes and failures of other states, perfecting the tool.[5]

Nevertheless, even the most organized state terror system cannot watch everyone, nor kill anyone at any time it pleases. Surveillance is expensive and labor-intensive. Processing and interpreting all the data from surveillance are even more demanding, and intelligence planners frequently have more data than they can effectively analyze. The state's omnipotence is never so complete, but it wants people to think so, since this belief prompts a self-regulation of political activity.

This supposed omnipotence is also limited by ideological factors. The same biases that bolster the state terror policy tend to filter information in ways that do not necessarily lead to accurate judgments. Policy makers tend

---

*This is not to say, of course, that Hitler and others were not psychopaths, but rather to point out that despite the mental state of any of its practitioners, terror is a policy with strategic coherence.

to pay attention to information that seems to confirm their preexisting ideas and to ignore data that might contradict them. Decision makers overwhelmed by demands and information tend toward oversimplifications and heuristic reasoning.*

Ideological blinders can do far more than filter information. In extreme cases, they can warp policy, causing terror to be exaggerated beyond any conceivable military or political benefit.[6] When these ideologies become institutionalized in bureaucracies, and vested interests evolve, the terror can continue long after its alleged justification is gone.

From Victims to Protagonists

When facing state terror policies, nonviolent organized action can be attempted only if there is some way to confront fear. Victims have faced attempts on their lives, threats over the telephone, or torture; they have seen their families or friends killed, mutilated, or disappeared. The Guatemalan, Sri Lankan, and Salvadoran military all used massacres, disappearances, and aerial bombing campaigns. The litany of barbarities that any human rights organization monitoring state terror can recite defies the imagination. The results are not "normal" or everyday fears. They are traumas of epic proportions, for which the psyche is utterly unprepared.

The psychological and psychiatric professions are also ill-prepared to address these concerns, since the victims of these traumas are usually too poor to seek treatment and live in societies where psychiatry is still considered anathema or is simply unavailable. The psychological profession's bias toward individual clinical work also limits its readiness to deal with what is essentially a collective psychosis. Political dynamics, combined with this lack of clinical experience and understanding, results in a dearth of academic research on the psychological effects of state terror, despite the vast quantity and frequencies of these traumas globally.[7]

Terror is designed to affect both the individual and the collective. The trauma of the entire society reinforces each individual's fear. Unspeakable tortures loom in people's minds. With assassination all around, even the politically timid citizen begins to recalculate the odds of survival.

The result is massive inhibition and suppression of the truth into the unconscious by the majority of the population. The victims' families are seen by their neighbors as tainted and dangerous and are socially ostracized. In defense against panic, people deny reality. Indifference becomes a survival

*Studies of high-level decision making in Israel before the Yom Kippur War or in the United States during the Vietnam War suggest that these problems of data processing, data filtering, and ideological limitations are common even in the most advanced intelligence-gathering systems in the world. Vertzberger, *World in Their Minds.*

mechanism.[8] The repression is internalized and becomes a part of the collective culture, affecting every sphere of social life. The victims are left with no "safe" social setting for a return to psychological health.

The family members of people who had been disappeared in Guatemala were still suffering these overwhelming effects even as they proceeded to organize the GAM. Blanca de Hernandez remembers:

> We couldn't even think at the time about practical things—we didn't know then where the organization was going. All we could think about was that primary goal: to find the person, because this was something completely new for all of us. There were many things I didn't understand. I just tried to stick to my work and watch out for my children. I had no idea where it would take me. The loss of my son changed my life completely, and intimately. It changes your family, your friends, your work companions, your whole society.[9]

Recovery

To recover, victims must confront the truth, find a community of support, and reestablish a sense of safety. Confronting the truth, though, means finding out who is threatening you, learning whether your disappeared daughter is alive or dead, or trying to understand how the state system functions. Such investigation can be dangerous.

Building a community of support is psychologically indispensable, and it is often achieved by joining others who have experienced similar trauma. Terror destroys the social fabric around the affected individuals, either by literally annihilating their family, friends, or community or by systematically isolating them. They have to rebuild this fabric themselves. Finding a supportive community breaks the isolation and helps to heal.

This new community, once it is found or built, also offers moral and ideological support. Activists attacked for political beliefs that they hold dear face a crisis of existential proportions: to continue on the path that gives their life meaning is now life-threatening. Abandoning that path can have massive consequences of guilt and doubts about self-worth. But continuing the struggle also generates guilt and doubt, since it puts the lives of their families and friends in peril, as well as their own. The role of a supportive and encouraging family and community is critical.[10]

During this recovery process, the recurrence of the trauma must be prevented. A mother cannot recover from the loss of a child while the threat of losing another hovers over her. Last year's life-threatening attack is relived with each new death threat.

The very process of regaining psychological health runs counter to the goals of the terror policy. It is not in the state's interest for people to confront reality or to know and speak the truth. The state fears these communities of mutual support, which are easily transformed into vehicles of political pressure. Consequently, the state opposes or targets those victims who are most actively trying to regain some semblance of psychological health.

This places the victims in an agonizing Catch-22. If they take steps toward psychological health, confront the reality of their trauma, and look for support from others, they may be increasing the risk of additional attacks on themselves and their families.

Confronting Fear with Accompaniment

People requesting international accompaniment are usually confronting real dangers. But with this danger comes a broader psychological context, affected by both the collective psychosis and the individual's past experience of fear and trauma. Julia Hernandez, former director of the Salvadoran archbishop's legal services office, asserts that the most critical factor enabling people to overcome fear is their solidarity with others in their organizations.[11] But the very act of forming such organizations may be dangerous. And when such a supportive organization does not yet exist, some level of fear must be confronted without it. We have seen with the GAM and the CERJ that accompaniment can aid in this process.

Once organizations exist that both offer support and seek the truth, they are inevitably delegitimized and demonized by the state, labeled "subversive" or "terrorist." These labels further inhibit participation. Accompaniment can lower the fear threshold, enabling people to overcome the early hurdles of democratic political activity, thereby promoting the growth of the group.

But accompaniment is also requested by democratic activists who have long since crossed such thresholds. They might be twenty-year veterans of the labor movement, or human rights activists who have been in and out of detention or torture repeatedly. The fact that such activists regard the facing of these threats as a daily moral imperative doesn't mean that they are not traumatized. Instead, they develop coping mechanisms: alternating or overlapping states of fear and recovery. They live with prolonged levels of high stress, from both the danger and the sense of responsibility, and their ability to manage this stress contributes to their effectiveness as activists. They worry about their families, and their families worry about them.

Medardo Gomez, the Lutheran bishop of El Salvador, was threatened and accompanied for several years, but he never slowed down his work. His wife explained to PBI in 1992:

> Once my little boy overheard the grown-ups talking about the threats against the bishop and the church. He stood there listening, and later when I saw

him, he was staring straight ahead. I talked to him and he responded, crying, "Mama, why are they blaming my papa?" And I told him, "Look, my son, don't worry. There are many people at his side who take care of him. Don't worry." This was a way I could calm him a little bit.[12]

Thus, in addition to providing a measure of real protection, the accompaniment serves many other purposes, from helping to confront fear and stress to reassuring loved ones, all of which contribute to the activists' ability to carry out their mission. Finally, just as an individual in a dysfunctional family is aided by supportive encouragement and solidarity from friends who are "outside" the problem, activists facing state terror in a dysfunctional society are helped by international accompaniment. The international presence legitimizes a struggle that the dominant society condemns. The volunteers are a supportive reminder that the activists are not alone in their search for truth and collective, even global, sanity.

Encouragement, Protection, and Political Space

The concept of *political space* is crucial to understanding how the incremental protection and encouragement provided by accompaniment interact with each other. Each actor in a complex conflict situation, whether a soldier or a human rights activist, perceives a broad array of possible political actions and associates a certain cost or set of consequences with each action. The actor perceives some consequences as acceptable and some as unacceptable, thereby defining the limits of a distinct political space (see figure 8.1).

Accompaniment alters this mapping of political space for a threatened human rights activist (see figure 8.2). It shifts the borderline upward, expanding the space of political action available to the activist. The middle ground is made up of actions that will no longer be attacked in an unbearable fashion. There are still actions that will provoke unacceptable consequences, even with accompaniment.

The notion of "acceptable" consequences can be fluid over time and varies greatly among individuals or organizations. For some, torture or death of a family member might be the most unbearable consequence. For others, a threshold might be crossed at the first threat. An organization might be willing to risk the death of a member, but not the annihilation of the whole group.

The political space of the aggressor is also affected by accompaniment, which tends to limit, or shrink, the available space for violent or repressive action—which we call "impunity space" (see figure 8.3). Again, there are still actions whose consequences are acceptable. As it is with the activist, so

Figure 8.1 Each Actor's Political Space

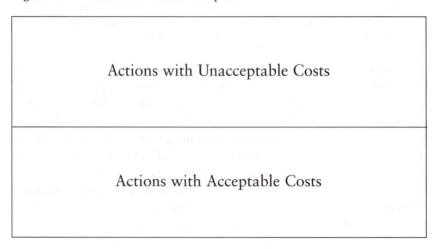

it is with the aggressor: the concept of "acceptable" is fluid and variable. One government official might be extremely savvy and sensitive to international criticism, whereas an independent death-squad leader might be relatively impervious.

Accompaniment is effective, in both figures 8.2 and 8.3, in the gray zone. If the aggressor's ability to attack has been significantly limited, the presence is a real protection. If the activists can carry out significant political activities that they otherwise would have avoided, then that accompaniment has contributed to the strength and growth of a nonviolent civil society.

But no one knows where the borders are. This is a critical complication, which requires an expansion of our analysis. All actors are guessing about the possible repercussions of their actions, and they are all making mistakes. Guatemalan security forces, for instance, might not have murdered GAM leaders if they had known that this would attract greater diplomatic support to the organization and increase its international profile and credibility. Meanwhile, the activists are also making mistakes. A young factory worker may think that it would be dangerous to be an outspoken union leader, but she figures that the odds are more in her favor if she is just a quiet rank-and-file member. Then she's dead. At the factory next door, everyone is too scared to even talk about unionizing. Yet maybe there would be no repercussions at all. They don't know. Nobody knows. Everyone learns by trial and error, and the errors are costly.

People are not only unsure of what the consequences of their actions will be; they also don't know the future acceptability of different consequences. Initially, a young activist might think that getting death threats on the

Figure 8.2 Accompanied Actor's
Political Space

Figure 8.3 Aggressor's Space for
Repressive Action

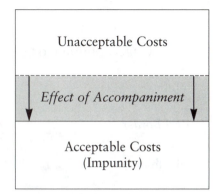

telephone would be an unbearable psychological torture. A year later, he may find that he's gotten used to getting such calls every week. One union may disband when its leadership is killed, whereas another may plan ahead for this potential cost and actually have two or three tiers of trained leaders ready to take over when one is wiped out. A dictator may look with chagrin at the risk of international rebuke from a massacre of peasants but later find that the rebuke could be handled if it doesn't last too long.

Everyone's choices are determined by this guesswork. They have only their own perceptions and projections of what consequences they might suffer. These projections might be based on substantial historical or political analysis, simple prejudices, an emotional reaction to a past trauma, or any number of other psychological factors. This uncertainty is illustrated in figures 8.4 and 8.6.

In space A in figure 8.4, the activist unknowingly walks into danger and suffers the consequences. In space B, fear has been instilled so effectively that the activist is inhibited from taking actions that are in fact relatively safe. In situations of state terrorism, this space can be huge: nearly all political or social action is feared; only passivity appears to have acceptable consequences. The darker gray area, then, is the only political space that is truly "available" to the activist. Space A is too dangerous, and part of space B has been eliminated in the activist's own mind.

The function of accompaniment is to expand this available space, by pushing both the "real" and the "perceived" borders upward (see figure 8.5). The actions in the dark gray shaded area are now available to the activists, but for a variety of reasons. Actions in B2, for instance, were not dangerous in the first place: the activist has simply overcome internalized inhibitions. Accompaniment in this case functions as encouragement rather than

Figure 8.4   Threatened Activist's Political Space: Reality and Perception

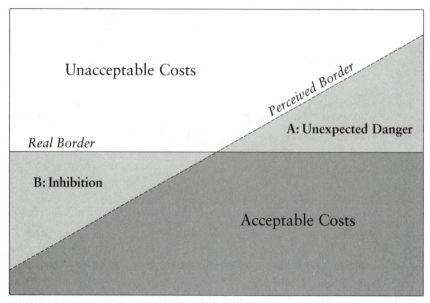

protection. Actions in A3 are now safer, but since the activist never saw them as unacceptably dangerous, the accompaniment here is serving as pure protection, not encouragement. In area F, both encouragement and protection are acting together: the activist is encouraged to take new action that was previously too dangerous and is now protected.

There is still fear: space B still exists with accompaniment. In fact, area B3 consists of additional actions that are now relatively safe, but the activist does not trust in this safety. Finally, area A2 represents the accompaniment volunteer's nightmare: the activist believes these actions to be safer now, but in fact they are not. The activist may walk blindly into danger because of the encouraging international presence.

The aggressor faces many different types of consequences for repressive action. Some are local, such as increased unrest if the aggressor is a state, or increased group loyalty or solidarity among the victims. International pressure is just one factor. Other perceived benefits might outweigh the costs. Getting rid of a troublesome activist, for instance, might seem to be worth a short-term embarrassment. Thus, "unacceptable costs" refers to the net effect of all these factors. Again, in figure 8.6, only the actions in the dark gray area are truly available "impunity space."

Protective accompaniment purports to deter violence and shrink this space (see figure 8.7) by moving both lines downward, eliminating the dark gray zone from the available space for repressive action. In the case of the

Figure 8.5   Activist's Political Space: Effect of Accompaniment

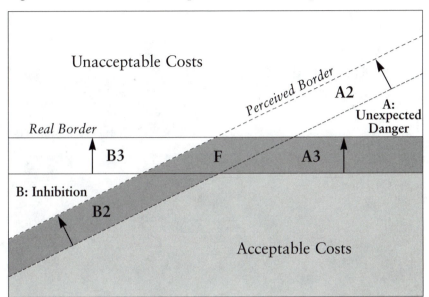

activist, we distinguished between protection and encouragement; with the aggressor, we speak of discouragement and deterrence. The aggressor is discouraged from acting in area D2, even though the real costs are acceptable. He overestimates the power of accompaniment and becomes even more overcautious. In area G, we come the closest to real deterrence: the accompaniment has raised the costs of repression; the aggressor recognizes this and holds back.

Sometimes, accompaniment helps the aggressor avoid mistakes. Thus, actions in area C2 are blunders, but the aggressor did not recognize them as such until the accompaniment was present. While discouraging the aggressor's "mistake," accompaniment is protecting the intended target. From the standpoint of the activist, repression by mistake is no less damaging.

International pressure is usually directly perceived only by the government leaders who receive and interpret it. It is effective only to the extent that it is transmitted, or "trickled down," to the direct instigators of violence against the threatened. In contrast, the physical presence of an international volunteer is visible to those who are directly watching the intended victim and is institutionally communicated to those at the top. This visibility is especially powerful for the relatively unknown potential target, whom decision makers would not expect to have international clout.

Going a step further, let us assume that the upper-level policy makers understand the political consequences of a human rights violation in the

Figure 8.6   Aggressor's Repressive Political Space: Reality and Perception

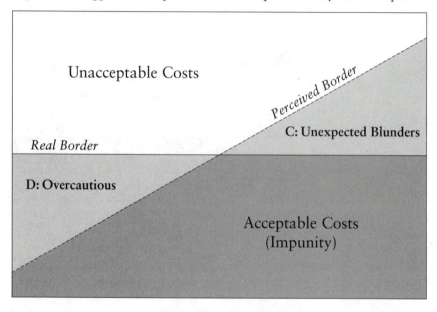

presence of international witnesses and wish to avoid these consequences. Is this analysis always transmitted effectively down to the street-level perpetrator? If not, then when a local death-squad thug comes to the door to abduct or kill someone and finds an unexpected foreigner, can we assume that he makes such a political analysis? Perhaps not; yet the accompaniment may be effective anyway. The local soldier, police officer, or thug may not be capable of a sophisticated international analysis, but he may perceive himself as relatively powerless and be concerned about getting into trouble. He also may have some qualms about carrying out immoral actions in front of judging witnesses.

In the final analysis, what determines decisions is not objective truth, but rather what the decision makers themselves perceive or believe to be true and how they analyze it. In other words, even if a small NGO may not be able to bring punitive pressure to bear for the actions witnessed by volunteers, what matters at the moment of decision is whether the potential aggressors think the NGO can punish them. Deterrence is all about perception.

Finally, returning to figure 8.7, the aggressor might commit a repressive act (area C3) and suffer unacceptable consequences because of accompaniment. In the immediate event, accompaniment has failed to deter, but over the course of time, such events should change the aggressor's perception of the available space. If he learns from his mistakes, the "perceived" line should move closer to the real line. Accompaniment thus discourages future

Figure 8.7 Aggressor's Repressive Space: Effect of Accompaniment

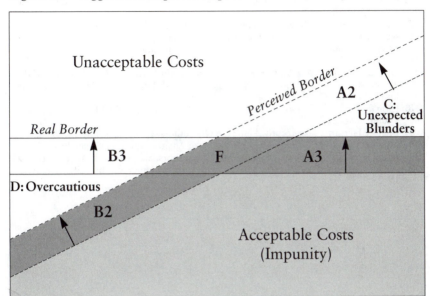

aggression, and the more severe the political cost, the greater the credibility of future accompaniment.

This model begins to synthesize some of the apparent paradoxes and uncertainties that human rights activists face. Accompaniment organizations need to understand deterrence strategy, appreciate how state terror strategy deliberately controls and manipulates fear, and be mindful of the trauma that activists are living through. Recognizing that perceptions and reality can sometimes be far apart, accompaniment and all human rights work need models to guide them through the ambiguities. With better analysis, accompaniment organizations can apply clearer strategies and exert greater pressure to protect both the activists and themselves. As we will see in the coming chapters, the volunteers must also measure the costs of their own actions and define a political space. They are vulnerable to terror and its debilitating psychological impact. And when the protection they provide proves to be effective, the aggressor will move to close the space for accompaniment.

Notes

1. Lebow and Gross Stein, *When Does Deterrence Succeed?*
2. Stohl and Lopez, *Terrible Beyond Endurance.*

3. Pion-Berlin, *Ideology of State Terror*.

4. Gabriel Aguilera Peralta, director, FLACSO/Guatemala, interview by authors, Guatemala, July 22, 1994.

5. Herman, *The Real Terror Network*, documents the role of the United States in consciously facilitating this mutual learning process, bringing Latin American military officers together to share techniques of torture and terror and to learn new ones.

6. Pion-Berlin, *Ideology of State Terror*.

7. Stohl and Lopez, *State as Terrorist*. See also Martin-Baro, ed., *Psicología social de la guerra*; Riquelme, ed., *Era de Nieblas*; Beristain and Riera, *Comunidad Como Apoyo*; Lira Cornfeld, "Guerra Psicologica."

8. Farina, "Terror de Estado como fantasma," p. 155; Lira Cornfeld, "Psicologia del miedo y conducta colectiva."

9. Ester de Herrarte, tape-recorded interview by authors, Guatemala, July 13, 1994.

10. Beristain and Riera, *Comunidad Como Apoyo*; Amati, "Aportes psicoanaliticos."

11. Julia Hernandez, tape-recorded interview by authors, San Salvador, August 11, 1994.

12. PBI delegation tape-recorded interview with Bishop Gomez and his wife, January 13, 1992.

9

Closing the Space

A S POPULAR ORGANIZATIONS began to surface after the 1985 election of President Cerezo, Guatemalan activists in exile also began testing this apparent political opening. The first organized and public group to return from exile was led by labor activist Miguel Angel Albizures and former student leader Tania Palencia in November 1987. After a few days of visits with the GAM and the union movement, they began receiving death threats. At the GAM's recommendation, they tried one day of PBI accompaniment. Then they cut their visit short and flew back to Mexico.

Albizures had been one of Guatemala's most visible labor leaders in the 1970s, but he was only one of hundreds of surviving leaders of the pre-1981 Guatemalan popular movement living in exile. The potential return of this huge resource of organizing experience was too big a threat to the Guatemalan elite, according to Albizures. A public return was still not "available" political space.

Nevertheless, Albizures came back to Guatemala a year later, quietly. Rather than seek a leadership position, he took the more low-key role of consultant and analyst for several labor organizations. Later he began working as a columnist for *Siglo Veintiuno*, a major Guatemalan newspaper.

> I had had direct conflicts with the elite groups who were investing in this new daily. I knew perfectly well that it was a bourgeois paper. But now they were trying to move into new political turf, and I needed to do the same, so for me it was a convenience and a protection. What I mean is that if I were attacked now it wouldn't just be Miguel Angel the labor activist anymore, but rather Miguel Angel of this newspaper. It raised the stakes of attacking me, and with this intention I started working with them, even against the opposition of many comrades.[1]

Instead of choosing accompaniment, Albizures limited his activities to minimize their confrontational impact. Meanwhile, he protected himself against attacks from the extreme Right by aligning himself with a newspaper of the more moderate financial and industrial elite.

Rigoberta Menchú Returns

Six months after Albizures' first attempted return, exiled Mayan leader Rigoberta Menchú made her first trip back to Guatemala. Her delegation was the first to use international accompaniment strategically as a protection for a visit from exile. It sparked a furious reaction in Guatemala.

Even in 1988, four years before winning the Nobel Peace Prize, Rigoberta Menchú was by far the most famous Guatemalan in exile. After her father, Vicente Menchú, was killed in January 1981 during the Spanish embassy massacre, Rigoberta became a leader of the Committee for Campesino Unity (CUC). She fled into exile after her mother was killed later in 1981. Her autobiographical account of repression in the Nebáj-Uspantán region of El Quiché, I, Rigoberta Menchú . . . , brought her to prominence in the field of international human rights. During the 1980s, she became the most eloquent, charismatic, and beloved voice of the Mayans and of oppressed indigenous people around the world. Only thirty years old, Menchú had already earned numerous human rights awards. She was working with other exiled activists in an organization known as the Unified Representation of the Guatemalan Opposition, generally referred to by its Spanish acronym, RUOG. The RUOG had built a credible reputation by testifying at international human rights forums.[2]

When Menchú was in Geneva testifying at the February 1988 UN human rights hearings, Guatemalan government representative Dr. Luis Chea accused the RUOG of being "out of touch" with the new democratic Guatemalan reality and challenged the organization to come see for itself. The RUOG chose to accept Chea's rhetorical challenge as a formal invitation.

Before the RUOG representatives arrived, Guatemala's oldest death squad, La Mano Blanca (The White Hand), issued a public death threat against RUOG members and any who accompanied them. The army accused the RUOG of being the political representative of the guerrillas. Newspaper columnists debated whether RUOG members should be arrested or granted amnesty. Minister of the Interior Rodíl Peralta insisted that they would be arrested upon arrival.

"All accompaniment is good and helpful, but some accompaniment is more helpful than others," said RUOG member Frank LaRue. "In this case we called on congressmen, parliamentarians, church leaders, etc. to come with us."[3] The delegation, which arrived in Guatemala on April 18, included four RUOG members; parliamentarians from Germany, England, Mexico, and Belgium; staff representatives of four U.S. congressmen; two journalists, including a CBS photographer; two representatives of the United Church of Canada; a U.S. Catholic priest; and five representatives of the

U.S. Sanctuary Movement.* In addition, they were met at the airport by three PBI volunteers; dozens of national and international reporters; a crowd of hundreds of Guatemalan students, unionists, and GAM members—and a battalion of 500 policemen on the runway.

Despite the heavyweight accompaniment, Rigoberta Menchú and her colleague, Dr. Rolando Castillo, were whisked into police cars the instant they stepped off the plane. PBI volunteers and the rest of the arriving delegation rushed to the airport pay phones to start an international human rights alert. In the next few hours, President Cerezo was barraged with telephone calls from the international and diplomatic community. Despite the government's stated intention of bringing Menchú and Castillo before a judge for "crimes against the state," charges were never filed. Several hours later, they were granted an amnesty they had never requested and were given legal liberty to travel in the country. Accompaniment alone did not prevent the arrests, but international pressure reversed them.

Cerezo and Rodíl were berated from all sides. The international community was upset over the arrests. The right wing was upset over the release. Newspaper editorials criticized the government's spineless capitulation in the face of international pressure. RUOG member Frank LaRue later stated that the arrests and release gave the visit far more legitimacy and publicity than they ever expected to receive.[4]

This apparent blunder can be understood only in context: Cerezo was under fire from the right wing for recent social policy accords he had signed with the union movement; the oligarchy was anxious over a recent Catholic bishops' letter calling for land reform; the army was suspicious of Rodíl's attempts to build an independent police force. Both politicians' positions were unstable, and by arresting Menchú and Castillo, they could send a message to the army and the oligarchy that they were "tough." The internal political benefit of sending this message to the army outweighed any consideration of the international impact. But when the force of the international pressure hit, they reversed themselves, using the legal artifice of "amnesty" to save face.

The RUOG spent a week meeting with popular movement organizations and Guatemalan politicians. Their accompaniment surrounded them on the street and in their cars, in fear of gunshots from death squads at any moment. Suspicious-looking men with ill-concealed weapons constantly loitered in their hotel lobby. Two of the delegation's parliament members

---

*Sanctuary was a church-based movement in the United States and Canada to protect Central American political refugees (who were not recognized as such by the U.S. government and were often deported), offering them sanctuary in churches, material support, and assistance in reaching Canada. See Golden and McConnell, *Sanctuary*.

*Rigoberta Menchú (second from left), with PBI accompaniment
(Liam Mahony, with camera), 1988.*

Photo by Marlyse Gehret

confronted one such man, only to find out that he was a policeman. Since it was impossible to distinguish between a plain-clothes policeman and a potential assassin, the RUOG members asked the government for a uniformed police escort—in separate cars—for the rest of their stay. The same day, they asked PBI to station volunteers in the hallways outside their hotel rooms at night.

On May 11, 1988, a few weeks after Menchú left the country, army hard-liners tried to oust Gramajo and Cerezo in a coup. Although Gramajo was able to quickly contain it, the coup attempt proved to be a successful pressure tactic by the extreme Right. An anonymous group calling itself Officers of the Mountain subsequently published a list of concerns and demands. Within the next few months, Cerezo reneged on his social pact agreements with union movement and later removed Rodíl Peralta from his post as interior minister.

That summer, violence increased. Rumors of coups continued throughout the autumn. In November, the country was shaken by news of the largest massacre since before civilian government: twenty-two campesinos in El Aguacate, Chimaltenango, disappeared and were found in a mass grave. The army blamed the guerrillas. Human rights groups blamed the army.

Human Rights Watch titled its 1988 Guatemala report "Closing the Space." Guatemalan columnist Hugo Arce ended the year with a column in *El Gráfico* entitled "International Image: The Edifice Is Crumbling."

Today, three years after the electoral triumph, Guatemala's image is deteriorating rapidly and irreversibly, so much so that even its most fervent allies are beginning to back away, some loudly and others quietly, without quite slamming the door. . . . Guatemala again takes its accustomed place on the bench of the accused.[5]

Attacking the Accompaniment

A process of polarization was beginning that was to deepen during 1989 and 1990, the last two years of the Cerezo government. The popular movement's growth and its drive to expand the political space available to it were on a collision course with the extreme Right. Where they collided, international accompaniment was vital to the popular movement and a major hindrance to the extreme Right. It was only a matter of time before attempts were made to remove this hindrance.

The first signal came on January 19, 1989. During an army press conference, self-professed guerrilla deserter Angel Reyes described to reporters how he had worked with the GAM and the guerrilla movement to discredit Guatemala, and how groups such as Amnesty International and Americas Watch had helped them do this. Reyes claimed to have personally assisted the guerrillas in founding the GAM. He called Amilcar Mendez a leader of the Guerrilla Army of the Poor (EGP—a guerrilla faction). Finally, Reyes named a former PBI volunteer as a guerrilla member and accused PBI of relaying messages between guerrilla contacts in Guatemala and Europe.

Reyes had been a member of the GAM, though not a founder, as he claimed. He joined after the disappearance of his brother in 1984 and fled the country during the period of the assassinations in the spring of 1985. Beyond this fact, which the GAM admitted from the start, Reyes could prove none of his assertions. Public-relations officer Colonel Isaacs later admitted to Americas Watch that the army had no corroborating evidence. Congressional deputies, jurists, and newspaper editorialists all criticized the Reyes press conferences as a political show.[6]

President Cerezo later assured us that the event had been mishandled:

There are always people who sympathize with the guerrillas inside the popular organizations. For that matter, there are sympathizers in the Christian Democratic Party as well. The frontier between popular organizations and guerrilla organizations is hard to distinguish. But the army was just trying to manipulate Reyes' information to try to link the guerrillas with the human rights groups, without evidence. . . . The Reyes thing was completely conceived and carried out by the army. If the information had been valid, and if the event had been managed by the government, I would have handled it quite differently. I would have gone and talked directly to the accused organizations and gotten some concessions from them.[7]

But at the time, Cerezo invited Reyes to repeat his presentation in the presidential press room, giving the charges his seal of approval. This expanded the political space for right-wing attacks against the named targets—the GAM, CERJ, and PBI. The civilian government's public collaboration lowered the political costs of such attacks.

In February, a new death squad, the Jaguar of Justice, began a reign of threats and killings, carving the initials JJ into the bodies of its victims. Several university students and faculty were threatened into hiding or exile. Four students in Quetzaltenango were killed or disappeared.

In contrast, the spring of 1989 brought the first of several "national dialogues," bringing together different social sectors to discuss the country's problems.* With government sponsorship, the dialogue seemed to offer relative safety, and the popular movement latched onto it to expand the available political space. Representatives of the refugees in Mexico and the exiled Guatemalan Human Rights Commission used it to shelter their first visits to the country. The government publicly cited these visits as proof of democracy. Despite such claims, all these groups asked for PBI accompaniment while they were in the country.

Rigoberta Menchú and the RUOG also returned for the national dialogue in 1989. On May 9, 1989, a year after the first coup attempt, anti-Gramajo troops again marched on the capital and were again quickly subdued. The dialogue was in process at the time, and PBI was busy accompanying participants. The afternoon of the coup attempt, PBI received the first of four threatening telephone calls: volunteers were instructed to tell the RUOG representatives and Amilcar Mendez to leave the country within forty-eight hours or they would be killed. The RUOG was threatened directly as well. Rigoberta Menchú and Frank LaRue's mother received anonymous Mother's Day bouquets with threats on the cards.

PBI volunteer Patty Mutchnick, an environmental activist and emergency rescue worker from Maine, was accompanying Menchú.

> The day was a waiting game. The RUOG proceeded with an intent of utmost normalcy. They were cautious, but not paranoid. . . . After the fifth threatening call of the day, I heard Rigoberta jokingly say, "I wish they'd get this straight. Do I have twenty-four hours from the 8 A.M. call or from the 10 A.M. call?" Rigoberta knew as well as I that when I went out to scan the

---

*The Esquipulas II Peace Plan had been signed in 1987 by all the Central American presidents and won Costa Rican President Oscar Arias the Nobel Peace Prize. It called for a formal process of dialogue in each country among all the sectors of society affected by the conflict. In principle, Esquipulas II recognized that the Central American conflicts were a product of deep structural problems and societal inequities and that their solution would require a consensus and cooperation across the political and economic spectrum. Cerezo was a firm supporter of Esquipulas II, and in 1988, he formed the Committee for National Reconciliation to plan the national dialogue.

street for snipers and dangerous men behind tinted windows, the actual physical protection I offered her was absurd, and to myself in that moment, laugh-
able. I was absolutely vulnerable, and so were they.[8]

On May 12, the fire department dismantled a bomb attached to a car
outside the RUOG residence. The same evening, PBI received a telephoned
bomb threat, but the police found nothing. Rigoberta Menchú left the
country within a few days, and the others within a week. None of them would
consider it safe to return for another two years.

The Bombings

The summer of 1989 was marked by several public-sector strikes, the longest
and largest of which involved up to 60,000 teachers by mid-July. July and
August also brought the beginning of a rash of anonymous bombings. The
targets at first showed no obvious pattern: a journalist and former army
officer's house, the university, a right-wing party office, the Belgian con-
sulate, the Camino Real Hotel, a bus stop, a bank, and a Texaco station,
along with eighty false alarms.[9] No one was killed in the bombings, but
everyone had the jitters. On August 1, Danilo Barillas, an intellectual leader
of Cerezo's Christian Democratic Party, was assassinated. Cerezo accused
the extreme Right of trying to destabilize the country.

In late July, one GAM member was brutally murdered, and another disappeared. In early August, Nineth was threatened in a restaurant. On the
seventh and eighth, she noticed armed men outside her home. PBI and
other international human rights groups mobilized international alerts to
express concern over the GAM's safety to the Guatemalan government.

At 5:30 A.M. on August 15, three armed men entered the home of GAM
member María Rumualda Camey. They fired shots in the air and took her
away while her children watched.* GAM leader Blanca de Hernandez went
down to Escuintla to evacuate the rest of the family.

> They had already kidnapped her brother Eliodoro the year before and killed
> two other relatives in July. . . . So we went back there to bring the family to
> the GAM house for refuge. When we were coming back in the evening there
> was a car following us. There was also a strange car parked near the house,
> and the man in the corner store told me later that it had been around since
> early afternoon, changing position now and then. We went in. We had only
> been there a few minutes when we heard shots outside.[10]

PBI volunteers Jennie Roitman and Laura Fernandez were up on the second floor, getting ready to spend the night with twenty GAM members,

---

*Maria Rumualda Camey never appeared. Her sister-in-law and sister's children fled to Spain.
Her husband eventually fled to Canada with their children.

mostly children, who were staying there. A little before 8 P.M., she heard the shots, and someone banged on the door. Jennie was on her way down the stairway to investigate the noise when a bomb exploded, destroying the room at the bottom of the stairway. Singed but uninjured, she went back up the stairs.

A mile away at the Peace Brigades house, the rest of the team had just sat down to dinner when two grenades were thrown over the garden wall. The explosions jolted the house, filling the air with smoke and glass. Everyone instinctively jumped under the dinner table. The force of the blast shattered most of the windows in the house, but luckily, the table was protected from the flying glass by a dividing wall. No one was injured. Spanish PBI volunteer María Gabriela Serra told the press, "If we'd been in the other room, we wouldn't be here to tell you about it."[11] Police who inspected the damage later stated that if the second grenade had been a few inches closer to the tanks of cooking gas, half the block would have gone up.

Shocked by the attack, yet grateful for their survival, PBI volunteers took turns spending the night watching for intruders—guarding the gaping holes that had once been windows. The next few days were spent frantically scheduling meetings with the diplomatic corps and government officials. Meanwhile, PBI's emergency response network barraged Cerezo with international telexes demanding that he investigate the attacks and ensure the safety of both PBI and the GAM. Unlike with previous PBI alerts, this time, European and North American citizens had been victimized. The resulting response was much greater. European and North American elected officials contacted Cerezo, demanding that their constituents be protected. Twenty-two members of the U.S. Congress wrote to Cerezo urging him "to investigate these bombings to demonstrate that attacks on human rights organizations will not be tolerated."[12]

On August 25, the PBI team held a reception in its newly repaired house. It was attended by the press, several ambassadors, and members of the Guatemalan Congress. Despite earlier insinuations by Interior Minister Valle Valdizan* that PBI and the GAM may have bombed themselves for publicity,[13] PBI diplomatically credited the government for its expressions of concern and declared unequivocally that it had no intention of leaving.[14]

The next day, the daily newspaper *El Gráfico* juxtaposed an article on the PBI reception with two other headlines: "U.S. Ambassador Condemns Attacks and Assassinations" and "USAID Gives $9.1 Million to Guatemala." Ambassador Michel did not say that funds from the United States were at

---

*Cerezo, in an apparent concession to those threatening him with coup attempts, had replaced moderate Interior Minister Rodíl Peralta with Valle Valdizan. Valle suggested that the late July international alerts over the GAM implied a prior knowledge of the mid-August attack.

risk, but he specifically took the opportunity of the signing of the U.S. Agency for International Development (USAID) agreement to express his concerns, naming, among other concerns, the attacks on PBI and the GAM.[15]

The violence kept increasing. On August 17, the army killed nine campesinos in the department of Alta Verapaz and then called it "a mistake." By August 25, seven student activists had been disappeared. Three more student activists disappeared in early September; some had been accompanied by PBI volunteers the previous spring when they had been threatened by the Jaguar of Justice death squad.

Sustained Terror

Meredith Larson, a U.S. volunteer, was twenty-three years old when she went to Guatemala. The daughter of a foreign service officer, she had grown up in suburban Virginia and had always been interested in political and international issues. After four years of student activism at Dartmouth, she began teaching health education at a high school. After hearing a former PBI volunteer describe his experience, she was inspired to go to Guatemala.

> Two weeks before I was to go down I found out the house was bombed. That was a little unnerving and I remember thinking, "Oh shit, this is pretty scary." PBI was cool about it: saying if I changed my mind that's OK. . . . I remember thinking, "How do I break this to my mother." She wasn't that pleased. Her first comment was: "Well, donating money is one thing, but donating a daughter is quite another."[16]

Meredith arrived in Guatemala in the midst of a spree of student killings and rumors of another coup. One of her first assignments was to accompany a young couple frantically trying to leave the country. The case didn't seem so dangerous at first, but when Meredith arrived at the house, the man had just received another death threat:

> The guy was already distressed 'cause he was trying to leave the country and now he was even more traumatized. So there I am with him in a mad panic trying to find his identity papers. When we left there were people watching us. I remember this white pickup truck nearby with no license plates, just the type of truck known to be used by the death squads.

Meredith realized that the situation was perhaps too serious for an inexperienced volunteer. She wanted to call PBI but, fearing surveillance on the telephone lines, didn't really know how much she could say about it. The Guatemalan woman went off alone to talk to the GAM and PBI but then didn't show up at either place.

> I was beginning to feel a little panicked, because we didn't know what had happened to her. The people I was with were unnerved thinking that the death squads had gotten her. They told me at one point, "we would be dead if you weren't here."

The Guatemalan woman eventually came back, unharmed, and Meredith spent the evening with them in a hotel.

> At midnight there was this banging at the door and we had all been dead asleep. Someone at the door was saying we had a phone call. We weren't expecting any calls, and I thought it was maybe someone trying to lure us out of there. So I just acted like I only spoke English until he went away. I was incredibly terrified at that point. All I could think was that they could break down the door with their machine guns, and I wasn't going to make a difference, they could do what they wanted. Later in the night it happened again.

Meredith found out later that one of the calls had been from the embassy, where the couple was making arrangements for asylum. They departed safely a few days later.

> After first being followed the day before, fearing the possible disappearance of the woman, the unexplained banging in the night, the incredible trauma of the people I was with—it was sustained terror for twenty-four hours.

On November 29, Guatemala and the international community were shocked by another high-profile attack: the abduction and brutal torture of U.S. nun Sister Dianna Ortiz. This attack garnered far more international pressure, and Ortiz was sheltered by the U.S. embassy before leaving the country. Ortiz, a missionary schoolteacher in rural Huehuetenango, testified that her kidnappers included not only uniformed Guatemalan police officers but also a North American who seemed to be ordering them about. (Five years later, retired General Hector Gramajo would be found guilty in absentia in U.S. Federal District Court of being ultimately responsible for Ortiz's torture and rape, along with several other attacks. Gramajo was judged to have "devised and directed . . . an indiscriminate campaign of terror against civilians" and was ordered to pay $47 million in civil damages. Gramajo scoffed at the ruling: "I don't have 47 million centavos!")[17]

Despite any doubts the bombings may have raised about PBI's effectiveness, requests for accompaniment increased during the fall. The national dialogue continued, and although Rigoberta Menchú and the RUOG considered it too dangerous to return, PBI again accompanied representatives of the Mexico-based refugees. In early December, the CUC, which had recently surfaced after nearly eight years underground, asked PBI to accompany one of its first large public events, a march of 600 campesinos from Chimaltenango to the capital.

The Knifing

At 7 P.M., on December 20, 1989, while U.S. troops were invading Panama, PBI volunteers Meredith Larson, Rusa Jeremic, and Mitch Goldberg were walking toward the PBI house in Guatemala City. Meredith wrote later:

> Less than a block from our house a dark figure appears three feet in front of me. He lunges at my chest. "NOOOOOOO!" I block. I feel the knife sink into my arm. Ohmigod, he has a KNIFE. I can't see anything. The light behind him is blinding. I swing my shoulder bag at him—I start to run, screaming. I run into the light and see the blood all over me. I trip and fall and lose my bag. Is he going to jump on me? It's not one but two, and they're running after my two friends, who have nothing to steal. The men are knifing, my friends are screaming. I jump up and start running again, yelling for help. There's more screaming. I don't know where it's coming from—then there's silence. The two attackers have gone: one running down one street, his companion down another.[18]

All three volunteers made it back to the PBI house. Mitch was wounded superficially in the hand, arm, and waist. Rusa received deeper wounds in the chest and shoulder. Meredith suffered serious nerve damage to her wrist. Other team members provided medical care and emotional support, but they also had to deal with the political implications of the attack and the fear it instilled. By now, they were certain that someone was trying to scare them out of the country. Team member María Serra noted: "After that I think they had to realize: if you knife them and they still don't leave . . . well, you either have to kill them, or accept that they're staying."[19]

A heated debate ensued among members of the steering committee of the PBI Guatemala project. Was PBI willing to risk such an apparently high probability of the death of a volunteer, for which it had no contingency plans? Did the risk make sense, since the protective value of the presence was in question? Meanwhile, everyone scrambled to right the balance—to stand the pillar of "protection" back up under the accompaniment edifice, with the most extensive campaign of international pressure yet attempted.

The week following the attack, PBI published an ad defending its work in every major Guatemalan newspaper. It was signed by dozens of members of the U.S. Congress, members of parliaments from Canada and Europe, international church leaders, and other well-known international figures. At the same time, ads condemning the attack on PBI were published by dozens of other Guatemalan organizations. Several embassies made public statements. U.S. Ambassador Thomas Stroock personally telephoned the families of the volunteers who had been attacked, and he visited the PBI house several times. Stroock condemned the attack publicly and told PBI volunteers that he suspected the same right-wing extremists who were trying to destabilize the Cerezo government. However, he also told visiting foreign delegations that the crime "was not political, just a street crime of passion, of Latin men getting excited over North American women."[20]

Meredith Larson returned to the United States for medical treatment. In January and February, she gave dozens of public presentations in the United States about her experience in Guatemala. She spent weeks going from one congressional office to another telling her story and urging the legislators to sign a letter to Cerezo. PBI's U.S. chapter organized its national network of supporters to barrage these same officials with constituent telephone calls. The letter sent to Cerezo was ultimately signed by 111 U.S. senators and representatives. Similar campaigns in Canada and Europe generated other high-level messages of concern.

U.S. Representative Theodore Weiss went on to submit an amendment to the 1990 appropriations bill conditioning military aid to Guatemala on the results of investigations of a list of human rights abuses, including the attack against PBI. Significantly, the text of the bill condemned human rights abuse in general, but four of the five specific cases named were non-Guatemalans, three of whom were U.S. citizens. A few months later, inn-keeper Michael Devine, another U.S. citizen, was murdered by Guatemalan soldiers, after which overt U.S. military aid to Guatemala was suspended altogether.*

The PBI team in Guatemala moved into a more secure house in April 1990 and held another reception for the diplomatic and press corps. The organization had achieved a new prominence both in and out of Guatemala. Through international organizing and local diplomacy, the image of "protection" was reclaimed. U.S. military aid to Guatemala had been directly threatened because of attacks on U.S. citizens. PBI now frequented government offices, and ambassadors visited the PBI house. The violent attacks against PBI stopped.

According to PBI volunteer María Gabriela Serra, "From the moment of the bombing, we achieved a legitimacy with the authorities that we'd never had before. . . . When you have government ministers and ambassadors coming to your house, that's sending a clear message to the death squads. They'd better take care, because this is who they're messing with."[21]

Volunteer Janey Skinner wrote home about the effect the whole series of attacks was having on the team:

*An internal U.S. Department of State memo, released in 1996 after pressure from Dianna Ortiz and Jennifer Harbury (wife of a disappeared guerrilla commander), accused the Guatemalan government of carrying out a high-level cover-up of the Devine murder, designed to "outlast Washington's anger" (*Reuters*, May 6, 1996). Despite the eventual "official" military aid cut-off, the United States continued to secretly train Guatemala's Kaibil forces. According to ex-Ambassador Stroock, the CIA kept numerous Guatemalan officers on its payroll, and the embassy and the Drug Enforcement Agency collaborated closely with the Guatemalan army well into the 1990s, citing the "war on drugs" as justification (letters from ex-Ambassador Thomas Stroock and investigative journalist Allan Nairn to *The Nation*, May 29, 1996).

Is it possible to be perfectly rational *and* incredibly paranoid? . . . A car slows down on the street, I go to the window to check what it is. Even in my sleep I can hear if a car is idling outside. A man follows me half a block on a city street, yelling "*Venga! Venga!*" [Come here!], and even though I know he probably just wants to sell me something, a special touristic deal just for me, I am frightened and duck into the first café. I am jumpy about all sorts of things, about using the telephone, about cars parked with people inside them, about people who stare at me in the airport. . . . Caution seems like a physical sense, like smell or hearing, a fear that has become corporeal.

The fear was no longer abstract or vicarious. The demands of political follow-up and continued accompaniment added the stress of mental burnout to the trauma of fear. For sanity, volunteers depended on the camaraderie of other team members and the encouragement of Guatemalan activists. Meredith remembered after the knifing:

So many Guatemalans came to our house after the knifing, saying, "We're so glad you're here. . . . You have helped. . . . You are important to us. . . . Because you've been there to watch, we've been able to go on with our struggle with less risk." It is some sick measure of our success that some people have been trying very hard to frighten us into leaving, with the death threats, bombing and this attack.[22]

This "sick measure of success" argument was echoed by many of PBI's contacts in the popular movement. They would point to their own history and say, "When you start to be really effective, they attack you." But of course, for PBI, the argument was self-contradictory: the whole notion of accompaniment as a protection is that you're effective because they *won't* attack you.

Prior to these attacks, PBI had been seen as the organization that had protected the rise of the GAM and the CERJ. Now it was the international group that had gotten bombed and knifed. Its "success rate" was slightly tarnished: the GAM, after all, had been bombed with PBI volunteers inside. For prospective team volunteers, the reassuring myth of immunity was now shattered. Some looked at the new reality of risk and changed their minds.

Guatemalans made jokes about "who is protecting whom?" but they respected PBI's steadfastness and kept asking for PBI accompaniment. If the bombing and knifing temporarily reduced the sense of protection that PBI's accompaniment offered, this was more than countered by the long-term increase in confidence in the organization. Union activist Sergio Guzman placed these doubts in perspective:

The violence in Guatemala has no borders, it's indiscriminate. At times it has neither ideology nor social position, because even the economic elite and politically powerful are sometimes touched by it, while the popular sectors are attacked constantly. . . . We always considered accompaniment only a minimal protection, but if the accompaniment itself is violated, no one can guarantee security.[23]

Political space perceptions are constantly changing, so the attacks against PBI did not necessarily imply a decrease in the protective value of its accompaniment. The attacks against PBI may have been symptomatic of an overall increase in violence and the closing of space for popular action. Within this changing context, everything was more dangerous, but accompaniment could still offer some protection to a threatened activist who chose to continue organizing. The lines were all shifting, but the dynamics of the decision were the same. (See figures 8.1–8.7.)

There are only two plausible theories as to who attacked PBI and the GAM: it was either an official arm of the security forces or one of the active ultra-right-wing paramilitary organizations. Shortly after the August bombings, a U.S. Department of Defense intelligence report—classified "secret" until 1996—stated that the "Special Operations" section of the D-2 (Guatemalan Army Directorate of Intelligence) was responsible. It went on to suggest that "the D-2 has used the recent disturbances as a cover to intimidate leftist opposition organizations."[24]

Nineth de García, citing anonymous sources, blamed the Department of Presidential Security. President Cerezo insists that this was the one security force whose activities he was fully aware of and that it could not have been them. He blames all the violence that autumn on the right-wing army officials who were supporting coup plans against him. Their motive, according to Cerezo, was to create a climate of governmental lack of control.[25] An arrest warrant was issued for right-wing activist Lionel Sisniega, leader of the Movement for National Liberation Party (the party of Castillo Armas after the 1954 CIA coup, which had openly admitted death-squad support in the past, earning the nickname "the party of organized violence"). Sisniega disappeared from sight for a few months. He was never arrested, but his son, a captain in that same Department of Presidential Security, was quietly packed off to the Guatemalan embassy in Venezuela, "until the situation concerning his father had been cleared up," according to another U.S. Defense Department report.[26]

An argument that the subsequent international pressure actually deterred continued attacks depends on the answers to two questions: First, were additional attacks planned? One might assume so if the motive behind the attacks was to frighten PBI out of the country, but there is no direct supporting evidence. Second, were such plans called off because of the international pressure? This pressure certainly affected Cerezo and Gramajo, who were scrambling to limit additional damage. But could they control the more extreme right-wing military or paramilitary groups?

"The Guatemalan army allows *no* armed competition," according to Guatemalan human rights lawyer Frank LaRue. Most human rights analysts we spoke with felt that the Guatemalan army was far too well organized to allow fringe groups to damage its program, even if there were some level of decentralization in the system or some "loose cannons." If the army approves of independent paramilitary actions, it might not intervene. But if such actions cause problems, it will. Even President Cerezo concurred with this analysis: "the government can always increase the control it has over such groups if it's pressured to do so."[27]

Nevertheless, we cannot discount the possibility that Gramajo and even Cerezo may have been fully aware of the attacks—or had, perhaps, ordered them. For the D-2 to bomb and potentially kill foreigners without superior orders would be a serious breach of discipline. Gramajo may have allowed these and other scandalous attacks in order to placate hard-liners who were threatening to replace him. The internal benefits of the attacks may have been judged to exceed the external political costs.

In any case, with or without superior orders, in the fall of 1989, internal schisms in the state terror system led to a temporary breakdown in centralized control, allowing for attacks against foreigners that were politically damaging to the Cerezo-Gramajo program. After several months of heavy international pressure and internal maneuvering in the military, the breakdown was mended and the pace of the attacks slowed.

From the perspective of the right-wing factions, attacking PBI may have been previously inconceivable: unacceptable space. But in the immediate context of dozens of other bombings, high-profile political killings, and internal conflicts in the army, it may have seemed, temporarily, more acceptable. When the situation calmed down, the political space mapping shifted again: the cost of such attacks again became unacceptable.

PBI did not have the luxury of waiting for the situation to calm down. Using international grassroots organizing and high-level diplomatic pressure, it worked to force that "impunity space" closed again and emerged from the process with greater legitimacy and recognition in Guatemala.

Expelling Murder Witnesses: The Olga María Incident

March 11, 1991: The scene is a large plantation known as Olga María near Tiquisate, on Guatemala's rich southern coast. A few kilometers down the access road from the highway, a driveway leads up to the owner's stately home. In the field across from the driveway is a mass of hastily erected shacks, temporary home to about sixty landless campesino families who invaded the land a month before. A hundred armed policemen are on the road, facing the families and their shantytown. Between them are two Peace Brigades volunteers, watching.

Through the hot, humid air, a policeman's voice over a megaphone gives orders for a forced expulsion. The riot police fan out on both sides and begin to close in, destroying the flimsy shacks in their path. When they launch tear gas into the crowd, tension erupts into chaos. The campesinos, surrounded, start to fight back, throwing sticks and whatever else they can get their hands on. There is a volley of shots. María del Carmen Anavisca Secaida falls to the ground, a bullet through her head. The police chief shouts, "Cease fire!" and orders a retreat.

The deed is done. María Anavisca, mother of five children, is dead. By intent or by accident, from a crowd of hundreds, the police have killed one of the few spokeswomen in the group. For Peace Brigades, a terrible precedent has been set: someone has been killed right in front of their accompaniment. The significance of this was not lost on the government.

The Olga María incident came during a political transition in Guatemala. In December, a massacre of fifteen civilians by the army in Santiago Atitlán had captured national and international attention, resulting in an unprecedented closure of a local military base by popular pressure. The same month, conservative Jorge Serrano won the presidential election with strong support from the South Coast, bastion of the traditional agricultural oligarchy. General Gramajo had retired, and under President Serrano, the leadership of the military high command shifted steadily toward the "hard-liners."

When the Olga María incident occurred, the Serrano government's delegation had just returned from its first UN human rights session in Geneva, where it had emphasized Serrano's commitments to human rights and peace negotiations. Serrano blamed previous governments for the country's problems and managed to come out of the Geneva session without the embarrassment of having the UN send a special rapporteur for human rights to Guatemala. In the U.S. Congress, though, aid to Guatemala was still drawing heavy fire.

While appeasing international human rights concerns, Serrano also had to respond to the demands of his conservative constituency in the army and the oligarchy. Army hard-liners did not like their bases being shut down by popular pressure. The oligarchy was even less happy about allowing poor campesinos to invade their land.

Meanwhile, the Peace Brigades team was frantically active. Threats had increased against the labor movement and the CERJ. Full-time accompaniment had started with the Communities of Population in Resistance (CPR). The national dialogue continued, with its heavy accompaniment demands. Because repression in the countryside was increasing, the team put a high priority on rural accompaniment.

The Southern Pro-Land Committee had organized the land takeover of a portion of the Olga María plantation on February 4, 1991. A few days later, fifty members camped out for three weeks in front of the National Palace, demanding that the government resolve their need for land. The Pro-Land Committee argued that the Olga María land had been stolen from some of their families in 1959, still contained their communal cemetery, and was illegally occupied by the current plantation owner.[28] On February 13, representatives of the interior ministry and the human rights ombudsman went to Tiquisate and managed to convince the campesinos to leave the land, promising them a meeting with Serrano. After that meeting, the government offered the families a plot in Alta Verapaz, which they rejected as too small.

Next the oligarchy got into the debate, with the Chamber of Agriculture denouncing all land invasions as illegal and criticizing the government for negotiating rather than enforcing the law. With negotiations stalled, the families reoccupied the Olga María plantation on February 26, asking PBI volunteers to stay with them. PBI paid a brief visit to the land that week.

Accompanying a land invasion put PBI in a legally ambiguous situation. The peasants claimed to own the land, but the plantation owner was recognized as such by the government and the courts. Therefore, the volunteers were going onto private property, a potentially illegal act. Sensing this risk, on each visit, the PBI volunteers went and spoke with the plantation administrator, explaining their presence and their role as observers. These meetings were friendly, and PBI was never asked to leave.

PBI visited again on March 8 and 9. Police arrived and ordered the families to leave. They refused. PBI volunteers spoke with the police, again explaining their role as observers. The police politely checked their IDs and left. Sensing that an expulsion was imminent, PBI kept a constant presence after that.

On March 11, the police attempted the expulsion, killed María Anavisca, and then retired to a position a few kilometers away to await further orders. Two PBI volunteers witnessed the shooting. One stayed with the families, and the other immediately left for the capital. That night, the team initiated an international human rights alert. The next morning, two other PBI volunteers set out to join their colleague at the Olga María plantation.

Before they got there, at about 8 A.M., a heavily armed detail of soldiers and police arrived at Olga María to complete the eviction. The families were in the midst of a wake for María Anavisca. Wanting no repeat of the previous day's tragedy, they quietly acquiesced, asking only that they be allowed to finish the wake. While the police and soldiers waited, the PBI volunteer and ten campesinos were told that President Serrano wanted to meet with them in the capital, and they were invited into a police vehicle.

The other two volunteers bound for the plantation were also picked up by the police. Though they were never informed of a formal arrest, by afternoon all three volunteers were being questioned in the office of Foreign Relations Minister Alvaro Arzú. Arzú met privately with the volunteers' respective ambassadors and then gave the volunteers fifteen minutes to choose among three alternatives: be legally deported; be handed over to the courts and charged with "illegal involvement in an event resulting in a woman's death"; or offer an act of diplomatic "goodwill" and agree to leave the country immediately, voluntarily, under the protection of their embassies. They were told in no uncertain terms that if they refused to leave or made a fuss, the entire PBI team would be expelled, and their lives might even be in danger. This was no choice at all, and at their ambassadors' insistence, all three signed a notarized statement agreeing to leave voluntarily and asserting that there had been no ill treatment or pressure of any sort.

The ambassadors brought the three home that evening and explained to the rest of the team that the PBI presence on the property was illegal and that their situation in the country was quite delicate. They pointed out that Arzú and Serrano were under pressure from hard-line sectors to respond much more severely and had actually offered them a good deal. The "deal" was that Arzú would keep PBI's name out of things and that there would be no further problems for the organization. The government would publicly defend the expulsion of three "foreigners" without reference to PBI. In exchange, PBI would make no public statement; for the team's own safety, they had to avoid speaking to the press, make no further contact with the Southern Pro-Land Committee, and avoid the Tiquisate region.

The ambassadors were emphatic. The team was dazed. Volunteers were facing a threat of expulsion and the possibility of legal indictment for partial responsibility for María Anavisca's death. They had three traumatized team members who had signed affidavits agreeing to leave. They were being told that their safety depended on their silence—in essence, their own ambassadors were transmitting death threats. The team knew that it had already alerted the organization's international alert network and that President Serrano was going to start getting pressure just when it had been advised to be quiet. Intimidated and paralyzed, unable to clearly analyze the situation, the PBI team called the project office in Toronto and insisted that the emergency alert be canceled.

All these events finally hit the headlines the next day, March 13: "Police evict the invaders," "One dead in eviction," "Three foreigners expelled for instigating the campesinos."[29] The expulsion of the "foreigners" got a great deal more coverage than the killing of María Anavisca. The afternoon paper, however, carried the intriguing headline, "Peace Brigades maintains complete secrecy," and the next day, "Diplomatic silence" at the embassies.[30]

PBI had witnessed what its presence was supposed to deter, but it was silent. This silence was confusing to popular movement organizations, many of which were making press statements daily, defending the land invasion, defending PBI, and condemning the killing. Government officials continued to accuse "the foreigners" of instigating the event, and they accused the campesino families of having fired on the police. Columnists and editorials condemned foreign agitators. Interior Minister Mendez Ruiz stated that María Anavisca had been beaten to death by the other campesinos.[31] Speaking to Congress, Mendez Ruiz hinted that PBI volunteers were responsible for the death.[32]

Outside Guatemala, PBI's "silence" was virtually impossible to achieve. An international alert cannot be stopped once it starts. It spreads like a wildfire, with each contact calling numerous others to generate a rapid response. The fact that PBI volunteers had witnessed a police killing was public knowledge internationally hours before Arzú and the ambassadors cautioned PBI to be silent. Nonetheless, PBI offices around the world tried to honor the team's request. They did not know the details of the risks the team faced, so even though many felt that it was a mistake, they did their best to reduce the response.

This process was probably useful to Serrano. For example, the Western Hemisphere subcommittee of the U.S. House of Representatives had a hearing on Guatemala scheduled for March 13. Upon receiving news of the killing, PBI offices in the United States had quickly contacted witnesses who were to testify at that hearing. When the alert was called off, the U.S. office had to call these witnesses back and ask them not to use PBI's name and not to assert that PBI had witnessed the killings.

As the days passed and the slander continued in the press, PBI realized that it needed to defend itself. By now, several members of the project's steering committee had flown in from Europe and North America to help out. Finally, on March 19, more than a week after the killing, PBI issued a public statement:

> [We] postponed any public declarations until [the volunteers] had left the country so as to guarantee their safety. We now consider it our responsibility—to the Truth and to our commitment to Peace and Justice—to publish an account of the events to which we were witness"[33]

The statement went on to confirm what everyone already knew: that PBI volunteers had witnessed the killing and that the national police were responsible. The expulsion was also explained, including the threats outlined by Foreign Minister Arzú. PBI defended its presence on the land, stating that neither the plantation administrator nor the police had ever objected.

With the silence broken, PBI began to regain its balance. In the next several weeks, volunteers visited embassies and government officials, emphasizing the organization's commitment to nonviolence, to nonintervention in the internal affairs of Guatemala, and, most importantly, to acting within the law. In essence, the PBI team had tried something new—the accompaniment of a land invasion—and this expansion of available political space had been sternly rebuffed. PBI now knew the boundaries of its political space, and the essential message of its postcrisis diplomatic effort was that the error would not be repeated.

Ex-President Cerezo later bluntly summarized the power relationships within which PBI was operating:

> In this country land is still the nucleus of power. The stockholders of three large banks own most of the land, which is the principal source of wealth. These landowners have great power locally as well: they chat with the local commanders and tell them that the guerrillas are supporting local land occupations. They convince them they have an enemy in common, and so the army acts against the campesinos. Then, with accusations against foreigners, they try to convert the local problem of land occupations into an international political problem. The occupations are then blamed on this myth of international subversives who are meddling illegally. Then of course the newspapers echo the accusations, because they're controlled by the same people.[34]

The Olga María invasion could not have been accompanied without entering onto private property. PBI had often accompanied labor union struggles in which factories had occupied, but the volunteers could stand across the street on public property or watch from the outside. That was impossible here. The plantation was huge: "outside" was several kilometers away and out of sight. The only way to observe the situation was to be right in there with the campesinos.

The moral argument for such accompaniment was compelling; the deadly expulsion of the campesinos only confirmed it. The political importance of the issue was equally compelling, since land inequities were at the root of Guatemala's centuries-old political crisis. The campesinos on the Olga María plantation represented millions of other landless Guatemalans facing the same poverty and frustration.

So PBI walked onto private property and opened itself up to charges of illegal action—the Achilles heel of an international organization. It is an ill-defined line, but once an organization crosses it, the host government no longer has to tolerate its presence, and embassies are less obliged to maintain support. PBI had faced accusations of being "instigators" and "troublemakers" for seven years, ever since the formation of the GAM, but the legal uncertainties in this instance gave those smears more credibility.

Serrano had a dilemma on his hands the moment the Southern Pro-Land Committee invaded the farm in early February. He resolved it by delaying action until the Geneva human rights meeting was over, and then proceeding with a violent eviction to appease the oligarchy. PBI's deterrence failed to prevent the eviction because Serrano had too much to gain from it. PBI failed to prevent the shooting as well, probably because in the heat of action, the police were no longer considering the accompaniment. Once María Anavisca was dead, Serrano faced another problem: damage control. The expulsion of the three PBI volunteers did not prevent the news of the killing from getting out, but it did give the national press a powerful diversion in the week that followed.

PBI learned a great deal from this painful experience. Foreign Minister Arzú, who would be elected president as a "moderate" in 1995, maneuvered PBI and the volunteers' ambassadors into a corner. In an example of effective but subtle state terror, Arzú, or Serrano through Arzú, threatened expulsion and criminal prosecution, frightening the organization into silence. Arzú convinced the ambassadors to back him up, arguing that it was the best deal available compared with the harsher, perhaps deadly, punishment desired by Serrano's ultra-Right supporters. The PBI team folded under Serrano and Arzu's swift offensive, and this weakness cannot have sparked confidence in the popular movement that looked to the organization for protection.

PBI's own damage control after the event resulted in an arrangement for special visas for PBI volunteers, sanctioned by the Guatemalan Congress—a considerable achievement. In April, PBI held a reception for the diplomatic corps and press: a public reclamation of lost political space. Arzú himself attended, perhaps as a peace offering. PBI volunteers and teams began to study more carefully the legal implications of each of their planned actions. PBI also worked more deliberately on team support and mental health, conscious that its own teams were as vulnerable to the debilitating psychological effects of state terror and political threats as the Guatemalans they hoped to serve.

In the flurry of press and government attacks, one columnist came to PBI's defense. Miguel Angel Albizures, the labor activist whose return to Guatemala PBI had accompanied in 1987, wrote a column in the *Siglo Veintiuno* entitled "Terrorists or Peace Brigades?"

> The Brigade members are not terrorists. . . . They are men and women who love peace; they are human shields. . . . The volunteers are present in countries where security forces are incapable of guaranteeing the safety of their people. . . . In Guatemala, many of us, committed to change and human rights—we are utopian. Utopian because we believe that the presence—the body of a foreigner beside our own will ensure that our lives are respected. We think that death squads and the authorities fear the political consequences were they to kill one of those human shields. . . . We are utopian because at the Olga María farm a bullet to the head killed a young woman defending a piece of land. . . . We are utopian because the hundreds of leaders and workers for social change can't possibly have as many human shields as they need. . . .

Only cavemen could accuse as terrorists those who merely wish another destiny for our country. If in Guatemala we want tourists instead of peace brigades, we'd better rid our land of terror. Public opinion leaders have a grave responsibility to stop writing from caves.[35]

Despite repeated efforts to close the political space for the popular movement and for accompaniment, the early 1990s was a period of rapid expansion for both. A new and powerful movement for Mayan rights developed, with dozens of new organizations. PBI began accompanying many of these new groups, while continuing its work with the GAM, CERJ, and the union movement. In addition, many organizations began setting up their own "private" accompaniment, in which volunteers unconnected with any international organization lived and worked in their offices, doing accompaniment, office work, and other support tasks. The Guatemalan popular movement was now embracing accompaniment wholeheartedly, and the demand could not be met by a single organization.

Notes

1. Miguel Angel Albizures, tape-recorded interview by authors, Guatemala, July 14, 1994.
2. Scott, *Two Years of Witness*. Scott was a volunteer with PBI, accompanying Menchú in 1988 and 1989.
3. Frank LaRue, interview by authors, Guatemala, August 1994.
4. LaRue interview.
5. *El Gráfico*, December 18, 1988.
6. Americas Watch, *Persecuting Human Rights Monitors*.
7. President Vinicio Cerezo Arevalo, interview by authors, Guatemala, August 1994.
8. Patty Mutchnick, letter to authors, 1995 (undated).
9. Americas Watch, *Messengers of Death*.
10. Blanca de Hernandez, interview by authors, Guatemala, July 13, 1994.
11. "Lanzaron Dos Grenadas a las Brigadas de Paz," *Prensa Libre*, August 16, 1989.
12. U.S. Congress, letter sponsored by Representatives Boxer and Foglietta, to Cerezo, September 6, 1989.
13. *La Hora*, August 16, 1989; *Prensa Libre*, August 17, 1989; *El Gráfico*, August 18, 1989.
14. PBI press release, August 25, 1989.
15. *El Gráfico*, August 26, 1989.
16. Meredith Larson, tape-recorded interview by authors, San Francisco, February 6, 1994. Subsequent quotes are from this interview unless otherwise noted.
17. Wilkinson, "'Democracy' Comes to Guatemala."
18. Larson, "Model Mugging Graduate Defends Herself."
19. Maria Serra, interview by authors. Barcelona, June 29, 1994.
20. Nairn, "Exchange."
21. Serra interview.
22. Meredith Larson, letter to friends, December 28, 1989.
23. Sergio Guzman, interview by authors, Guatemala, July 18, 1994.
24. Intelligence Oversight Board (IOB), "Report on the Guatemala Review," U.S. State Department, June 28, 1996.
25. Cerezo interview.
26. IOB, "Guatemala Review."
27. LaRue interview; Cerezo interview; Oswaldo Enriquez (Guatemala Human Rights Commission), tape-recorded interview by authors, Guatemala, August 1994.

28. Comite Pro-Tierra Del Sur, press release, February 20, 1991.
29. *Prensa Libre*, March 13, 1991, p. 2; *El Gráfico*, March 13, 1991, p. 1; *Prensa Libre*, March 13, 1991, p. 1.
30. *La Hora*, March 13, 1991, p. 1; *El Gráfico*, March 14, 1991, p. 5.
31. "Castigarán a responsables," *El Gráfico*, March 14, 1991, p. 4.
32. "Their own ambassadors denounced their compatriots as instigators, which is why the three foreigners were captured and handed over for deportation, after SIPROCI had come to the farm and found a dead body" ("Mendez-Ruiz en el Congreso," *Diario de CentroAmerica*, March 14, 1991).
33. PBI, press release, March 19, 1991.
34. Cerezo interview.
35. Miguel Angel Albizures, "Terroristas o brigadas de paz?" *Siglo Veintiuno*, April 4, 1991.

10

The Refugee Return: The Institutionalization of Accompaniment

O N JANUARY 20, 1993, a caravan of seventy-eight buses carrying 2,480 refugees crossed the border back into Guatemala. International volunteers were inside every bus. Over the next few years, the "returnees" resettled in dozens of small communities in northern Guatemala, frequently in war zones, and always with international accompaniment. "The Return," as it was called in Guatemala, was a milestone in the national struggle to overcome fear. Salvadoran refugees had set the example four years earlier, returning en masse to their homes despite government resistance.[1] Learning from the Salvadoran experience, Guatemalan refugees went a step further, negotiating conditions of their Return in advance. The result was also a turning point for the role of international accompaniment. For the first time, the Guatemalan government signed an agreement accepting a threatened population's right to have accompaniment of its own choosing.

The returning refugees, survivors of the army's scorched-earth campaigns in 1981 and 1982, were among the most traumatized people in Guatemala. Many had suffered or witnessed torture and village massacres. With little more than the clothes on their backs, they had fled north across the border. To them, the Guatemalan government *was* that army of 1982—an inhuman enemy who had tried to annihilate them and who, even as the Return was under way, continued to threaten them and label them "guerrillas." Against this threat, the refugees saw international accompaniment as an essential shield.

The army, meanwhile, saw the refugees as supporters of the guerrilla movement. It knew that guerrillas frequented refugee camps in Mexico. The army saw refugee propaganda apparently echoing guerrilla demands. The refugees were choosing to return to the areas where the guerrillas had maintained their most consistent operations for over a decade—specifically, the Ixcán jungle region, the northernmost municipality of the El Quiché province. Future returns were also planned for other areas, particularly Huehuetenango, Alta Verapaz, and the Peten, but the largest and earliest returns all went to the Ixcán, which is the focus of this chapter. The army

believed that the guerrillas wanted the refugees to repopulate that region in order to re-create the friendly civilian "cover" that had been so brutally eliminated in the early 1980s. The army's theory of guerrilla manipulation explained the apparently self-destructive decision to return to the Ixcán, the most dangerous area in the country, when the government was offering the returnees alternative lands in other regions.

The army did not want the refugees to return to the Ixcán. Nor did it want international accompaniment getting in the way of what it perceived to be essential military operations. Military leaders knew that every casualty of their operations would be labeled an innocent civilian victim. "Crimes," which the army considered legitimate acts of war, would be broadcast worldwide by the foreigners in the region. The army also feared that international NGOs and volunteers outside of military control would become a conduit for logistical and material support for the guerrillas.

International realities, however, conflicted with this tactical military analysis. The government was still trying to clean up its international image, and the Return could be either a windfall or a scandal. The world was watching the refugees in a way that no other Guatemalan population had ever been watched. A solid international base of support for their return extended from the highest levels of foreign governments to mainstream development agencies. So the Guatemalan government had the additional incentive of knowing that the Return would bring with it considerable foreign development aid.

The refugees had originally colonized the Ixcán region in the late 1960s, drawn by the availability of land and the possibility of two harvests each year. Cut off from most of Guatemala by impassable mountains, they faced relentless heat, malaria and other diseases, and a constant struggle against a dense and fast-growing jungle. With no roads and no government services, they built their own clinics, schools, and markets. Supported by the Catholic Church and Maryknoll missionary Bill Woods, they formed cooperatives and marketed their crops to other regions using small planes.

The army approved the colonization, seeing the need for a labor force to develop the region. But the growing strength of the cooperatives and the leadership of the church were threats to army control over the development process. Father Bill Woods was assassinated in 1975, and his successor was later expelled. Other cooperative leaders were killed or threatened.

The army strategy of economic and political control changed to one of widespread terror and extermination in response to the growing strength of the guerrilla rebellion in the early 1980s. In the scorched-earth campaigns of 1981–83, the Ixcán was only one municipality among dozens destroyed in rapid succession. In his book *Massacres of the Jungle*, Ricardo Falla details the army's relentless 1982 sweep of the Ixcán, documenting the deaths of 773 civilians during ten distinct massacres.[2]

The scorched-earth policy resulted in a dramatic exodus. From the Ixcán and other regions near the border, Guatemalans fled north into Mexico. Funded by the United Nations High Commissioner for Refugees (UNHCR), the Mexican government set up a refugee commission, known as COMAR, and began establishing temporary camps. Two thousand refugees were registered in 1981. By the end of 1982, there were over 30,000 registered refugees in the border state of Chiapas. By the time of the Return in 1993, there were 43,500 registered refugees in COMAR/UNHCR camps. Estimates of additional unregistered refugees in Mexico ranged from 50,000 to 160,000.[3]

Guatemalan newspapers as early as mid-1984 discussed the government's efforts to get the refugees to repatriate in order to improve its image. Later, the Cerezo government set up a Special Commission for Attention to

Repatriates (CEAR) and encouraged a return. But military leaders were still accusing the refugees of supporting the guerrillas, and the news of ongoing human rights abuse in Guatemala was reaching the camps in Mexico. Fear and distrust were preventing a mass return.*

Negotiating the Return

In Mexico, conditions were difficult, but the refugees were safe and free to organize—more so than in most civilian communities in Guatemala. From the patchwork of surviving remnants of different ethnic groups, they regained a sense of unity and organization. In 1987 and 1988, the Permanent Commissions of the Guatemalan Refugees in Mexico (CCPP) were formed— a democratically elected leadership body that represented all the official refugee camps in Chiapas, Campeche, and Quintana Roo. In March 1988, the CCPP sent a letter to President Cerezo outlining five conditions for their return: that their legitimate right to their original land be recognized, that they have the unrestricted right to organize upon their return, that the government guarantee their safety, that only civilian government authorities be allowed on their lands and that the army be excluded, and,

> That we be allowed to have both international governmental and nongovernmental organizations accompany us on our return to the country, and that they be allowed to stay with us as witnesses to the fulfillment of our petitions and as support for the achievement of our full economic, social, and political participation in the country.[4]

These conditions were to change only slightly over the next five years. It took four years just to get the Guatemalan government to start discussing them with the CCPP.

The 1989 national dialogue prompted the refugees, through their Permanent Commissions, to attempt their first formal visits back to Guatemala. The UNHCR initially declared that the moment the refugee emissaries crossed the border, they would lose their individual refugee status and be subject to Guatemalan repatriation law. Then both the UNHCR and the Guatemalan government insisted that the refugees could not make independent contact with other popular movement organizations. Such "meddling in internal politics," they said, was inappropriate for those who were maintaining refugee status.

*Between 1984 and October 1990, 5,785 persons were repatriated. UNHCR lists later repatriation numbers as only 964 in 1989, 740 in 1990, and 1,765 in 1992. This is less than the birthrate in the camps; thus, the refugee population was increasing (U.S. Committee for Refugees, *El Retorno*).

Since a key objective of the visits was to forge links within Guatemala in order to build sufficient pressure to force the government to negotiate, the refugees insisted on their right to contact other groups, and the government and UNHCR relented. But the refugees concluded from this struggle that the UNHCR could not be counted on to protect their interests, as it was either aligned with, or controlled by, the government. This understanding reinforced the refugees' later demand for control over the choice of non-governmental accompaniment for the return process.

When the first five CCPP members came into Guatemala in early March 1989, they brought with them representatives of the Mexican and Spanish solidarity movements. They were met at the border by PBI volunteers and escorted for the next ten days. UNHCR accompaniment was important and carried greater political weight, but the refugees had more trust in the volunteers who had no governmental connection.[5] The national dialogue continued in 1990 and 1991, and with each visit, the CCPP gained greater support within the popular movement. On every visit, the members were accompanied by foreign NGOs.

In 1991, a mediating commission was established consisting of the UNHCR, the Guatemalan Catholic Church, the governmental human rights ombudsman, and the exiled Guatemala Human Rights Commission. After the first formal meeting, Guatemalan Vice President Gustavo Espina insinuated that the return process was being manipulated by the guerrillas.

While the government stalled, international pressure was building. Momentum was also growing within the refugee camps. The primary motivation for the refugees was the possibility of getting their land back. In addition, many refugee children had never seen Guatemala, and their parents were concerned over the loss of cultural identity in Mexico. The refugees also felt pressure from Mexico and the UNHCR. Humanitarian support for the camps was diminishing, as was the refugees' access to jobs in the region.

In November 1991, a "letter of understanding" between the Guatemalan government and the UNHCR guaranteed security and free passage to NGOs to carry out humanitarian and nonpolitical work during the repatriation, on the conditions that they have legal status and be "duly authorized" by CEAR. Such conditions might seem reasonable were it not for the fact that access to legal status in Guatemala is under tight political control. PBI, for instance, had been struggling through red tape and deliberate political roadblocks in the legal registration process since 1985, with no success. Other accompaniment organizations had not even bothered to attempt it. The government wanted to control *which* NGOs would be allowed to participate.

In February 1992, a new level of international observation came into the negotiation process with the formation of GRICAR, the International

Group for Consulting and Support of the Return. GRICAR consisted of representatives of the Canadian, Swedish, Mexican, and French embassies; the International Council of Voluntary Agencies; and the World Council of Churches. GRICAR was authorized to sit in on the negotiations—without voting power—and to move informally behind the scenes to bring the two sides closer together. GRICAR's diplomatic clout had a major impact on the negotiations.

The demand for accompaniment was not the most difficult of the refugees' conditions. One of the toughest was the proposed demilitarization of the returnee communities. The refugees wanted no part of the civil patrol system and wanted exemption from military recruitment, privileges denied to the rest of the highland population. But they went much further, demanding the absolute exclusion of the military from their communities. This was inconceivable to the army, which was still fighting a war in the region.

The other seemingly unresolvable problem was land access. The refugees who had owned land wanted their own parcels back. They also expected the government to find land for those who did not own parcels, and they wished to stay together as whole communities. The Guatemalan legal system was inept at dealing with land tenure problems even under normal circumstances. Parcels commonly have multiple titles. The refugees' land had often been deliberately recolonized with army supporters. It might take decades to straighten out the land needs of 40,000 refugees. Any agreement with the refugees would call attention to the vastly larger—and potentially explosive—problem of land access for the over a million internally displaced Guatemalans.

In the years to come, not surprisingly, these two thorny issues—demilitarization and land access—would cause most of the conflicts that international volunteers witnessed. The accompaniment condition, in contrast, seemed easy at first: agreement "in principle" was reached at the first negotiation in March 1992, though without specific wording. No one questioned whether the return would be accompanied. What was at stake in the ensuing months of discussions was *who would control and select the accompaniment.*

The refugees, walking back into the lion's den, were adamant. They would not go without international accompaniment of their own choosing. The UNHCR was ambivalent. Some of its staff were insulted that the refugees publicly doubted the UNHCR's ability to protect them, and additional accompaniment seemed unnecessary and costly. They considered it their traditional role to stand up for refugee demands, but their support was erratic. The government was satisfied with NGOs bringing funding or infrastructure projects, but it did not want foreigners along for purely "political" reasons. Claiming a legitimate right to control the NGO presence, the government argued that it couldn't do a responsible job of protecting the returnees without carefully monitoring any outside parties that got involved in the process.[6]

The government wanted to limit the negative image that international observers would project to the outside world. According to Mediating Commission member Anantonia Reyes, "They didn't want to lay themselves bare for that sort of inspection."

> It took a lot to convince them that this was simply a cost they would have to bear. In the event that things went wrong, the accompaniment was undoubtedly going to point it out, but the accompaniment had other dimensions beyond mere criticism. I have to emphasize that GRICAR, and especially the Canadian representative, lobbied to convince the government. GRICAR pointed out to them that there would be much worse criticism and denunciation for denying the refugees access to accompaniment than for accepting it.[7]

On October 8, 1992, the final accords were signed, paving the way for mass returns. Many were skeptical of the government's commitment or its ability to fulfill its end of the bargain, but the refugees had nevertheless accomplished a historic victory. They controlled when and where the returns would occur.

The accords exempted returning refugees from military service for at least three years. The best they could achieve regarding overall demilitarization, however, was a sentence stating that "the Government of Guatemala recognizes the civilian and peaceful character of the returnee population, and is committed to observe that in all stages of the Return process, regulations which the government establishes be in concordance with this peaceful and civilian nature of the population." The accords did not prohibit the army from entering or passing through their communities. The returnees would have to keep struggling on this issue.

The final text of the accompaniment accord was specific, yet it left vast areas open to interpretation:

> Accompaniment for the Return is understood to mean the physical presence of the Human Rights Advocate, the Church, the UNHCR, and the International Consultation and Support Group for the Return (GRICAR), as per their respective mandates, as well as governmental and non-governmental international organizations, governmental and non-governmental national organizations, governmental and non-governmental religious or lay national and foreign organizations, and individuals, in the stages of the journey, resettlement, and the reintegration of the returnees.

It went on to specify that the Permanent Commissions would provide lists of accompaniment volunteers' names to CEAR, and that organizations lacking legal standing could register through CEAR if their presence was endorsed by another legal organization. The government, meanwhile, was committed vaguely to "facilitat[ing] the stay of members of international organizations and foreign individuals."[8]

For the first time, the Guatemalan government formally recognized the role and existence of nongovernmental accompaniment. The refugees themselves had fought for this recognition of accompaniment, with broad support from the diplomatic community through GRICAR. The government had openly stated its resistance and then given in. The agreement explicitly allowed organizations with no legal status in Guatemala to participate. Their participation was legitimized through the long process of resettlement and reintegration. Finally, although CEAR could "register" the accompaniment, it had no explicit power to veto or screen participants. The refugees had negotiated an open door, strengthening the position of accompaniment organizations throughout Guatemala.

NGOs did not know how the government would handle the formal authorization process. Some volunteers, out of a habitual or ideological distrust of the state, did not want to hand over their names to CEAR, contradicting the public and legal strategy of the Permanent Commissions. Others feared that the government might limit participation by slowing down the registration process with red tape and bureaucratic mismanagement. Right up to the day the refugees crossed the border, accompaniment volunteers wondered how they would be treated by the government.

La Victoria

Every aspect of the first return was unpredictable and confused. In November, the Permanent Commissions announced an "operative plan" for a return of 2,500 people on January 13 to a parcel of land called "Polígono 14," in the Ixcán jungle right on the Mexican border. A bus caravan would take them in a wide circle, south through Guatemala City and then up to the Ixcán. Both the UNHCR and the government preferred a shorter route through the Chiapas jungle directly into the Ixcán. The refugees felt that for the sake of their security and long-term reintegration, they needed to be seen and welcomed by Guatemalan society and not spirited in surreptitiously through the jungle.

In late November 1992, the army carried out a military offensive in the Ixcán, bombing areas just a few kilometers from the intended return site. In December, Defense Minister General García Samayoa announced the discovery of guerrilla documents allegedly proving that the Return was a guerrilla strategy to unite the refugee population with the nearby Communities of Population in Resistance (CPR) and form a civilian base for its operations in the Ixcán. The army's threatening behavior cast doubt on the possibility of return.

No one could tell if or when the first Return would really happen. The Permanent Commissions insisted that the refugees would cross the border on January 13 and requested that accompaniment prepare for that date. Given the army's increasingly menacing attitude and the logistical difficulties involved, the UNHCR and the Mediating Commission doubted that such an early date was possible. Accompaniment organizations in Europe and North America, trying to prepare, found these uncertainties exasperating.

PBI was by now only one of several international groups planning to accompany the return. The U.S. accompaniment and solidarity organization Witness for Peace now had volunteers working with the refugees in Chiapas, Campeche, and Quintana Roo; others in Guatemala were preparing accompaniment for the returnees, and there was a standby list of over 100 people in the United States waiting to accompany the Return journey. Witness for Peace had sent dozens of short-term (two to three weeks) accompaniment delegations from the United States to visit refugee camps in the previous years. These delegations were a hybrid between short-term accompaniment and guided tours, in which small groups were brought to visit refugee camps and popular organizations. Although the primary goal was education and empowerment of delegation members, these visits also demonstrated visually the numerical strength of the accompaniment organization, contributing to its protective image.

Project Accompaniment united a Canadian coalition of solidarity organizations to support the return. Funded by this coalition and the Canadian government, it had placed staff in Mexico, prepared short-term delegations for the Return journey, and planned to maintain ongoing medium-term accompaniment (in shifts of one to three months) with the returnees in Guatemala. Numerous Mexican organizations, which had worked for years with the refugees, also had accompaniment ready for the trip. Meanwhile, in Spain and Germany, other NGOs were organizing to send accompaniment volunteers. (Once the returns were under way, similar organizations sent volunteers from France, Sweden, Switzerland, Austria, Norway, Netherlands, United Kingdom, Denmark, and elsewhere.) Inside Guatemala, ad hoc accompaniment groups were forming among foreigners studying in the country's many language schools. Finally, many unaffiliated volunteers arrived to do accompaniment simply as individuals.

The Permanent Commissions, overwhelmed by the logistical needs of the refugees and the demands of the continuing negotiation process, left the foreigners to organize themselves. As January 13 approached, international volunteers from all over the world arrived daily in Comitán, Chiapas. In an ad hoc process, at the last minute they tried to make sure that enough volunteers were sent to each point of origin of the refugee caravans. Some had experience, and some did not. Some spoke Spanish well; some did not. They did not know one another, and no one had either the authority or the capacity at that moment to define or implement selection criteria for accompaniment. They were not sure if COMAR would let them onto the buses with the refugees. They were not sure if the Guatemalan authorities would let them cross the border. No one was sure of anything. Urgency, chaos, and hope drove the process.

At a January 5 meeting, the government did an about-face and blocked the Permanent Commissions' Return plan. It would not allow a mass caravan through Guatemala. It would not agree to the date. It would allow no more than 500 refugees a day to enter the country, and they would have to travel directly from Mexico into the Ixcán via the shorter and publicly invisible jungle route. The Mediating Commission was shocked, and the refugees left the meeting angry and desperate. The UNHCR was paying for everything from buses to food and would not take a step without Guatemalan governmental approval. The Return seemed doomed.

A few days later, the Permanent Commissions announced that the refugees would return on January 13 regardless, with or without government agreement, with or without UN support. It was an impossible notion, yet on January 9, refugees and their accompaniment in Quintana Roo began walking toward Chiapas, 800 miles away. In Campeche, the refugees hired private buses with their limited community funds. They went with NGO accompaniment, but without the UNHCR. The effect was electrifying: immediately, the Mediating Commission convinced the government negotiator to get in a helicopter with them and fly to Mexico. They zoomed from camp to camp, trying to convince the refugees to change their minds and give the negotiations one more chance.

Neither the government, the UNHCR, nor the Mediating Commission comprehended the refugees completely. The refugees had lived through unbelievable horror. They had survived flight through the jungle. They had lost parents, husbands, wives, children, friends, and homes. They had struggled ten years in Mexico to rebuild their communities and their dignity. They were prepared and committed to bring that dignity home despite the danger. They had a profoundly different understanding of the word "impossible" than any Guatemalan government or UNHCR official. In their experience, the mere lack of a bus was hardly a major impediment. Lack of food was a frequent experience. Walking all the way to the border could hardly seem more difficult than what they had already survived.

What the refugees considered impossible was to give up hope, or to live without dignity. The government's betrayal of the October 8 accords was seen as a demand that they crawl home submissively, contrary to everything they had struggled for. The government was completely taken off guard by the refugees' resolute response. The prospect of weeks of sympathetic publicity for the refugees as they marched toward the border was a nightmare for both the Guatemalan and the Mexican governments, as well as for the UNHCR, all of which would be condemned if any mishaps occurred en route. It took only three days for the Guatemalan government to capitulate. It did not have the political capital to back up its bluff. The government negotiator agreed on January 12 to the CCPP operative plan in its entirety, with the sole condition that there be a one-week delay to prepare the logistics in Guatemala. With that green light, Mexican authorities released the buses and the refugees gathered in Comitán, Chiapas.

The January 20, 1993, return was the most accompanied event in recent Guatemalan history. Seventy-eight buses, each with one or two international volunteers inside, inched up the mountain and crossed the border at La Mesilla. They were met by hundreds of Guatemalans, foreign accompaniment, diplomatic officials, and news reporters. Official vehicles of the United Nations, Doctors Without Borders, Doctors of the World, and the Mexican government were interspersed between the buses. Lavishly decorated with banners declaring the refugees' right to return home in peace, the caravan spent several days inching through the densely populated Mayan highlands. The road was lined with welcoming crowds, and thousands flocked to events held in the cities, including two days of celebration in the capital.

> From inside the bus the power of the crowds on the road really was moving. I was sitting next to a man who seemed to feel impelled to affirm every show of welcome—he was literally waving his hand out the window nonstop for hours. He was tired, sick, and almost half asleep at times, but he wasn't going to let a single greeting of welcome go by without showing his gratitude.[9]

The day the caravan left the capital, an anonymous woman telephoned the PBI house, saying, "Do you hear me? Those who protect the traitors are communists. All the communists will die!" The threat did not name PBI and seemed to refer to all the accompaniment. The team alerted its international response network and spent the next two days visiting embassies and the UN office to report the threat.

The caravan made it to the Ixcán jungle a week later and christened the first returnee community "La Victoria 20 de enero" (Victory of January 20), in honor of the day they crossed the border. Together with dozens of international volunteers, the 2,500 refugees built makeshift shelters of plastic sheets and started clearing the land and building a town.

Some felt that the amount of accompaniment was excessive. Michel Gabaudin, UNHCR head in Guatemala, assured a PBI delegation that with all the international attention at that moment the army would be crazy to lay a hand on the returnees. "I'm more worried about what will happen three years from now when there's no one watching." Others worried that all those short-term volunteers were unprepared and would not take the risks seriously.

The accompaniment did not always put its best foot forward: the volunteers couldn't stop bickering among themselves. Cultural, ideological, and strategic differences among the volunteers were difficult to overcome in such a short, intense period. The Guatemalan government refugee commissioner even accused the accompaniment of using illicit drugs and stealing food and blankets, and some volunteers admit that this may have occurred. One UN worker, while praising the seriousness of several established accompaniment groups, suggested that for some participants it was more of a vacation than an earnest act of service.

> These people get into buses that we paid for. They sleep on mattresses that had been given to refugees. They are eating [the refugees'] food. They are really tourists or hippies, joining the movement. I don't think they really represent a real protection, because you don't know who they represent, seriously, coming on their own like that.[10]

For the refugees, "excessive" accompaniment was a long-term investment. Every volunteer who came with them, or even visited them briefly, might go home and tell the world about their fears and their needs, encouraging others to keep coming in the future. If some volunteers were troublesome, it was a cost the refugees accepted. Some accompaniment organizers wanted the Permanent Commissions to screen the volunteers, but the refugees kept an open-door policy. If years later they found themselves without accompaniment, they wanted the army to know that there were lots of international allies to stand up for them when needed.

In La Victoriá, in just a few weeks the returned refugees built shacks, planted corn, and set up community centers, schools, flour and lumber mills, bakeries, and stores. The pace of development kept the international volunteers' heads spinning. And on every errand that took a refugee outside the confines of the village's populated zones, an international volunteer went along.

The returnees embraced the accompaniment and wove it into the community structure. Each new volunteer arriving in the community was registered in the town office and shown to special huts built just for the accompaniment. A different returnee household was responsible each day for bringing food to the volunteers' huts. Around the muddy town square were rugged, thatched wooden shelters for official offices: the town council, the women's organization "Mama Maquín," the school, and an accompaniment coordination office. This "office" consisted of a few rough-hewn log benches, a table, some rickety shelves, and an old manual typewriter. Between accompaniment assignments, volunteers met here, typed up reports on their activities and the events of the week, and watched the rain.

While La Victoria built itself up out of nothing in the first months of 1993, the army carried out a military offensive in the Ixcán, trying to flush out the guerrillas from around La Victoria and the nearby CPRs (see chapter 13 for more on CPRs). Military patrols camped on or passed through the returnees' land. Helicopters flew over La Victoria constantly. Machine-gun fire and aerial bombardments were heard nearby at night. The refugees were certain that the army was deliberately trying to terrorize them.

Their response was to confront the army head-on. The Permanent Commissions office released an endless stream of press releases denouncing the army's helicopter overflights and nearby bombardments. When someone noticed soldiers on La Victoria territory, the community would immediately pull together a delegation, complete with several accompaniment volunteers, and go out to find the soldiers and protest. Jack Fahey, a Boston volunteer with the Seva Foundation, a private North American development NGO that maintained a constant presence of two volunteers in La Victoria, describes one such incident:

> Five La Victoria commission members, Manuel the boatman and I took the boat down the Xalbal river to near the border and then proceeded on foot, following the trail of the soldiers for about a mile through the cornfields and jungle. As we were chasing down the trail after the Army, me with my video-camera, Francisco with his machete, I was wondering what would happen when we found them: 200 soldiers armed to the teeth.
>
> When we caught up with the end of their column, [commission member] Francisco and the others demanded to speak with the officer in charge to find out the reason for the incursion. The soldier said he was too far ahead. Francisco insisted, saying we would issue a denunciation to the colonel at the Playa Grande military base. After a while, some officers arrived. Everyone was pleasant, shaking hands, giving salutations. When they saw me video-taping, one of them started taking pictures of us and asking our names. . . .
>
> Quite a discussion then took place about the role of the Army, about them not respecting the rights of the community by coming in and scaring people, about their role defending the country. At one point, when the Army was accused of defending the rich, they became animated and said, "Who here is the son of the rich?" as if that were the point. They were all campesinos. It all ended in "friendly" handshakes. . . . The soldiers said "good-bye" to me in English.[11]

The soldiers almost always insisted that they were merely following orders. But the refugees complained to the Government Human Rights Office and sent delegations to visit the commander of the nearby Playa Grande military base, demanding that the army stop crossing their land and

Photo by Piet Van Lier

PBI volunteer Beth Hewson (US) with returned refugee children in La Quetzal, El Petén, 1995.

stop the helicopter overflights, and calling both acts violations of the October 8 accords.

The army flew helicopters over every other civilian community in the country and had the legal right-of-way to cross any private property in the fulfillment of its mission. It justified every move based on the continued activity of the guerrillas in the region. It was not explicitly violating the accords.

The refugee leadership knew that they had lost this point at the negotiating table, but they had no intention of giving it up. Starting with a press release right after the accords were signed, they argued that army incursions on their land would violate the *spirit* of the accords. They repeated the charge so many times that many people began to believe it.

Most international volunteers arrived predisposed to believe the refugees, and few had carefully studied the accords. Even if they had, the refugees argued that the military sought to terrorize them because the army believed that the refugees were guerrillas. Therefore, they were not being treated as "civilians" as the accords demanded. Accepting this reasoning, many volunteers and NGOs transmitted the returnees' denunciations verbatim to the international community. These denunciations were not based on the explicit wording of the accords and sometimes seriously misinterpreted them, damaging credibility.

The NGOs and the UNHCR were trying to maneuver between two different visions of reality. From a legal perspective, helicopter overflights and troop incursions in a war zone could not be called abuses of human rights or breaches of the accords. Closer inspection of other denunciations by the Permanent Commissions often revealed exaggerations or factual errors. The diplomatic community and established human rights networks depended on high-level credibility for their effectiveness and could not accept the returnees' statements as objective truth without evidence.

In contrast, the accompaniment volunteers were out in the jungle sharing the fears and hardships of the returnees. They were under those helicopters, listening to the machine guns nearby, remembering with every shot what they knew of the army's past massacres. Now they were building friendships with the survivors, who detailed their grisly testimonies as though the massacres had happened only yesterday. The sound of a helicopter was unsettling to the volunteers, but it was horrifying to the returnees. A helicopter meant only one thing: death. Those bombs might be landing on the returnees' friends and families. Seeing that fear, volunteers were not going to say, "Oh, don't worry. It's not *legally* a human rights abuse." Instead, accompaniment volunteers were often aghast that anyone would insist on sticking to the letter of the law when faced with what they perceived to be the overwhelming moral truth behind the returnees' fear and vulnerability.*

There being no simple reconciliation of these two visions, different groups chose different strategies. The UN, for instance, would not publicly denounce actions that did not explicitly contradict the accords. Instead, it went behind the scenes, asking the army, "Look, can't you just fly your helicopters in a wider circle around La Victoria? It will be less trouble for all of us."[12] Development NGOs avoided human rights denunciations altogether. At the other end of the spectrum, many of the new ad hoc accompaniment groups and individual accompaniers gave priority to solidarity with the returnees' vision of the truth, sometimes issuing more outspoken condemnations than the returnees themselves.

Established accompaniment NGOs wanted to maintain credibility both nationally and internationally. They sometimes doubted the Permanent Commissions' strategies, but, consistent with their organizational commitments to noninterference, they recognized the returnees' democratic right to interpret the accords, and even the facts, as radically as they chose. The accompaniment would inevitably be perceived by other parties as supporting returnee decisions and denunciations. But when the Permanent Commissions pushed for more active and compromising collaboration in their international denouncements, some organizations chose to say no.

---

*Psychological consequences of the process of exile and return often affect this dynamic. Some common repercussions include a heightened sense of anxiety, danger, and mistrust, mixed with some level of survivors' guilt. (See Aron, "Gender-Specific Terror," pp. 37–47; Goldberg, "Efectos psicologicas," p. 403; and Weinstein, "Problematica psicologica.")

The Jiménez Incident

Joaquin Jiménez Bautista was a member of the Association of Dispersed Guatemalan Refugees in Mexico, those refugees not registered in UN camps. In late August 1993, he took part in a delegation into Guatemala to investigate possible land purchases for refugee resettlement. On August 27, he visited his hometown of Todos Santos in Huehuetenango to secure valid personal documentation. He was accompanied by a Guatemalan lawyer for the Catholic Church and Randy Kohan, a volunteer with the Canadian Project Accompaniment.

Upon leaving the municipal building in Todos Santos, all three were detained by the local civil patrol, which accused Jiménez of being a guerrilla. They were beaten and eventually handed over to the police. An angry crowd surrounded the police, threatening a lynching. People in the crowd identified Jiménez as "Comandante Leonel," a notorious guerrilla responsible for assassinations in the village between 1980 and 1982.

Randy Kohan escaped and took refuge in the telephone company office, where he made some calls. The lawyer was released and continued on to the capital to report the incident. Jiménez remained in the custody of the police. But the police were surrounded by a crowd that wanted to lynch Jiménez. Minister of the Interior Arnoldo Ortiz Moscoso got directly involved and negotiated his release. On Sunday the twenty-ninth, Jiménez was handed over to representatives of the UNHCR and the Government Human Rights Office and received a police escort to the Mexican border.

Kohan stated later in an interview, "they held [Jiménez] . . . and beat him quite badly, but we like to think that my presence stopped them from doing anything worse."[13] Ortiz Moscoso commended Kohan's courage and resourcefulness and maintains that his presence and response most likely saved Jiménez's life.[14] International organizations, in turn, praised Ortiz Moscoso for his professional and prompt handling of the incident.

The army leaped at the opportunity to support the local residents who were denouncing a refugee leader as a guerrilla criminal and cited military intelligence confirming the accusation. They accused Ortiz Moscoso and the UNHCR of illegally helping Jiménez escape. Nevertheless, the army did not directly intervene: Jiménez could never have been moved all the way from Todos Santos to the border without the army's acquiescence.

This incident could not have happened at a safer political moment. Only a few months earlier, hard-line President Jorge Serrano had suspended the constitution and declared a state of emergency in what was later called a "self-coup," modeled after Peruvian President Fujimori's similar move the previous year. It failed dismally, and after a week of public and international protest, Serrano fled to Panama and the congress named Ramiro De

Leon Carpio, the former human rights ombudsman, as interim president. After this unprecedented and embarrassing political defeat of military hardliners, popular and high-level support for the rule of law was in fashion. Reform-oriented Minister Ortiz Moscoso and the national police surprised the international community. Whether or not Jiménez was a guerrilla, they argued, he was in the country under the protection of the UN, and as long as no one was filing criminal charges against him, it was their legal duty to protect him and escort him out.*

The incident raised important political questions for accompaniment. Jiménez came from Todos Santos, and people there knew him well. Their accusations were quite specific, and Jiménez's denials were often unconvincing. The ambiguity left the UNHCR, the accompaniment, and the other permanent commissioners on unsteady ground. Accompaniment volunteers usually know very little about the past of those they accompany. So what are the risks and implications of accompanying a former guerrilla leader, if that's what Jiménez was?

Humanitarian law and human rights law apply to ex-combatants and their right to participate in civil society. The refugees have the right to make their own choices of leadership. And even assassins have the right to protection from human rights abuse. Accompaniment organizations can argue, as Ortiz Moscoso did, that whether the person had been a guerrilla is irrelevant. Anyone carrying out a civilian function nonviolently deserves protection and due process.

But this was an extremely radical and dangerous argument in Guatemala in 1993, where in thirty years of war, the army had supposedly taken no prisoners. The label "guerrilla" was still a death threat, and the army did not distinguish between "combatant" and "sympathizer." In this context, few could risk making a legal argument about the rights of ex-combatants. The UNHCR, for instance, immediately defended Jiménez and denied the accusations, rather than risk being seen as protecting guerrillas. The Canadian Project Accompaniment declined comment, consistent with their posture of noninterference.†

---

*The army eventually regrouped and put pressure on President De Leon to replace Ortiz Moscoso and other reform-oriented officials in November 1993.
† The issue of humanitarian law in Guatemala was burst wide open in 1994 and 1995 by U.S. lawyer Jennifer Harbury. Harbury pressured Congress, the U.S. embassy, and the Guatemalan military to investigate the fate of her husband, Efrain Bamaca, a guerrilla commander who was captured and disappeared. The case, notorious for its shocking revelations about the role of the CIA in Guatemala, opened the political space for discussion of humanitarian law and the rights of prisoners of war and combatants. Bamaca was the first confirmed guerrilla to be treated publicly and sympathetically by the press and by U.S. government spokespersons as a "victim" whose human rights had been violated. The fact that Harbury was a U.S. citizen and a Harvard Law School graduate obviously helped open this space and demonstrated once again the sensitivity of the Guatemalan state to the treatment of foreigners.

Meddling Foreigners

The uncertainties caused by Serrano's mid-1993 self-coup delayed the return process temporarily. But in early December, with the more moderate De Leon Carpio in office, another 1,000 refugee families returned from Mexico to the temporary village of Veracruz, Ixcán. Their final destination was the nearby village of Tercer Pueblo, where the army still had a base. On December 12, the returnees in Veracruz organized a peaceful accompanied march of 200 to deliver a letter to the commander demanding its removal.[15]

At a press conference the next day in Guatemala City, army spokeswoman Major Berta Vargas falsely accused the returnees of provoking the base, throwing firecrackers, and yelling slogans aggressively. She noted that the march had included various foreigners, "mostly Spaniards." The same day, President De Leon Carpio ordered an investigation of "the participation of foreigners, together with returnees, in acts of provocation against the Tercer Pueblo military base."[16] On December 14, Foreign Minister Arturo Fajardo Maldonado declared, "We're collecting information about who these foreigners are and what their motives are for participating in the repatriation process, since they have no right to be there. . . . If we can prove any anomalies, we will expel them." Finally, on December 18, the daily newspaper *Siglo Veintiuno* published a frenzied column that accused foreign volunteers of having links to the guerrillas, the Sandinistas, the ETA (Basque separatists), the Shining Path, and the Palestinian Liberation Organization and urged the president to "throw them all out!" All this fury came after one of the more peaceful interchanges to date between returnees and the military. No investigation occurred.

The accusations, though false in this case, revealed a general animosity that could not be ignored nor dismissed out-of-hand. Disrespectful or provocative behavior by volunteers or inappropriate "activist" intervention, though infrequent, certainly occurred. Some volunteers probably did have links with the guerrillas. Hundreds of unscreened volunteers were passing through the region, some with no organizational affiliation, many with no training or preparation. Even within well-intentioned and legitimate accompaniment organizations, there was no consistent definition of what was appropriate behavior for accompaniment volunteers. In one case, a group of accompaniment volunteers felt that they had to physically restrain one of their own from intervening in a verbal confrontation between returnees and civil patrols.[17]

The returnees probably did not pay much attention to such behavior by foreigners, but neither did they actively discourage it. The army stereotyped the accompaniment as a unit, so the behavior of a few individuals compromised everyone's credibility. Although some organizations disdained the confrontational behavior of volunteers over whom they had no authority, they did not publicly condemn it. The accusation of manipulation was an insult to the returnees' intelligence and independence that accompaniment organizations did not want to legitimize. Threatened, and fearing that the army would only take further advantage of any sign of disunity, the accompaniment organizations closed ranks, publicly anyway, to defend their right to accompany the returnees. This only confirmed the army's belief that all the accompaniment endorsed disrespectful and meddlesome behavior.

Some UNHCR staff thought that many accompaniment volunteers were too biased, that they had made a naive "good guy versus bad guy" analysis of a complex situation, and that they reinforced confrontational attitudes among the returnees—attitudes the UNHCR considered unproductive. Nevertheless, collective attacks on foreigners hurt the UN as well. The UNHCR, for example, was accused of transporting weapons for the guerrillas, and received anonymous threats.[18]

There was no easy solution to the problem of inappropriate volunteer behavior. A single organization with a consistent mandate might exercise some control over its own volunteers, but no single organization could have provided the Return with such a vast variety of services, international contacts, and audiences. The Permanent Commissions did not want to cede control over such a vital aspect of their security to any single outside group. The moral authority to impose uniform criteria for accompaniment behavior rested with the returnees themselves, and they didn't do it. Eventually, the various accompaniment organizations formed the Accompaniment Forum, a monthly meeting at which they shared their experiences, concerns, and future plans. Although it was not a vehicle for developing unified policies, the forum was a step toward greater coherence and respect among the different organizations.

Righteous Indignation or Provocation?

Accompaniment organizations also had problems responding to the behavior of the returnees themselves. The massacres had left more than a legacy of fear—they had also left anger and hatred. The returnees' political strategy of assertive political confrontation won them many victories. But in the heat of the moment, the line between assertiveness and aggression can be easily crossed.

In one incident in the spring of 1994, two civil patrollers—one with a gun—tried to walk through the returnee community of Veracruz. They were immediately surrounded by a hundred angry returnees who verbally harassed them to such an extent that accompaniment volunteers perceived a real risk of violence. In the end, however, with the UNHCR, CEAR, and accompaniment watching every move carefully, the two men agreed to withdraw.[19]

On August 5, 1994, at 4:30 A.M., 300 to 400 soldiers from the army outpost at the nearby Xalbal River attempted to pass through Veracruz on the public road, on their way to relieve the soldiers stationed at Mayalán. The community's night watch sounded a general alarm, and a large number of returnees got out of bed and moved to the highway to confront the soldiers. Tempers flared. The returnees insulted the soldiers and accused them of having murdered family members. Then they formed a human barrier blocking the army's advance. The army commander ordered his troops to return to the Xalbal River outpost. According to accompaniment eyewitnesses:

> As the soldiers were leaving, returnees became physically aggressive, pushing, tripping and kicking the soldiers. . . . Soldiers were heard requesting authorization to open fire on the returnees, but the Army commander refused to give the order. Several soldiers threatened that they would return in the future to even the score after the international accompaniers are gone.

This accompaniment report, published in an international solidarity periodical, went on to say:

> Many returnees do not agree with the community's assault on the soldiers. Many agree that the Army does have the constitutional right of free movement, and that nothing good will result from this incident.[20]

These two incidents in Veracruz illustrate how international accompaniment volunteers can find themselves in ambiguous situations. Who is the "aggressor" in this second scene? The soldiers, on their way to maintain an armed occupation of land that belonged to the returnees, were the ones with the guns. They were legally on the only public road leading to their intended destination, but they had to have known that marching through this town at 4:30 A.M. would upset people. The returnees, however, were violently provocative. As long as that commander maintained discipline and refused to authorize his soldiers to react, his soldiers were angrily and illegally assaulted, in the presence of international accompaniment. The accompaniment did not protect the soldiers from this assault. It may even have emboldened the returnees to express their anger. They may have assumed that the accompaniment would take their side regardless of their actions, and that the army would not react with violence in the presence of accompaniment.

Perhaps the accompaniment did influence the commander's restraint. Nevertheless, some of his soldiers sought permission to fire. A less intelligent and disciplined commander might easily have been rattled. Every soldier in the

Ixcán is taught that the returnee communities are rife with armed guerrillas. An armed response would have been an illegal and immoral use of excessive force, even under provocation. But the soldiers may have claimed self-defense. The returnees' security hung by a thread. The accompaniment, with no influence over the provocative behavior, hung on that thread with them.

The international distribution of a critical accompaniment report through a solidarity periodical (cited above) is in itself an important step in the development of the accompaniment relationship. The report emphasizes that neither the periodical nor others in the community endorse such aggressive behavior. Criticism of this sort is rare in international solidarity movements. The report's implicit message to all sides of the conflict is important: accompaniment purporting to protect cannot endorse or encourage actions that unnecessarily increase the risk of violence. In its recognition of the legal rights of the army, the report's criticism represents a political cost to the returnees, encourages greater discipline in the future, and hinders the army from holding the entire community responsible.*

The La Aurora Massacre—An Unknown Future

As the returns continued, the growing network of accompaniment organizations stretched its resources to maintain a presence in each new village. By mid-1995, over 11,000 refugees had returned to over a dozen new communities in the Ixcán, Huehuetenango, Alta Verapaz, and the Petén, and accompaniment had expanded to include the neighboring CPRs.[21] The number of available accompaniment volunteers gradually decreased, but not nearly as quickly as many had feared. In the third year of the return, the returnees and the CPRs were still well-accompanied, more so than any other communities in the country. The returnees faced hardships, lack of resources, sickness, and disorientation, but they persevered and began rebuilding their lives. The army carried out propaganda campaigns to turn neighboring communities against them. Nevertheless, for two and a half years, the returnees escaped their worst fears: killings and disappearances. Popular movement organizations in other parts of the country continued to suffer deadly attacks. The returnees seemed protected.

On October 15, 1994, 441 returnees relocated from La Victoria to a plantation in Alta Verapaz called Xamán. They christened their new home

---

*This argument assumes that the returnees and the army would be aware of the message that was published. In the returnees' case, these concerns were communicated informally. The Guatemalan intelligence service does indeed monitor what is published about Guatemala in the international press and in solidarity publications. We do not know how thorough this monitoring is, nor how effectively the information is processed through the chain of command.

La Aurora 8 de Octubre, commemorating the date of the original return accord. They built their homes, a school, and a clinic and restored a pre-existing rubber plantation. La Aurora gained a reputation as one of the most trouble-free returns. There were no conflicts with neighbors, no struggles over land, no civil patrols nearby, and no confrontations with the army. Accompaniment volunteers from Spain and North America lived with them throughout their peaceful first year.

In early October 1995, for the first time in a year, all the foreign volunteers were temporarily away from the community. On the morning of October 5, schoolchildren alerted the community that there were soldiers on community property. By 1:30 P.M., a patrol of twenty-six soldiers led by a lieutenant were in the center of town, surrounded by an angry crowd of over 200 returnees. The returnees complained that the soldiers were not allowed to enter the community and demanded that they lay down their weapons and wait for the United Nations (MINUGUA* and UNHCR) monitors to arrive to verify this alleged breach of the accords. Tempers flared, and the soldiers began to push their way out through the crowd. A woman grabbed a sergeant's rifle, apparently trying to take it away from him. The sergeant immediately ordered his men to fire, without conferring with his commanding officer. The soldiers, in a panic, began shooting in all directions. The crowd scattered, and the patrol left carrying three wounded soldiers shot by their own comrades. Behind them in La Aurora were thirty wounded and eleven dead civilians: six men, three women, and two children.[22]

The UN arrived quickly to evacuate the wounded in helicopters and verify what had happened. Within a day, President De Leon accepted the resignation of Defense Minister Mario Enriquez, and all the soldiers in the patrol were arrested. The subsequent UN report concluded that there had been no prior orders to attack. It confirmed that although the soldiers had indeed felt intimidated by the surrounding crowd, they had committed several deliberate murders on their way out of town. Finally, the report placed full responsibility on the army for having systematically trained its troops to believe that the returnees were armed guerrillas, thus creating paranoia and a predisposition to use deadly force.

The accompaniment volunteers who had just left La Aurora could not help but ask themselves, "What would have happened if we'd stayed?" We saw in the Veracruz incident that the presence of accompaniment did not inhibit the returnees from aggressive action against the soldiers. The La Aurora shooting began spontaneously, and it seems doubtful that the

*MINUGUA, the United Nations Mission to Guatemala, had placed several hundred human rights monitors in Guatemala in November 1994, in fulfillment of the human rights accord signed earlier that year between the Guatemalan government and the guerrillas. Its mandate was to investigate all human rights abuses committed by either the government or the guerrillas after the date of signing.

presence of a foreigner would have been on the mind of the sergeant surrounded by the apparently threatening crowd when his gun was grabbed. One might hope that an accompaniment presence would have calmed the returnees' fears that the soldiers would "escape" before an official report was filed or perhaps would have led the officer in charge to try to calm his men as the tension rose. No one will ever know.

The La Aurora massacre frightened all the returnee communities, as well as those refugees still waiting in Mexico. It confirmed everyone's original fears: that the returnees' peril was long term, and that civilian government leadership could not control the army. But the Return did not slow down. In 1996, thousands more refugees returned, and accompaniment organizations redoubled their efforts to find volunteers for each new community.

The Guatemalan refugee return brought accompaniment to a new level of legitimacy, both in Guatemala and internationally. It spawned a dozen or more new accompaniment organizations, many of which offered their presence to other communities of displaced and disenfranchised Guatemalans as well. By 1996, the UN human rights monitoring mission (MINUGUA) was also offering accompaniment in some situations, with the goal of preventing abuses rather than only reporting on events after they occurred, as had been the practice of previous missions. Meanwhile, the growing network of international volunteers became a credible source of information for both the UN and the diplomatic corps.

In a span of ten years, protective accompaniment developed into one of the key security strategies of the Guatemalan civilian popular movement. The government, meanwhile, learned to accept this outside interference, gradually shifting its tactics from blunt attacks to more subtle manipulations. Through the accompaniment process, hundreds of volunteers came to Guatemala, offered themselves for brief periods, and returned to inform and strengthen the network of human rights and solidarity organizations in their home countries.

In the late 1990s, violence and economic inequality continue, but Guatemala has changed considerably. The guerrilla war is over. The "national security" ideology of the extreme right-wing oligarchy has been replaced with the free-market economic ideology of the moderate financial sector. Selective repression continues. Poor Mayans are still starving, but they aren't being massacred. Achieving economic and social justice, however, will take far more than immediate physical protection. Guatemalans need broad strategies for structural change.

A vibrant civilian movement is now developing these strategies, proposing changes at all levels of government and society, and electing representatives

Photo by Didier Varrin

May 1993—Amilcar Mendez, Rigoberta Menchú, and Nineth Montenegro de García take to the streets during President Serrano's 1993 coup d'etat.

to congress. A government whose only tool of control had been disappearance and assassination is learning to live with the international concept of human rights—albeit unwillingly and erratically. These changes were won by hundreds of courageous Guatemalan activists, many of whom died in the struggle. Those international volunteers who stood by them can be rightfully proud of their contribution to this process.

Notes

1. See chapter 11 and Compher and Morgan, *Going Home*.
2. Falla, *Masacres*. Drawing on exhaustive interviews with survivors of the massacres, Falla chronicles the step-by-step escalation of violence in the area, from the sporadic assassinations of cooperative leaders in the late 1970s to the massacre of 324 people in the village of Cuarto Pueblo in February 1982.
3. U.S. Committee for Refugees, *El Retorno*; Americas Watch, *Human Rights in Guatemala During Cerezo's First Year*.
4. *PBI Project Bulletin*, October 1988.
5. Alfonso Paiz Bauer (lawyer for the Permanent Commissions) and Anantonia Reyes and Oswaldo Enriquez (Guatemalan Human Rights Commission and members of Mediating Commission), tape-recorded interview by authors, Guatemala, July 1994.
6. Interview by authors with pre-return refugees in Mexico, returnees in Guatemala, members of the Mediating Commission, and officials within the UNHCR.
7. Reyes interview.
8. "October 8, 1992 Accords Between the Guatemalan Government and the Permanent Commissions of the Guatemalan Refugees in Mexico."
9. Liam Mahony (coauthor), letter to friends, February 7, 1993.
10. UNHCR official (name withheld), interview by authors, Guatemala, July 1994.

11. Jack Fahey, La Victoria accompaniment log (Seva Foundation), January 1995.
12. UNHCR/Guatemala official (name withheld), interview.
13. "Canadian Solidarity with Guatemala's Refugees: An Interview with Project Accompaniment," *Reunion* 1, no. 8 (February/March 1995).
14. Arnoldo Ortiz Moscoso, interview by authors, Guatemala, July 1994.
15. Report from accompaniment volunteers in Veracruz, Ixcán, December 15, 1993; also, "Repatriados efectuaron protesta en interior de destacamento militar," *Siglo Veintiuno*, December 13, 1993.
16. "Refugiados: De León ordena investigar participación de extranjeros en retorno," *Siglo Veintiuno*, December 14, 1993.
17. Incident witnessed by Fermín Rodrigo (a volunteer with Entrepobles, a Catalan NGO), tape-recorded telephone interview by authors, April 1995.
18. UNHCR/Guatemala, interview.
19. Curt Wands, tape-recorded telephone interview by author, June 1995.
20. NCOORD newsletter, September 1994. NCOORD (National [U.S.] Coordinating Office on Refugees and Displaced of Guatemala) is a coalition of U.S. organizations, based in Chicago.
21. For a moving account of the experience of the CPRs, see Falla, *Historia de un Gran Amor*. For a summary of these communities' campaign's for legitimacy and the gradual opening of links with greater Guatemalan society, see the EPICA/CHRLA report *Out of the Shadows*; see also chapter 13.
22. Report of the United Nations Mission to Guatemala (MINUGUA), October 10, 1995.

PART II

11

A Tenacious Grip: Accompaniment in El Salvador, 1987–91

*I*N EL SALVADOR, the experience of accompaniment was significantly different from that in Guatemala. After six months of steady accompaniment, Herbert Anaya, the most well-known Salvadoran human rights activist, was gunned down on one of the few days he stepped out of his house alone. Humberto Centeno, an outspoken and high-profile union leader, was captured by the armed forces right in front of eight foreign volunteers. When Salvadoran refugees tried to come home from Honduras, their international NGO accompaniment was stopped at the border. For over a year, the government carried out a systematic campaign of harassment, detention, and expulsion against foreigners.

El Salvador's military leaders hated foreigners, made no secret of it, and made little effort to avoid scandalous incidents. Yet the more the army harassed foreign volunteers, the more the Salvadoran popular movement valued the accompaniment. Lutheran Bishop Medardo Gomez, who himself was extensively accompanied, explained this apparent contradiction to a PBI delegation:

> Hope can only be kindled where there is solidarity. It is much easier to throw yourself into any commitment when you have someone with you, protecting you. . . . I can throw myself from a high place, if I know that there is someone there to make sure I am not destroyed by the fall. You give us the force to be able to throw ourselves into our work.
>
> You have been expelled. You have suffered some of the same problems as those whom you have helped. When you look back on this work, do not forget that it is precisely because you have suffered with the people that you have been able to support them in building their resistance.[1]

El Salvador is a small, densely populated country on Guatemala's southern border, sharing a similar precolonial, colonial, and military history. In contrast, though, its indigenous population was reduced to a small minority as a result of colonial pressures and massacres. During *La Matanza* (the killing) of 1932, dictator Maximiliano Hernandez obliterated a campesino rebellion, exterminating over 30,000 people, most of whom were indigenous. Salvadorans have never forgotten *La Matanza*.

With a recent history of cyclical repression similar to that of Guatemala, El Salvador reached a crisis in the late 1970s. The civilian opposition was strong despite a heavily repressive government financed and advised by the United States. By 1979, under the government of General Humberto Romero, the news of hundreds of deaths, disappearances, and torture began to reach the international community. Amnesty International, the Inter-American Commission for Human Rights, and eventually even the U.S. State Department issued public condemnations. Fearing another Sandinista-type guerrilla victory, the United States supported a coup against General Romero in 1979, putting in place a civilian-military "revolutionary junta." At the same time, the United States promoted other measures intended to diminish popular discontent, including an increase in economic and military aid and a timid agrarian reform. These measures did not slow the growth of the opposition, however, and the Salvadoran armed forces continued their repression.

During this period of repression, several attacks in 1980 and early 1981 had major international repercussions. On March 24, 1980, Salvadoran Archbishop Oscar Romero was assassinated while saying mass. A massacre at his funeral, witnessed by numerous international mourners, resulted in 26 deaths and over 200 wounded.*

Next, on November 27, six of the principal leaders of the opposition Revolutionary Democratic Front (FDR) were assassinated shortly after completing a series of international tours to build support for their movement. On December 2, four U.S. women, three of them nuns, were tortured, raped, and killed near San Salvador. The slogan "U.S. dollars murder U.S. nuns" became a rallying cry of the movement opposed to U.S. support of the Salvadoran regime. At the end of December, an American freelance journalist disappeared, and on January 5, 1981, two U.S. agricultural advisers and a Salvadoran coworker were assassinated in the Sheraton Hotel in San Salvador. Pressure from U.S. citizens led to a temporary suspension of $25 million in aid.†

According to Salvadoran human rights activist Mirna de Anaya:

> Ever since they killed the four American nuns and the two U.S. agricultural
> advisers, it's as if they received a prohibition. The security forces understand
> very well that they can't kill an American, and for that reason we're safer

---

*Nevertheless, the day after the funeral, the International Operations Subcommittee of the U.S. House Appropriations Committee approved $5.7 million for equipment for the Salvadoran security forces (Armstrong and Rubin, *El Salvador*, p. 144).

†When an investigatory commission sent by U.S. President Carter returned with no proof of military involvement in the nuns' assassinations, Carter renewed part of the suspended aid and pushed for yet another change in the ruling government junta (Armstrong and Rubin, *El Salvador*, p. 166).

with the accompaniment. They're not quite as frightened of Europeans, because Europe hasn't exerted as much pressure. But gringos are different. You can't kill a gringo in this country.[2]

These events defined the terms of debate in the United States: for the rest of the 1980s, economic aid to El Salvador would be approved only after overcoming a steadily increasing resistance in Congress and heated debates over Salvadoran human rights violations.

But the administration of President Ronald Reagan (1981–88) was rigidly committed to finding a military solution to the Salvadoran conflict. Secretary of State Alexander Haig declared categorically that El Salvador faced a dangerous attempt at penetration by international communism into Central America.[3] In February 1981, the U.S. government removed the condition of investigating the killing of the women missionaries from its economic and military aid decisions.[4] Congress responded in April with new restrictions, demanding that Reagan certify every six months that the Salvadoran government complied with a series of requirements in the areas of human rights and democratic reform.[5] These mixed messages signaled to Salvadoran leaders that they could depend on steady support from the Reagan administration for their counterinsurgency operations as long as they avoided high-profile scandalous attacks that would raise the ire of the U.S. Congress.

During 1982, 4,419 Salvadorans were assassinated, and 1,045 disappeared.[6] By the end of that year, the civilian opposition movement was crushed and forced underground. At the same time, the guerrilla Farabundo Marti National Liberation Front (FMLN) carried out military campaigns, consolidating its presence in several rural provinces. In response, U.S. training and financial support increased dramatically, and U.S. military advisers were sent to El Salvador, violating congressional restrictions. To maintain the facade of a formal democracy, elections were held in 1982 and again in 1984, although no genuine opposition could risk a campaign.

Meanwhile, international attention to El Salvador continued to increase. In the United States, a movement opposing support for the Salvadoran government was growing, including CISPES (Committee in Solidarity with the People of El Salvador) and more loosely connected movements such as the Pledge of Resistance and the religious-based Sanctuary Movement. These movements sent delegations to visit El Salvador, carried out educational activities with the U.S. public, and vigorously lobbied for changes in U.S. foreign policy.

Under increasing pressure, the Reagan administration began favoring those Salvadoran officials who supported the U.S. strategy of "low-intensity warfare."* The United States tried to limit the actions of hard-line officers who supported what they called the "Guatemalan solution" (referring to the scorched-earth campaigns that had recently been carried out with considerable military success in Guatemala). The Salvadoran military, becoming increasingly dependent on U.S. funding for survival, was forced to defer to outside pressure.

The figures on human rights violations began to decrease after 1983, in part due to this pressure, and in part because the popular movement's activities had been so drastically curtailed by the repression. Systematic violations continued in rural areas, but overall, massive repression was replaced by more selective attacks, frequently carried out by death squads rather than by uniformed soldiers.[7]

Despite continued assassinations and disappearances in 1984 and 1985, the opposition movement regrouped. Various new organizations protested the deterioration of living conditions due to the war and demanded a negotiated solution and an end to the repression. In 1986, many of these organizations coalesced under the umbrella of the UNTS (National Unity of Salvadoran Workers), which mobilized mass demonstrations that year in San Salvador.[†]

In rural areas, a parallel process led to the formation of the Christian Committee for the Displaced (CRIPDES) and the National Coordination

---

*Low-intensity warfare is a term coined by the U.S. military, referring to a level of conflict in a foreign country with a minimal direct implication of U.S. forces. Local forces implement military, political, economic, and psychological tactics in the furtherance of counterinsurgency strategies favored by the United States. The strategy was favored at least in part as a result of the United States' high-intensity debacle in Vietnam. See Klare and Kornbluh, *Low Intensity Warfare.*

†The UNTS was a broad-based umbrella organization encompassing labor, church, peasant, and student organizations.

for Repopulation (CNR). Both began to organize the return of the displaced population to the homes they had fled during the military operations of 1980–83.

As the Salvadoran opposition grew, so did the presence of internationals in El Salvador. Delegations from international labor unions, church groups, and other humanitarian organizations began visiting El Salvador regularly after 1985. Also, an increasing number of foreigners began living in El Salvador, working with churches and other organizations.

The Marin County Interfaith Task Force

The first accompaniment requests arose in 1986, from the Nongovernmental Human Rights Commission of El Salvador (CDHES), which set up a partnership with a small church-based solidarity committee in northern California, the Marin County Interfaith Task Force on Central America. The CDHES had been a pioneering voice for human rights throughout the violence of the 1980s. It had a strong reputation for providing documentation of abuses to international organizations. Of the eight people who founded the CDHES in 1978, three had been assassinated and several others were imprisoned from 1986 until February 1987, when they were freed through a government amnesty program. According to CDHES activist Mirna de Anaya, whose husband, Herbert, was one of those being released from jail:

> We did not want to go back into hiding. Most people who come out of jail do not come out in public again, but if we really wanted to continue to open up democratic spaces, we had to be willing to be in the public eye. We saw that doing this, we could be killed at any time. That's when we decided to ask the people at Marin for accompaniment. . . . Really, when we were accompanied by the Americans, we were never hassled. They didn't even stop the cars.[8]

Marin volunteers accompanied the CDHES from 1987 through 1991; they came from all over the United States, staying for a month to a few years. They accompanied CDHES activists to events and meetings in San Salvador and on investigations in rural communities. The CDHES leaders took charge of their training and orientation. The volunteers often drove the cars and helped with office work, computer work, and translations.

The Marin Interfaith Task Force entered El Salvador incognito. Reasoning that they would be less vulnerable to deportation, the CDHES and Marin decided to present the volunteers to neither the Salvadoran government nor even the U.S. embassy (as U.S. citizens are generally expected to do).[9] Thus they limited the accompaniment message to pure physical presence.

Herbert Anaya, CDHES coordinator, was the best-known human rights activist in the country and was respected by the international human rights community as well. After leaving jail in February, he threw himself into his work and became one of the few voices in 1987 who dared to openly denounce military violations of human rights. He trusted his security to accompaniment, although he did not use it consistently. Once, for example, when he was alone, he noticed that he was being followed. He immediately went into someone's house and telephoned to have one of the Marin volunteers come and get him.

The next time, Anaya didn't get the chance. At 6:35 A.M. on October 26, 1987, he was assassinated in his driveway while waiting to drive his children to school. He had no accompaniment with him.

Because of the CDHES's high profile, there was an immense international outcry. The CDHES accused the death squads and security forces of the killing, but the army denied any responsibility. On January 4, 1988, after a few months of pressure, the government made public a confession to Anaya's murder by a supposed guerrilla named Jorge Miranda. Shortly afterward, Miranda retracted, claiming that he had been tortured into a false confession. He was sent to prison. The next session of the Geneva UN Human Rights Commission in February 1988 demanded that the Salvadoran government investigate attacks against human rights organizations.[10]

The assassination was a severe blow to the CDHES. It also provoked serious questioning of the embryonic work of accompaniment in El Salvador. CDHES workers were then the only activists receiving regular personal accompaniment, yet their most prominent leader had been killed. Marin volunteer Kate Bancroft wrote, "I feel like the project is a failure. They killed Herbert. We thought that our mere presence would protect the human rights workers. It didn't. It couldn't."[11]

Although Anaya had frequently been followed by suspicious vehicles, his widow, Mirna, stated later: "When they killed Herbert, he had no accompaniment with him; this was an error, he had gotten too confident."[12] But she admitted that her husband might not have been safe even with accompaniment. "They might just as easily have killed a foreign volunteer." As CDHES activist Celia Medrano expressed it, "Threats, blackmail, torture, and jail hadn't stopped him. What else could they do to him?"[13]

The government was under pressure from the United States to control the ever-more-embarrassing human rights clamor, and Anaya's international work through the CDHES was a major force behind this clamor. Anaya's attackers may have felt so harassed by the CDHES's work that the benefits of eliminating him outweighed the possible political cost—costs they may have underestimated. The threats against Anaya had gone so far as to say "even if you're with gringos we will kill you." The threat was realized with full knowledge of the accompaniment but carried out when he was alone. The resulting international outcry forced the government, in a botched attempt at damage control, to contrive an alleged guerrilla assassin.

As Celia Medrano explains, CDHES activists still trusted in accompaniment.

> They're going to think twice, because they don't want the political cost of killing a foreigner. . . . If the political decision has been taken to assassinate you, they're going to do it, in front of a foreigner or not. But now, if the situation is purely circumstantial, the international presence could have a big influence on a spontaneous decision to kill someone.[14]

On January 10, 1989, Celia Medrano and Marin volunteer Jack Hammond were detained while investigating abuses in rural Usulután. Although there is no way to determine if Hammond's presence ameliorated official treatment of Medrano, the arrest resulted in considerable outcry from the international solidarity movement. Medrano was held for forty-eight hours and subjected to all-night interrogations while blindfolded. Hammond was also held but was treated less roughly. Upon his release, he was refused a visa renewal and was forced to leave the country.[15]

The Marin Task Force accompanied the CDHES through 1991, sending thirty-three volunteers for periods of anywhere from one month to four years. When the CDHES decided that accompaniment was no longer needed, Marin initiated a similar relationship in Guatemala with the National Widows Council (CONAVIGUA).

Office Work

In late 1987, a few months after the Marin group had arrived, Peace Brigades International began a steady presence in some of the other offices that were then focal points for opposition activities. These included the UNTS, CRIPDES, and COMADRES. These offices were all in San Salvador. They were simple places with little furniture or equipment—perhaps in the basement of a building or a one-family house. Nevertheless, they fulfilled a variety of functions: a reception space for the public, a meeting place, a storage space for materials, a home for threatened members of the organization, and a refuge for members who came in from the countryside.

The security forces often broke in without a court order, demanding identity papers, searching the premises, and sometimes detaining members. Similar incursions were also carried out by unidentified armed men in civilian dress. Each office was facing constant surveillance; the COMADRES office had recently been bombed.

Accompaniment was still a new idea in El Salvador. Some Salvadorans grasped it immediately, but many members of these organizations did not understand the volunteers' function. Salvadorans were also suspicious, because many foreigners were working in the country at the behest of the U.S. government and its aid programs, and they were suspected of reinforcing counterinsurgency policies. There were also constant rumors that the U.S. embassy was trying to infiltrate the popular organizations. So there was always a certain reserve with foreigners once the conversation went beyond certain bounds. But as volunteers passed countless hours in these offices, friendships and trust developed.

The international presence was valued more when repression increased. One day in April 1988, when a large demonstration had been called at the University of El Salvador, the security forces blocked the streets to isolate several popular movement offices. Spanish PBI volunteer Luis Enrique Eguren was on his way to the CRIPDES office:

> As I approached, I saw quickly that there were two checkpoints, one at either end of the little street, stopping everyone walking towards the CRIPDES office. But they were still letting cars through, so I decided to try a taxi. I paid him in advance, so I'd be able to get out quickly. . . . As we approached the checkpoint, the taxi driver gave me a questioning look. I thought he was going to stop, but instead he accelerated slightly. As we passed, the soldiers were looking at me, doubtfully. When the taxi stopped thirty meters down the street, one of them started coming towards me. I got out quickly and went up the few steps to the door. It was opened for me before I had to ring the bell, and as it was shut behind me, I saw that the taxi had gone and the soldier was on the steps, looking surprised. It had taken only a few seconds, and the people inside the CRIPDES office had watched the whole operation. I could see in their smiles their satisfaction—shared—that we had broken the isolation that they had been submitted to for several hours.[16]

In another incident, Spanish PBI volunteer Ramon Ballester accompanied some organizers for the telephone workers' union (ASTTEL) while they handed out leaflets in a telephone office.

> The police surrounded the building, closed the doors, and told everyone to leave except us. An officer began to aggressively interrogate one of the ASTTEL members, asking what they were doing there, and why they were disrupting the office. Then he demanded they all identify themselves. They refused, asserting that what they were doing was entirely legal and that he had no right to close the office. At this point I came over and asked the officer innocently, "Is there any problem, sir?" He stared at me, and asked, "Are you a foreigner?" I said yes, that I was accompanying these people, and I didn't understand what was happening, or why he had locked us in here. At this point his aggressive attitude changed. He responded that nothing was wrong and these were routine procedures in a country at war. Then he said, "OK, you can all leave now," and they opened the doors and we left. The ASTTEL workers

commented later that the situation had been fierce and they joked about how I had kept innocently asking the officer, "What's happening here?" I understood from them that my presence had made a big difference.[17]

Humberto Centeno

Humberto Centeno was one of the most threatened people in El Salvador. He was also one of the first popular movement leaders to grasp the potential of international accompaniment. He put PBI to work immediately and became a trusted adviser. By 1988, the forty-seven-year-old union leader and journalist had been tortured, jailed, and exiled several times and was the most visible member of the Executive Committee of the UNTS, the National Unity of Salvadoran Workers. We asked him how he dealt with the risks he faced.

> I've been a union activist for a long time. Measuring risk is basically the same as doing an analysis of levels of repression. . . . From 1987 to 1989 were really difficult years. So what are the symptoms for this thermometer? First: bombings of union offices and attacks against leaders. Second: machine-gunning of houses and people in the street. Third: being followed by armed men. You start to develop a sixth sense—you watch every movement of everyone around you, and you reach a moment where you know you're being followed. . . .
>
> It's a whole atmosphere that you can sense when they are getting ready to kill you. It's hard to explain this feeling. First you have this foreboding sense, then you notice them following you, or hanging around near your home.
>
> At the same time, we stay very alert to the declarations of those in power: the military, the [cabinet] ministers, etc., and you see who they are blaming and targeting in their propaganda. They try to turn public opinion against you in advance. So later, if you're dead, they can just say "He was a bad one, anyway."[18]

One of these declarations occurred in March 1988. It was an especially volatile moment: a weakened government led by Christian Democrat President Napoleon Duarte faced strong opposition from the right-wing ARENA party (Nationalist Republican Alliance, principal party of the Salvadoran hard line) in the upcoming legislative and municipal elections. On March 9, Minister of Defense Eugenio Vides Casanova claimed that FMLN documents had been captured outlining a guerrilla campaign, including mass mobilizations of the labor movement. The UNTS immediately called the announcement a justification for continued captures and assassinations.

Around 5 P.M. the next day, a busload of union activists, including Centeno, was heading toward the Labor Ministry near Ilopango air force base to meet another group of unionists who had been occupying the building. With them on the bus were six members of a solidarity delegation from the United States and two Spanish PBI volunteers. As the bus approached Ilopango on the main highway, it was stopped by an air force barricade. An officer told Centeno that they would have to turn around. Centeno assured him that they had every right to stay there. The officer left shortly thereafter in a car with other soldiers.

An hour later, when it was almost dark, two truckloads of camouflaged soldiers arrived from the air force base. The soldiers surrounded the group, grabbed Centeno, and threw him into one of the trucks. The soldiers then forced the rest of the group back into the bus at gunpoint, screaming at them to leave. The truck carrying Centeno drove off. The soldiers kept their guns trained on the group, and eventually a shot was fired through one of the bus windows, grazing one of the unionists in the ear. The bus headed back to the UNTS office.

At the UNTS office, everyone launched into feverish activity to publicize Centeno's capture. The foreign volunteers notified their contacts in North America and Europe. The next day, after interrogating and beating Centeno, the air force handed him over to the treasury police, who immediately checked him into a private hospital in downtown San Salvador and notified his wife. After his release, Centeno lodged a protest before the Inter-American Human Rights Commission.

A group of soldiers had captured Centeno in plain sight of international witnesses. The air force had had plenty of time to consider the foreign presence and make a decision. The accompaniment had not stopped them.

The order for capture had to have come from General Juan Rafael Bustillo, commander of the Salvadoran air force, or someone close to him. Bustillo had close ties to the extreme Right and played a fundamental role in implementing counterinsurgency strategy against the FMLN. The air force under Bustillo's leadership (1979–90) became the primary recipient of U.S. military aid and a stronghold of power within the Salvadoran armed forces. He maintained a privileged relationship with the U.S. military and political establishment.*

Bustillo's relationship with the Duarte government, though, cannot have been very good: in early 1988, the right wing was working against the ruling Christian Democratic Party. The capture of an important labor leader a mere ten days before the elections would inevitably cause problems for the government. According to Centeno:

> At that time, a delegation from Harvard spoke with Defense Minister Vides Casanova, and in his talk about human rights he told them, "Look at the

---

*For example, in 1989, Bustillo was the only Salvadoran military officer invited to President George Bush's inauguration. See Charles Lane, "El tiburon piloto de El Salvador: la crueldad y corrupcion de Juan Rafael Bustillo," *El Diario Latino* (San Salvador), September 24, 1990; and *Proceso* (San Salvador), March 18, 1992, p. 12.

case of Centeno: an official in the air force captures him and practically kills him. We didn't give that order! How could we?" I believe him: I don't think they would have given an order to do that in front of so many people and foreigners.[19]

According to Felix Ulloa, president of the Institute for Juridical Studies of El Salvador and formerly a lawyer for the UNTS:

I don't think the military had enough analytical subtlety to consider whether their violations of human rights would weaken the government. They took decisions by instinct, an instinct for repression, aggression, or, from their perspective, survival.[20]

In these cases, there are different spheres of decision, with a certain autonomy between them, yielding sometimes contradictory results. If indeed General Bustillo ordered Centeno's capture, acting outside the legitimate authority of the civilian government, he wasn't going to suffer the political consequences. It would be difficult for the United States to reprimand a man who had been a pillar of their military strategy and was also closely associated with the right-wing groups expected to head the next government. Thus, whether Bustillo spontaneously took advantage of having Centeno right on his doorstep or considered the costs carefully, he probably would not have been discouraged by the presence of international witnesses.*

Centeno was tortured by the air force, but the treasury police immediately put him in a private hospital—and paid his expenses. This special handling suggests that the government was trying to undo the damage caused by Bustillo's unauthorized action.

Throughout 1988 and 1989, Centeno remained one of the popular movement's more visible leaders, and threats against him continued. With increasing frequency, he turned to PBI for accompaniment. By August 1989, he was being accompanied twenty-four hours a day.

I'm certain that the fact that I went around with foreigners is one of the reasons I am still alive.

The armed forces sent me scores of messages in those years. Sometimes they grabbed one of my kids and said, "How's your dad? Listen, tell him to stop talking about the military. People are getting upset with him." A little friendly advice.

The way I lived it was this: if Humberto Centeno, condemned to death since 1985, so to speak, had gone around with a police escort—if I asked the state to protect me—I wouldn't have lived thirty days. . . . If Humberto Centeno had only depended on the accompaniment of fellow unionists or church workers, I also have no doubt that we'd all have turned up dead in

---

*Bustillo would later be named as one of the primary initiators in the assassination of the Jesuit leaders of the University of Central America in November 1989.

some alley. . . . But, when Humberto Centeno goes around with someone from the United States, Canada, or Spain—well, to kill us together would bring the state a heavy political cost.[21]

Centeno's days were absorbed in public organizing. When night fell, he and his accompaniment would head somewhere to hide and sleep. Centeno usually didn't decide where to go until the last minute; he had dozens of different places where he could sleep with no advance notice. One night he might stay in the house of a friend, the next in a union office. This tactic gave the death squads too many possibilities, thus diluting the chances of finding him on any given night to carry out their constant threats to kill him.

Semiclandestinity and accompaniment are both valid security strategies when used separately, but the combination is somewhat problematic. The mere presence of the foreigner makes hiding more difficult, and the protective function of the accompaniment is lost if the potential attacker is unaware of it. But Centeno wanted to get the most out of every possible strategy. By hiding, he could minimize the probability of being found by the security forces or death squads. But if hiding failed, he wanted the accompaniment on hand when the encounter occurred.

Accompanying Against Bombs

The military often surrounded the offices of the popular movement with checkpoints, harassing everyone heading toward them. As more checkpoints and encirclements sprang up, more accompaniment was requested. U.S. PBI volunteer Carolyn Mow remembered spending a lot of time in these offices:

> You sit there all day and every day, and nothing happens; you feel a little bit like a piece of furniture. And it's not clear that anyone really knows or cares that you're there. But during moments of crisis, I felt that all that time maybe really did matter, so that you would be there at the moment when you were needed.[22]

These offices were bombed repeatedly. In defense, the UNTS set up rows of sandbags in front of its office entrance. After one bombing, the UNTS asked PBI volunteers to stay outside the building where they could be seen. According to Spanish volunteer Ester Domenech:

> When we headed over to the UNTS office in the morning to relieve the PBI volunteer who had been there overnight, we would have to climb over the sandbag barricades. . . . As we passed we would always greet "Good morning" to the soldiers, and then walk down the street to the other sandbag

barricades, which UNTS had set up in front of its office. There we would stay, in front of the office, as visible as possible.[23]

Carolyn Mow recalls:

Sitting on the sandbags, in front of a place that had just been bombed, I felt more useful than I had felt inside. There were soldiers there all day. We were watching, making sure that people from the office didn't get arrested. They might not have continued to come and go from the office if we had not been there to walk them a certain distance.[24]

The timing of each bombing seemed directly linked to the progress of the war on the military front. For example, according to Centeno:

One day the FMLN attacks the First Brigade, and the next day we get a bomb. Then the FMLN attacks the high command—someone else is bombed. The security forces couldn't figure out how to bomb the FMLN, so they would bomb *us*.[25]

Sometimes the link was publicly announced in advance. At the end of December 1988, for instance, a new death squad calling itself ARDE (Anticommunist Revolutionary Action for Extermination) announced to the press that "for every car-bomb the guerrilla explodes we will put at least one bomb in the houses of the Communist leaders." The next day, another death squad, calling itself the Committee for Eastern Solidarity (COSOR), announced that "for every terrorist attack committed by the [FMLN's] front organizations, there will be an implacable and direct punishment of the political leaders of the extreme left and the contaminated unions."[26] Both death squads included foreigners in their threats, referring to the "infiltration of our country" and "death to international Communists."

On February 14, 1989, the military set up checkpoints encircling the UNTS office, questioning everyone going near the building. Early the next morning, a bomb destroyed the entranceway of the building. A PBI volunteer and several Salvadorans were sleeping inside. The popular movement and the international solidarity movement denounced the bombing vehemently, but PBI never publicized the fact that one of its volunteers had been inside. The possible injury of a foreign citizen might have strengthened the force of the international pressure after the event, but PBI was afraid that publicity might provoke the volunteers' immediate expulsion. This silence directly contradicts the strategy of deterrence and shows how tenuous the volunteers felt their presence was.

Bombings with volunteers inside raised hard questions. Was the army aware of the international presence and measuring the consequences? PBI volunteers were not sure. The security forces could certainly see them coming and going, but whether these movements were carefully traced and communicated to superiors or between shifts was unknown. And given that the army always denied responsibility, it is hard to establish the chain of command for the bombing orders.

If the bombings were explicit reactions to FMLN attacks, such a stimulus-response spiral would leave little space for effective deterrence by accompaniment in an individual case. The military objective of the bombings—to punish and deter FMLN attacks—may have seemed to outweigh the political costs implied by a foreign presence.

There was really no way of knowing if the international presence could prevent bombings. As attacks increased, the increasing demand for accompaniment was a statement of faith and hope. Alicia de García of the COMADRES summed it up simply:

> Look at what they did while you were there, and just imagine what they might have done if you weren't![27]

The CRIPDES Assault

CRIPDES worked with refugees and the rural displaced populations, aiding in their resettlement to the areas they had been expelled from by the scorched-earth strategy of the army. Since many of these resettlement areas were contested by the FMLN, the army was extremely belligerent with CRIPDES. PBI maintained a regular presence in the CRIPDES office and traveled with activists outside the capital.

On the morning of April 19, 1989, Attorney General Jose Roberto García Alvarado was assassinated by an FMLN commando unit. The security forces immediately encircled the offices of three popular movement organizations, CRIPDES among them. The other two offices were quickly invaded and their leaders arrested. At CRIPDES, the door was barricaded, with sixty people inside: CRIPDES workers; people from the countryside wounded in army attacks and waiting for an appointment at the clinic, including a blind man and an amputee; a seven-day-old baby; an eighty-six-year-old woman; and three foreigners: a U.S. church worker, a German journalist, and Australian PBI volunteer Eve Scarfe. When soldiers banged on the door at 3 P.M., CRIPDES leaders refused to let them in without a court order.[28]

The military encirclement of the CRIPDES office lasted over eight hours. Salvadoran and foreign journalists arrived, as well as members of other Salvadoran organizations and three more PBI team members. Various members of CRIPDES kept up a constant verbal barrage over megaphones,

PBI volunteers (seated) observing outside while police prepare to storm the CRIPDES office (April 19, 1989).

denouncing the encirclement and assuring the authorities that there were also foreigners inside. Eve Scarfe remembers:

> Anti-riot police arrived as reinforcements, and they started preventing journalists from getting close enough to see what was going on. . . . The journalists protested, and while CRIPDES leaders debated with a sergeant, they [the journalists] came up to the building and began taping interviews through the windows, and taking photos of the newborn, the wounded and the old women. I never thought the soldiers would break in after that.[29]

PBI volunteer Carolyn Mow was outside:

> There were all these police and military outside, just standing there, not letting anyone go in, but not actually going in themselves either. At one point, one of them said to us, "So when are you all leaving, anyway?" So we felt that they were waiting for the crowd to die down before they forced their way in. They could have gone in whenever they felt like it. By 11 at night, many of the press had left, but we were still there. We couldn't stop them, but I think they had been hoping that we would leave, too.[30]

A little after 11 P.M., the soldiers forced open the door and put everyone inside into a military truck, which took them to treasury police headquarters. Once there, the older men, the women with small children, and the German journalist were separated from the rest and released. Eve Scarfe was kept standing up for sixteen hours with no food or water and then handed over to the British consul.

> A few times I was threatened, for instance one man said to me, "If I were the president of this country, old women like you would not exist." Or, "British lady, soon we'll do this": and draws his finger across his throat, like a knife, and makes a choking sound. Another time they told me, "Your soul is poisoned. All the foreigners who come here have poisoned souls. You're all condemned."
> Such hatred! Towards the Salvadoran prisoners and towards the foreigners. The hate, palpable in a way I had not experienced before. A feeling of being in the hands of someone who would like nothing better than to hurt you, and only held back—precariously?—by some sense of political expediency.

The rest of the Salvadorans were released a few hours later, except for six members of the CRIPDES directorate, who were tortured and imprisoned for four months.

Miguel Mejía, a CRIPDES member, believed that PBI's presence was important, despite the arrests:

> When they captured us, I remember the woman from Peace Brigades. We could see that when she spoke with her tormentors she was very brave. She asked why they were doing it, and she explained to them what respect for human rights meant.[31]

Eve was skeptical.

> I don't think the international presence in the office made much difference. They had already searched several other offices. . . . We saw them coming and barricaded the doors. That may have slowed them down somewhat. But they were getting in one way or another.

It wasn't the barricades that slowed them down. Whereas other offices had been broken into at once, at CRIPDES, the military had delayed entry for eight hours, probably calculating the political cost of the international and media presence. As night wore on and the press left, the calculation changed: PBI alone was not sufficient.

Nevertheless, Eve's presence throughout the process of arrest and detention made a difference. Even during the standoff, PBI supporters all over the world sent hundreds of messages to the authorities. This pressure—from other urgent action networks as well—continued until everyone captured was released or accounted for. In fact, after Eve's release, the treasury police published a list of those still detained. The list omitted the name of CRIPDES leader Inocente Orellana, and it was feared that he might be disappeared. Eve's testimony that she had seen him in custody contributed to minimizing this risk.

This event strengthened the relationship between PBI and CRIPDES. PBI volunteers visited regularly those who were imprisoned. In addition, despite the apparent failure to deter arrests, the remaining CRIPDES members were even more appreciative of the ongoing presence. According to Carolyn Mow, "After the capture, they went right back the next day to clean up the ransacked office, but first they came up to us and said, 'We're going back. Are you coming with us?'"[32]

The international outcry after the CRIPDES roundup may have contributed to more restrained government decision making in subsequent events. A month later, after the FMLN attacked the headquarters of the First Brigade, the national police barracks, and the Transportation Bureau, the police requested court orders to search the offices of the National Federation of Salvadoran Workers (FENASTRAS), CDHES, and CRIPDES. In each case, the judge ruled that there was no evidence to justify the searches.[33]

The Salvadoran Refugee Repatriation

Tens of thousands of Salvadorans spent most of the 1980s in refugee camps in Honduras, after fleeing army bombings and massacres in 1981–83. In late 1986, however, the UNHCR announced its plans to close the Honduran camps: the Salvadorans would have to either go home—to a military government that didn't want them—or accept Honduran citizenship. They chose to go home, but on their own terms: they would return in large groups, and to their original homes. After a difficult and rushed negotiation process with very little political support from the UNHCR, the first caravan of buses and trucks, carrying 4,000 Salvadoran refugees, arrived at the border on October 10, 1987.[34]

The refugees knew that it wouldn't be easy to reconstruct their lives in a war zone, especially when the army was openly hostile to their presence. They hoped that international presence would help, but they had no guarantees from the Salvadoran government. With the support of international NGOs that had visited the Honduran camps and the work of CRIPDES and the CNR inside El Salvador, the refugees arranged for the first mass return to be accompanied by dozens of foreigners. The Salvadoran government was prepared; unhindered by any sort of formal agreement such as was later achieved in Guatemala, it simply closed the border to the accompaniment. CRIPDES and CNR were ready for this and arranged for dozens of other foreigners to travel up to the border from San Salvador to replace those who couldn't get in from Honduras.

Continuous accompaniment of the return voyage was thus achieved, somewhat surreptitiously. Maintaining an ongoing international presence in returned communities, popularly known as "repopulations" (*repoblaciones*) in El Salvador, was an arduous process. The government went out of its way to prevent foreigners from getting to the repopulations. The accompaniment effort was uncoordinated and improvised from one day to the next, combining short-term visits by delegations from European and North American solidarity groups with longer-term stays by church workers, humanitarian aid groups, and others. Although the obstacles and disorganization resulted in some lapses, most of the repatriated villages, as well as the subsequent return of thousands more refugees, were consistently accompanied. The experience, both of government opposition and improvisation, was a learning process that directly informed the Guatemalan return several years later (see chapter 10).

The Army Against the Foreigners

The Salvadoran army was much less confident and strategically capable than its Guatemalan counterpart, and it suffered from debilitating levels of corruption and a subservient dependence on the United States for both resources and guidance. Salvadoran officers shared the same ideological blinders and biases described in chapter 3, only more so. Salvadoran General Orlando Zepeda described the modern era as follows:

> We're seeing a period of romanticism, for more than 200 years now, where we're living under the philosophical influence of socialism of "the masses." We simply have to put up with it. We may not be completely in agreement, but this is the current fashion: "human rights" and "democracy."
>
> But 2,000 years ago, Plato and Aristotle were enemies of democracy. They referred to it as anarchy, which was but one step short of dictatorship. Because democracy necessarily degenerates to dictatorship in order to correct the errors in behavior of the people: this formless mass without direction, completely polarized and anarchic—where everyone yells, and he who yells the loudest leads. You lose that vital principle of order and harmony, because everyone demands his rights, but no one fulfills his duties.
>
> But you can't say anything in these times against the democratic system. We were born into it. It permits greater liberties, which at times turns into licentiousness. So we have to put up with all these criticisms. But some way or another we must find mechanisms of self-defense against this tendency.[35]

As the war intensified in 1988 and 1989, more foreigners came to El Salvador, either on short visits or for long-term work stints with humanitarian or political organizations. In a later interview, General Mauricio Vargas, one of the Salvadoran army's foremost counterinsurgency experts, described how the military felt about foreign and local NGOs:

Here in El Salvador there were NGOs in industrial quantities! Their objectives were not humanitarian, but political. . . . They were really anarchic: they come in to work in one place, and then they're somewhere else. They never asked permission. They did whatever they wanted, breaking rules and laws. It was a constant confrontation. . . . The ICRC [International Committee of the Red Cross] came with clear institutional functions, an area of competence, and well-defined procedures. All the rest was just a complete carnival.[36]

General Zepeda accused some members of the NGOs Doctors of the World and Doctors Without Borders of being guerrilla members and of helping to organize the FMLN system for caring for the wounded. He added:

I told these foreign groups, "All you're doing here is extending the suffering. The more logistical aid the guerrilla receives, the longer it will take them to give up and negotiate." Any armed force will die without a logistical apparatus: food, medicines, clothes, weapons. You don't have to defeat them in combat if you can attack their supply routes. But there were so many of these organizations! . . . At one point I made a list of about thirty-five different supposedly "humanitarian" organizations who were helping [the FMLN] in the conflict.[37]

Zepeda was the highest-level officer responsible for controlling the movements of humanitarian aid and foreign visitors to the rural refugee repopulations. He established a system of "safe-conduct" passes, without which access was difficult. This mechanism achieved two military objectives: it limited accompaniment, and it threatened the communities' material survival and thus, from the army's viewpoint, the FMLN's logistical support.

The hostile attitude of the Salvadoran government toward foreigners in general made it particularly difficult to judge the effectiveness of the growing accompaniment presence. It was not merely a case of individual xenophobia: it was a matter of policy. Government spokesmen, quoting the constitution, deplored the alleged foreign intervention in sovereign affairs.[38] The chief of the high command, General Onecifero Blandon, declared on August 16, 1988:

The Army is warning all internationalists: all foreign agitators who come here to immerse themselves in internal Salvadoran politics and provoke disorder will be expelled or consigned to the tribunals.[39]

Systematic Detention and Expulsion

Beatrice Chantal was a French nurse who had worked for a year with the health programs of the Catholic archbishop of El Salvador. In late September

1988, she planned a trip to Paris. When her baggage was searched in the Salvadoran airport, the police found what they called "communist literature and propaganda for clandestine groups connected with the FMLN-FDR." Chantal was handed over to the French embassy and expelled. The treasury police declared it "a new case of foreigners intervening in internal affairs. She was posing as a religious missionary, but she was really a nurse and activist of international communism."[40]

From 1985 to 1987, security forces detained only thirty-five foreigners and deported only two.[41] In 1988 alone, they detained at least 108 and deported 35 of them. Various factors may have caused this shift. The popular movement was becoming more outspoken, and large numbers of organized refugees were returning from camps in Honduras with foreign accompaniment. There were more foreigners in the country now, but this expanded presence could not account for the drastic increase in the number of detentions and deportations.

The majority of those detained had come to El Salvador to support the repatriations. Most detentions took place in rural areas under tight military control. It is conceivable that the military, unaccustomed to and unwilling to tolerate the presence of so many meddlesome foreigners, was reacting with exaggerated anger, forcing the civilian government to acquiesce in the expulsion of foreigners without considering political costs. The army's fear that material aid was reaching the guerrillas may have outweighed any concerns about image. In any event, the abrupt change in 1988 (six times as many detentions and seventeen times as many deportations compared with previous years) and the continual official declarations against foreigners suggest a high-level policy change, approved or at least consented to by the government.*

In addition to detention and deportation, immigration authorities were authorizing extremely short lengths of stays when foreigners first entered the country, sometimes as little as twenty-four or forty-eight hours. During this brief time, they needed to report to immigration headquarters in San Salvador for intensive interrogations.

Some foreigners could not get in at all. The government set up a system of "blacklists" at each entry into the country. Acting President Castillo Claramunt† declared in 1988:

---

*The detention and deportation figures dropped significantly again from 1989 to 1991, to an average of twenty-five detentions and eight deportations a year (excluding the November 1989 offensive and state of siege, to be discussed later). This decrease is more difficult to explain. The ascent of the right-wing Republican Nationalist Alliance (ARENA) party to power with the March 1989 elections provoked a series of changes in policies, as well as in the leadership in the armed forces and the immigration department. The change in treatment of foreigners could have been the result of a combination of bureaucratic factors or policy shifts.
†President Duarte, dying of cancer, was in the United States undergoing treatment.

The procedure is that foreign agitators should be rounded up and brought before the authorities for expulsion. Sometimes we are not 100% successful, but that does not mean we're tolerant: Immigration has orders to proceed, as well as not to let such people into the country.[42]

For example, on November 25, 1988, Peggy O'Grady landed at the San Salvador airport with her visa and papers completely in order. She was working for the archdiocese of San Francisco. She was not allowed into the country. After considerable pressure from San Francisco Archbishop Quinn and several U.S. representatives, the director general of immigration confirmed that there was a restriction against O'Grady for having participated in activities opposed to the Salvadoran government.[43]

Jorge Martinez, former vice-minister of the interior, the ministry with direct oversight over immigration, spoke with us quite matter-of-factly about the blacklists:

In Latin American countries, the offices of immigration are always closely linked with the military intelligence apparatus. When NGOs start saying that the military is behind the human rights violations, immigration control becomes one means of neutralizing these groups. Our country is no exception. The military objected to specific individuals for their political activities which violated the constitution.[44]

According to Felix Ulloa, of the Institute for Juridical Studies:

There was no legal reason to block access to the people on these lists. It was unconstitutional and in violation of international law. The names were selected and calculated not to damage the country's access to international aid: no functionaries of major agencies were on the lists . . . only *certain types* of foreigners.[45]

Immigration director Daniel Guerra declared in 1988 that "the U.S. Embassy is in complete agreement with our procedures."[46] In fact, several U.S. citizens accused the U.S. embassy of actually sending names to the Salvadoran government to add to these lists.[47] Such collaboration, though difficult to prove, would be consistent with the high level of U.S. influence over all matters of Salvadoran security. In fact, given the government's utter dependence on U.S. support, it is difficult to imagine the implementation of such a policy against U.S. citizens without embassy permission. Despite considerable pressure from U.S. citizens, the embassy never made a formal complaint about the blacklists during the years they were used, between 1988 and 1992.

The Killing of Jurg Weiss

On August 28, 1988, the dead bodies of two Salvadorans and a Swiss citizen were found in the department of Cabañas. According to the official army report, Carlos Linares, Carlos Mendez, and Jurg Dieter Weiss belonged to the FMLN and were killed in combat.

Weiss was on a short visit to El Salvador to investigate human rights violations, representing the Zurich Secretariat for Central America, a Swiss NGO. Although the Swiss government accepted the army's official explanation, an investigatory delegation (promoted by NGOs and including forensic experts) was sent from Switzerland with the support of the European Parliament. Its report concluded that Weiss had been captured by the national police, tortured, and then killed by several bullets. After his death, his face was mutilated, apparently to prevent recognition.

Exactly who killed Weiss and why were never clarified. The report suggested that the intelligence services of the army had been following him, but the motives for the surveillance and the assassination were unknown. It also alleged that high-level officials were involved in either the assassination decision or the subsequent coverup.

In September, the European Parliament condemned the Salvadoran government for Weiss's murder, citing a conscious campaign of repression against the civilian population. It accused the Salvadoran army of deliberately blocking the humanitarian work of international organizations and independent observers.[48] The resolution was one of the harshest condemnations of El Salvador in several years, and it called on the member states of the European Community to pressure for a permanent UN human rights observer in El Salvador. The Inter-American Human Rights Commission later condemned the Salvadoran government for Weiss's murder.[49]

This murder sent an eerie message to all foreigners in El Salvador and multiplied the psychological impact of every subsequent detention or threat. Whether deliberately intended or not, the effect was a classic element of state terror, applied to foreigners in the country.

PBI: Immigration Processes, Detentions, and Deportations

> Your work is clearly political . . . the military will never understand, and they will always consider you subversive.

Such was the prognosis of President Napoleón Duarte in a December 1987 meeting with PBI, shortly after the organization arrived in El Salvador. Events proved it accurate: between 1987 and 1991, no fewer than fourteen PBI volunteers were arrested and unofficially expelled.

Like many other foreigners, PBI volunteers were legally "tourists" in El Salvador. Work visas were hard to obtain, making it even more difficult to establish some sort of stability in the country. PBI volunteers needed to constantly renew their short-term visas. To avoid attracting attention by constant trips to the immigration office, some volunteers got into the habit of making short trips to Guatemala when their permitted time was up. Each time they came back in, their time would be prolonged by fifteen days or a month—more if they were lucky. There didn't seem to be any sort of centralization of information among the different border crossings and the main immigration office. Some volunteers managed to stay over a year through this constant process of extension.

Apart from official policy, visa decisions seemed to depend on the arbitrary decisions of immigration officers. PBI volunteer Karen Ridd, a professional clown who had previously worked in child therapy at a Winnipeg hospital, had to make three visits to the immigration office in 1989. Accused of FMLN collaboration the first time, she convinced (and distracted) the office workers by teaching them how to make balloon animals. On her second visit, she taught them how to juggle. Later, when Karen was reentering the country at the border and facing similar doubts about her hospital experience, a Salvadoran man in the office had an epileptic seizure. When Karen finished helping him through it, border officials happily let her in.

PBI's aim was to stay in El Salvador. As the pressure against foreigners increased in 1988, the PBI team decided to seek legal recognition from the government. What with the time-consuming bureaucratic demands of this legal process and the volunteers' individual efforts to keep their visas in order, the PBI team estimated that during certain periods it spent more than 50 percent of its time simply trying to stay in the country.*

But the official harassment was more than just time-consuming. It also affected important tactical decisions. We've already seen how fear of expulsion prevented PBI from capitalizing on the presence of a team member in a bombed building to increase international pressure. At another point, the team decided to limit its public accompaniment of popular movement demonstrations. These events were so public—and so closely watched—that the team feared that the volunteers seen at them would be more easily identified and expelled. At the same time, they reasoned that there was safety in numbers at these demonstrations, as well as significant press coverage, lessening the need for PBI protection.

Thus, for the two years prior to the November 1989 FMLN offensive, international volunteers in El Salvador lived a tenuous existence. They were insulted and threatened publicly by the army and the press, interrogated

---

*PBI finally achieved legal recognition in El Salvador in 1991, a year before leaving the country.

daily at checkpoints, detained, deported, sometimes even tortured, and, in rare but significant instances, killed. In principle, with each attack, their power to deter violence was called into question. But it wasn't questioned by the Salvadorans they accompanied. On the contrary, according to Salvadoran Episcopal Father Luis Serrano:

> The proof of effectiveness is in the persecution. It's like a church: a church that does not have problems during twelve years of war is a church which has betrayed its people. A volunteer who faces no problems is a volunteer who has not seriously confronted the truth. He has no effect.[50]

The November 1989 Offensive

On November 11, 1989, the FMLN attacked San Salvador at various points simultaneously, as well as various other large towns. It was the beginning of a general offensive that pushed the Salvadoran government and army against the ropes. The situation and the resultant repression closed all space for political activity in El Salvador for several weeks.

The offensive was to some extent announced in advance through rumors and preparatory actions. In the preceding months, the negotiations between the government and the guerrillas had stalled. The war had heated up in San Salvador, with several attacks against the civilian opposition movement and the FMLN's assassinations of several right-wing leaders and families of military officers. In October, a bombing of the COMADRES office wounded four people, including Brenda Hubbard, a U.S. woman who had been accompanying them. Immediately after an October 30 FMLN mortar attack on the high command, the office of the labor federation FENASTRAS was bombed, leaving eleven dead and dozens wounded. This bombing prompted the FMLN to walk away from the ongoing negotiations with the government. Rumors about an offensive now became silent preparations. People began closing offices and storing foodstuffs for a siege. Many activists went into hiding. Others fled the country.

The impending armed offensive against the capital raised hard questions for the PBI team. What would be the role of international accompaniment in the context of open street battles?

> We discussed it a great deal. It wasn't merely a question of whether our accompaniment would be useful or not. We also had to think about our own survival if things got really bad. We consulted with several trusted Salvadoran advisers. They wanted to leave us free to decide for ourselves, but it was clear that they wished us to stay. They felt that an international presence would be important, even during an offensive. In the end we decided to stay.[51]

A powerful factor in this decision was a sense of moral solidarity, which led the volunteers to view the option of leaving the country as a sort of desertion or abandonment of Salvadorans in their time of greatest need.[52]

A few days after open combat began on the streets of San Salvador, the team split up. Some went to accompany popular movement leaders who were in hiding, including Humberto Centeno. The rest of the volunteers provided an international presence at the refuge centers set up by the churches for civilians displaced by the violence.

As the FMLN attack progressed, the Salvadoran army faced one of the most difficult moments of the war. The army responded with aerial bombings of the poorest neighborhoods in San Salvador, killing hundreds of civilians.[53] The army countered international rebuke with the argument that the FMLN had attacked first and was using these neighborhoods as its base. PBI volunteers sometimes ventured out during the daytime to deliver messages, contact the press, or travel to where someone needed accompaniment. At night, after the 6 P.M. curfew, they would sit and listen to the planes flying low overhead and the bombs falling. As PBI volunteer Karen Ridd recalls:

> The two things I remember as strong feelings; one was a sense of closing of space. Like a cat was cornering a mouse. But the overriding sense was grief and horror of knowing what was happening to Salvadorans . . . seeing people walking out of those bombed areas with a few belongings in a plastic bag and a white flag.[54]

On November 16, an army commando unit entered the University of Central America and killed four prominent Spanish Jesuit priests and two Salvadoran women who worked there. The army and the government asserted that the guerrillas were responsible, an allegation that right-wing observers initially believed, since they couldn't see how the army could have expected to benefit from the murders. According to Waldo Salgado, president of the extreme right-wing Institute for Liberty and Democracy: "It was the most stupid act of war that anyone could imagine. . . . The killing of the Jesuits detroyed the army and raised the guerrillas to the status they now have."[55]

The accusation against the guerrillas did not hold up for long. Once army responsibility was confirmed, the international reaction was tremendous, signaling the final and total deterioration of the army's reputation. The high command would suffer the repercussions of this fiasco for years to come.

For the PBI team in the midst of the offensive, the death of the Jesuits was a psychological bombshell. According to Karen Ridd:

> That was a huge sign that foreigners were fair game. I mean, the Jesuits were very important foreigners compared to us. We might have had a little bit of a sense of immunity before. At this point that was not realistic.

Meanwhile, the security forces began to search and sack over a hundred different local churches and popular organization offices, detaining dozens of activists.[56] One specific objective was the systematic detention of foreign workers. During November 1989, at least sixty foreign citizens were officially detained. The treasury police later released a list of fifty, over 90 percent of whom were accused of "suspected terrorism" or "collaboration with terrorism." Most were released with deportation orders. For some reason, with its back against the wall and military control of San Salvador in question, the army diverted valuable time and resources into rounding up foreigners and dismantling the civilian opposition.

Accompanying One Another

One by one, church refuges were searched, and foreigners were arrested. On November 16, soldiers arrested fifteen Lutheran church workers, including twelve foreigners. The PBI team knew that the Episcopal refuge would soon follow. On the nineteenth, the Episcopal refuge was denounced on the evening news. PBI members awaited their arrest. At 5:30 A.M., November 20, a detachment of soldiers arrived at the church, looking for "the foreigners." According to Colombian PBI volunteer Marcela Rodriguez:

> The lieutenant started to explain to us that he was concerned for our security. "We have information that the guerrilla wants to kill all the foreigners in order to incriminate us, the security forces, and damage the image of the country. We must protect you, and to do this we need to keep careful track of all foreigners in the country. We also know that there are some foreign terrorists who have come into the country in recent months to support the offensive." (Later on, at the National Guard barracks, when someone there asked this same officer who we were, he responded, "terrorists from the Episcopal church.")[57]

The soldiers were relatively civil during the arrest, so PBI volunteer Karen Ridd asked permission to make a telephone call. She called the Canadian honorary consul. Serena Cosgrove, a U.S. PBI volunteer staying at the Camino Real hotel making press contacts, called in at that moment, and Karen told her that their arrest was in progress. Serena immediately called the PBI regional office in the United States. PBI's international emergency response network was activated before the captives were even taken out of the church. The group of captives included Zea Melendez, a Guatemalan; Josephine Beecher, a U.S. religious worker; and five PBI volunteers.

At the National Guard barracks, Spanish PBI volunteers Ester Domenech, Francesc Riera, and Luis Perez were handed over to their embassy. The other two PBI volunteers, Canadian Karen Ridd and Colombian Marcela Rodriguez, were loaded into a truck with Beecher and Melendez.

At the treasury police compound, the soldiers took Marcela and Josephine out of the truck, handcuffed together, and began walking them across the parking lot. Marcela, still blindfolded, sensed that Karen was not with them. Unwilling to leave her comrade behind, she instinctively turned around, dragging Josephine back with her toward the truck, until the soldiers assured her that Karen would follow as soon as they found a blindfold for her. Because of Marcela's resistance, the soldiers simply draped a sweater over Karen's head and brought them all in together.

After some initial processing and questions, they were loaded into another truck. A soldier told them that they were on their way to the "Puerta del Diablo," a well-known dead-body dump. But instead they were simply driven across the compound to the interrogation center. From this point on they were separated. Karen recalls:

> I remember having something run across my throat and being told, "next time that will be a knife." Shoved around. Hit a bit, not real hard. Back of the hand, in the ribs. The handcuffs were too tight. I asked that they be loosened, and they were. Marcela asked the same, and they refused.
>
> The most frightening moment was when they took me aside and told me to pull my shirt up and my pants down. They claimed they had to check for battle wounds and register any marks so we couldn't blame them later, but the sexual threat was obvious.

Karen and Marcela were interrogated for several hours about their alleged connections with the FMLN. According to Marcela's later testimony:

> On repeated occasions, when I am silent and don't accept their accusations, they hit me in the back with some object. . . . I get threats like "I'm going to have to put 'the hood' on you if you don't cooperate!" Then for ten minutes there are no questions, and I can hear the beatings and the screaming of women and men who are being tortured near me. Sometimes I pick out Karen's voice. I hear metal doors opening and closing. Then another minute of silence; then more screams, more weeping.[58]

Five PBI volunteers had been detained during the previous two years, and Karen had studied their experience. She had talked with other Salvadorans, studied the testimonies from other detentions. The team had discussed strategies for dealing with different interrogation tactics. Karen felt well prepared: her interrogators asked few questions for which she had not already prepared answers.

> The whole interrogation took about five hours. As curfew hour approached, they were suddenly in a big hurry to get me out of there. In their hurry, they

took my blindfold off at a place where I was able to see that Marcela was still there in the hall. It was really horrible to see her blindfolded and facing a wall with her hands behind her back. But it was good to know where she was.

Just before curfew, the treasury police released Karen and sent her across the parking lot to meet her Canadian embassy representative:

I felt a great responsibility for Marcela. I had a strong sense of her vulnerability. . . . The soldiers told me that her embassy people were outside as well, and that I should go out. I wasn't sure what to do. I felt like a betrayer every step across the parking lot. Then when I saw that there was no one there for her. . . . I felt sick. I felt like I had blown it.

Karen told her embassy official she wouldn't leave without Marcela. The Canadian official, worried about the approaching curfew, was angry with her, but she insisted. She had to insist even more firmly with the treasury police officials. They were a bit puzzled but decided to let her stay. The Canadian official left, saying simply, "Well, we'll see you whenever they let you out."

As I walked back towards the jail I felt a sense of triumph. But back in the interrogation room reality hit with a thump. What would be next? Torture? Then they handcuffed me again and took me to a different hallway which was full of people in various states of post-torture. I could see it under the blindfold. I saw some faces of people I vaguely recognized. . . . I felt an enormous sense of their misery.

My captors were abusive at first, and ridiculed my decision to stay. But when I reminded them of the importance of loyalty, and pointed out that they would have done the same thing for a comrade in distress, their attitude became much more respectful.

Marcela Rodriguez remembers this moment:

At one point I heard Karen's voice and then steps approaching me. Someone forced my head against the wall and said, "Some white bitch had a chance to leave and didn't take it. Now you're both going to see the treatment a terrorist deserves!" He threatened me some more, knocked my head against the wall again, and then left. Again I heard Karen. Someone asked me if I was frightened. They took off my handcuffs and I took Karen's hand. I was still blindfolded. They opened a door, took off our blindfolds, and told us to walk straight ahead without turning to look back.[59]

When she was pushed out the door, still blindfolded, Karen felt cold air,

I thought, "Oh God, here's the air-conditioned cell I've heard about."* Under my blindfold, I could see a drain in the concrete under my feet. Then they pulled the blindfold off, and I looked up and I could see all these stars. We

*A common torture, keeping the captive naked in a cell at a low temperature.

were out. Back in the parking lot. We walked back across the parking lot holding hands.

Karen and Marcela were driven to the Camino Real hotel in a military convoy and handed over to Canadian embassy officials. Within a few days, the entire PBI team was in "exile" in Guatemala. Josephine Beecher, the American religious worker detained with them, had been released earlier. She later revealed that she had been threatened and beaten and had been forced to sign a document in the presence of a U.S. consular official declaring that she had not been mistreated.[60] The Guatemalan in the group, Zea Melendez, was also beaten and was held for two days before being deported.

There are actually very few previously documented cases of mistreatment of foreigners in detention in El Salvador. During the November 1989 offensive, there were not only a massive number of deportations but also frequent reports of physical mistreatment. In another case, two U.S. citizens, Brenda Hubbard and Eugene Terril, were captured in the COMADRES office and severely beaten and threatened until their release. U.S. religious worker Jennifer Casolo was held for eighteen days on charges of having FMLN weapons buried in her backyard. Her arrest was initially supported by the U.S. embassy. Later, a judge found no legal basis for the charges against her, and she was released, but only after considerable U.S. congressional pressure.

During the guerrilla offensive and government state of siege, out of thirty-seven Europeans and North Americans detained, 75 percent were held for less than twenty-four hours, and nearly all were handed over to their embassies. In contrast, out of seventeen South American and Central American foreigners detained, 60 percent were held for over four days and then summarily deported. PBI volunteer Marcela Rodriguez, with Karen Ridd's accompaniment, was the only Latin American to be freed the same day she was detained.[61]

More Space, Continued Harassment

The FMLN November 1989 offensive was a turning point in the evolution of the war in El Salvador. The attack was finally repelled by the army, but it showed the degree of military stagnation of the conflict. Internal and external forces pressured the government and the FMLN toward negotiation. The investigation of the killing of the Jesuits led to prosecutions of military officials for the first time in the history of El Salvador. Although only a few officers were condemned, the parallel political investigation implicated the highest-level officials, many of whom eventually resigned their positions in government. This case also led the U.S. Congress to place serious limitations on military aid.

After diplomatic negotiations with the government, PBI installed a new team in El Salvador in April 1990. The demand for accompaniment persisted, especially in rural areas, where the war continued in force and the struggle of the displaced for land intensified. The political space was much more open, and PBI managed to achieve legal status in 1991. But harassment continued: military attitudes don't change so quickly.

The Salvadoran popular movement consistently defended its accompaniment in the face of harassment. In resettled refugee communities, for instance, villagers sometimes prevented detentions by surrounding their accompaniment with no more than their bodies: unarmed men, women, and children saying no to the army.

On November 5, 1990, PBI volunteers Sharon Bernstein and Luis Miranda accompanied Episcopal Reverend Edgar Palacios to a prayer service for peace in the main plaza in Chalatenango. The army demanded that the Salvadorans cancel the event and surrounded the crowd with tanks and soldiers. The tension was so high that Reverend Palacios feared a massacre. At the edge of the crowd, a frustrated army officer launched into a screaming tirade against Sharon Bernstein, "Get out of this country, you fucking gringa!" and then hit her with the butt of his rifle.

> I remember thinking, "obviously I can't leave your country right this minute. What do you want me to do, disappear?"
>
> After he hit me, he pushed me back into the crowd, which sort of absorbed me. That was the aspect I most remember, because it was, well, an incredibly peaceful experience. . . . I was enveloped into the crowd, and slowly sucked back, for my own safety, to where he couldn't see me anymore.[62]

The officer's harassment suggests that he found Sharon's presence more provocative than deterring. But his singling out of a visible foreigner for such harassment shows that the presence weighed heavily on his mind. Sharon may have been a buffer, a deflection of the officer's frustration at being unable to control the rest of the crowd. Compared with the more deadly violence that Reverend Palacios feared, the blow on the shoulder was relatively minor—though sufficient to prompt an immediate protective reaction from the Salvadorans around her.[63]

Three more PBI volunteers were arrested in 1991. The seesaw of official harassment and international protest generated an unstable equilibrium: foreigners could never feel secure, but neither could the government get rid of them entirely. With each arrest of a volunteer, PBI activated its international emergency response network, and in several cases, evidence shows that this external pressure helped bring about the release not only of the PBI volunteer but sometimes also of the Salvadorans arrested with them. When U.S. PBI volunteer Phil Pardi was arrested along with Salvadoran activists Gloria and Ernesto Zamora in August 1991, within a few hours he got a visit from the U.S. embassy. According to Phil:

> Actually the first thing he said to me was, "Well, Phil, you're very popular, you ever think of running for mayor of Cambridge, Massachusetts? I think half the town of Cambridge has probably called me." He was also asking me why the people who were calling him knew Ernesto and Gloria. That told me that the phone calls and the faxes were also about Ernesto and Gloria. This embassy guy just wanted to get me out of there. He kept saying, "Well, Phil, you're just in the wrong place at the wrong time." And I kept saying, "No, I was in the right place at the right time." But he just didn't get it.[64]

Phil and Gloria were released that same afternoon. Ernesto was freed the next day, with no charges.

In 1990 and 1991, the Salvadoran government and the FMLN signed a series of peace accords, prompting the July 1991 arrival of 150 UN observers (ONUSAL) and, in January 1992, a final cease-fire. The political opening, cease-fire, and UN presence brought by the negotiating process resulted in a virtual termination of protective accompaniment requests. The war was over, and although violence and inequality continued in many forms, protective accompaniment was no longer the service Salvadorans wanted from foreign NGOs. After holding on for five precarious years, PBI closed its project in El Salvador.

Notes

1. Bishop Medardo Gomez, interview by Liam Mahony with PBI delegation, San Salvador, January 13, 1992.
2. Mirna de Anaya (Salvadoran lawyer and human rights activist since the 1970s, widow of Herbert Anaya, former president of the CDHES), tape-recorded interview by authors, San Salvador, July 28, 1994.
3. ECA, *La Guerra de Baja Intensidad*.
4. Gettleman et al., *El Salvador*.
5. ECA, *La Guerra de Baja Intensidad*, p. 276.
6. ECA, *La Guerra de Baja Intensidad*, p. 285.
7. UCA, "La resistencia noviolenta," pp. 117–8, 121–3.
8. Mirna de Anaya interview.
9. Bill Hutchinson, former director, Marin Interfaith Task Force, tape-recorded telephone interview by authors, April 22, 1995.
10. "Deterioro de la situación de derechos humanos," *ECA* 473–474 (March–April 1988), p. 298.
11. McConahy, "Well-Meaning American."
12. Mirna de Anaya interview.
13. Celia Medrano, interview by authors, San Salvador, July 29, 1994.
14. Medrano interview.
15. Susan Greenblatt (Marin volunteers), letter to friends, January 30, 1989.

16. Luis Enrique Eguren, author's notes from personal experience.
17. Ramon Ballester, tape-recorded interview by authors, Trier, Germany, September 9, 1995.
18. Humberto Centeno, tape-recorded interview by authors, San Salvador, August 11, 1994.
19. Centeno interview.
20. Felix Ulloa, tape-recorded interview by authors, San Salvador, July 29, 1994.
21. Centeno interview.
22. Carolyn Mow, tape-recorded interview by authors, June 26, 1994.
23. Esther Domenech, tape-recorded interview by authors, San Salvador, August 13, 1994.
24. Mow interview.
25. Centeno interview.
26. "ARDE Amenaza," *El Mundo*, December 27, and "Tercer Grupo Anticomunista," December 28, 1988.
27. Alicia de García, tape-recorded interview by authors, San Salvador, July 29, 1994.
28. *PBI Project Bulletin*, April 1989.
29. This and subsequent quotes from Eve Scarfe are taken from a 1989 personal letter to friends (undated photocopy) and from Scarfe's testimony before the Central America Human Rights Commission, San Jose, Costa Rica, April 27, 1989.
30. Mow interview.
31. Miguel Mejía (member of CRIPDES directorate), tape-recorded interview by authors, August 8, 1994.
32. Mow interview.
33. IDHUCA, *Los derechos humanos*, p. 40.
34. For more on the Salvadoran repatriation, see Compher and Morgan, *Going Home*.
35. General Orlando Zepeda, interview by authors, July 28, 1994.
36. General Mauricio Vargas, interview by authors, San Salvador, July 29, 1994.
37. Zepeda interview. Zepeda was later accused of planning the November 1989 massacre of Jesuit priests and retired in disgrace.
38. *El Diario de Hoy*, August 12, 1988. Article 97 of the constitution of El Salvador, as well as Article 8 of the Salvadoran Immigration Law, prohibits the direct or indirect participation of foreigners in the internal politics of the country or in illegal actions.
39. "Ejercito advierte a internacionalistas," *El Diario de Hoy*, August 16, 1988.
40. "Falsa misionera capturada," *El Diario de Hoy*, September 29, 1988.
41. All statistics on detentions and deportations compiled from databases of the CDHES, Tutela Legal (human rights legal support office of the San Salvador archbishop), PBI and other NGO reports, and Salvadoran press and army reports.
42. "Piden expulsion de agitadores," *El Diario de Hoy*, August 12, 1988.
43. Letter to Ligia Segovia (Foreign Ministry) from Daniel Guerra, director general of immigration, December 9, 1988.
44. Jorge Martinez, tape-recorded interview by authors, San Salvador August 11, 1994.
45. Ulloa interview.
46. *El Diario de Hoy*, December 21, 1988, cited in PBI–El Salvador special report, "*Internacionalista* Incidents in El Salvador: A Media Summary for the Latter Half of 1988," San Salvador, 1989.
47. Lindsay-Poland, "Unwelcome in El Salvador."
48. European Parliament Resolution #B-2-670/1, B-2-733/1, September 14, 1988.
49. Report no. 3/94, case 10242, Inter-American Commission for Human Rights.
50. Fr. Luis Serrano, tape-recorded interview by authors, San Salvador, July 28, 1994.
51. Luis Perez, tape-recorded interview by authors, San Salvador, August 13, 1994.
52. Ballester interview; Francesc Riera, interview by authors, Barcelona, December 1994.
53. For a detailed analysis of the FMLN offensive, see "La Ofensiva de Noviembre," *ECA* 495–496 (January–February 1990).
54. Karen Ridd, interviews by author, May 25, 1996 (tape-recorded by telephone) and November 9, 1996, Philadelphia. Subsequent quotes from Ridd are from these interviews.
55. Kirio Waldo Salgado, tape-recorded interview by authors, San Salvador, August 9, 1994.
56. IDHUCA, "Los Derechos Humanos y la ofensiva del 11 de noviembre," *ECA* 495–496, (January–February 1990).
57. Marcela Rodriguez (member of PBI El Salvador), testimony before the Central America Human Rights Commission, San Jose, Costa Rica, November 27, 1989.
58. Rodriguez testimony.
59. Rodriguez testimony.

60. *Washington Post*, November 30, 1989, p. A16, cited in *Central America Update*, November–December 1989.
61. Policia de Hacienda, public document, "Nomina de personas extranjeras detenidas del 1 al 25 noviembre," San Salvador, November 25, 1989.
62. Sharon Bernstein, tape-recorded telephone interview by authors, January 18, 1995.
63. Rev. Edgar Palacios, tape-recorded interview by authors, San Salvador, August 8, 1994; Luis Miranda, tape-recorded interview by authors, San Salvador, August 12, 1994.
64. Phil Pardi, tape-recorded interview by authors, Orleans, Massachusetts, June 26, 1994.

12

Bitter Tea, with Sweetener

THE ISLAND NATION of Sri Lanka lies twenty-five kilometers off the southeast coast of India, on the other side of the world from Central America, geographically and politically. After two millennia of relatively peaceful coexistence between its Tamil and Sinhala population and a calm transition from "civilized" British colonialism to successful parliamentary democracy, this beautiful island became a hellhole: rival armies were killing civilians by the thousands, throwing them in the ocean, leaving them in the street, or sticking their victims' heads on poles to "teach a lesson" to others. In late 1989, when PBI's accompaniment model was being sorely tested in both Guatemala and El Salvador, the request came to try it in this far more complex conflict, with utterly different political and cultural underpinnings.

Sri Lanka's 17 million people are descendants of pre-European migrations from the Indian mainland: 74 percent are Sinhala and mostly Buddhist, with a Christian minority; 18 percent are Tamil, mostly Hindu; 7 percent are Tamil-speaking Muslims; and a small remnant (less than 1 percent) are original indigenous peoples of the island. Sinhala and Tamil people speak separate languages, with distinct alphabets, but they have many common-alities of culture and caste. Tamils are the majority population in the northern part of the island, yet 47 percent of the Tamil population is distributed around the rest of the island in majority Sinhala towns. Muslims are largely concentrated in the capital city of Colombo and the eastern province around Batticaloa.

Dubbed "serendib" by Marco Polo, the island's lush beauty and agricultural promise attracted several waves of Asian, Arabic, and eventually European colonization: Portuguese, Dutch, and then British, between 1796 and 1948. The British colony, renamed Ceylon, became one of world's major tea exporters.

Ceylon was granted independence without rebellion or violence in 1948. Colonial governing structures were quickly transformed into a base for a socialist welfare state, and for the next two decades, this democratic country seemed a model of stability. Literacy rates, education, and health services were among the best in the postcolonial world. Sadly, through a series of tragic but sometimes deliberate political maneuvers and popular

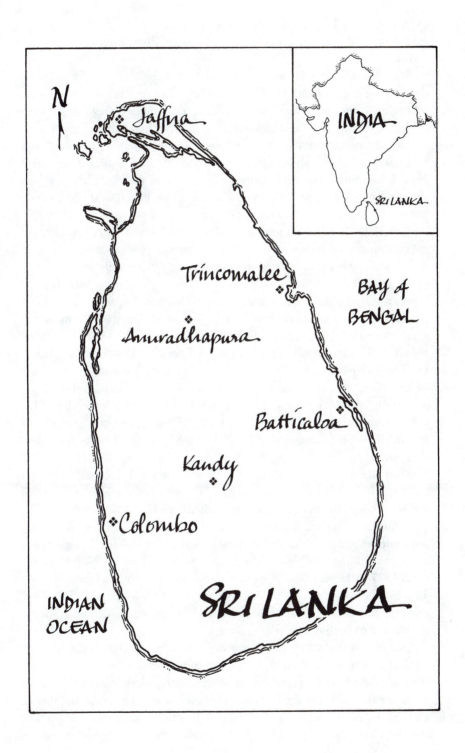

explosions, Sri Lankan democracy was effectively dismantled, and its ethnic diversity was transformed into blatant discrimination and then civil war.

With political stability and good education, expectations after independence were high for rapid economic growth. But it didn't happen. In the 1960s, an economic crisis began with a drastic drop in global prices of tea, rubber, and other key exports. With an economy still based on export agriculture, the possibilities for work or career advancement were limited, and many well-educated and politically sophisticated Sri Lankans remained poor. Consequent frustrations attracted many educated Sinhalese youth to the ultra-nationalist Marxist People's Liberation Front, more commonly known by its Sinhalese acronym: JVP. Capitalizing on poverty and discontent, the JVP launched an armed rebellion in 1971 that was quickly suppressed, giving rise to the first state of siege. Emergency status was maintained for six years, the first of a series of inexorable steps toward state terror.

Meanwhile, other Sinhala political factions exacerbated ethnic tensions by scapegoating the Tamil minority for their economic woes. Increasing economic and legal discrimination prompted the first strong Tamil separatist movements, the largest of which was the Liberation Tigers of Tamil Eelam (LTTE), frequently called simply the Tigers. Sporadic terrorist attacks by these groups were used by the government to justify the 1979 Prevention of Terrorism Act, allowing for forced confessions and detention without charge. In July 1983, after an ambush of government soldiers by the LTTE, the government tacitly encouraged an orgy of rioting and killing of Tamils by Sinhala mobs. Thousands of Tamils were killed, and many more lost their homes.

After the riots, many Tamils saw the separatist rebellion as their only recourse. By 1987, a much stronger LTTE controlled the northern part of the island, and the Sri Lankan army was incapable of dislodging it. The government shifted more and more of its economic resources into the military budget and used the civil war as a justification for further emergency measures eroding civil rights. The United National Party (UNP), in power from 1977 to 1994, based its electoral appeal to the Sinhalese majority on anti-Tamil chauvinism, citing the need for self-defense against "Tamil terrorism" rather than dealing with the legitimate economic and political grievances of both ethnic populations.

One reason that such chauvinism was effective, and that the Sri Lankan conflict is now so intractable, is that the country has a "double-minority" complex: Tamils feel threatened and discriminated against by the country's Sinhalese majority, but the Sinhalese also claim to be oppressed and threatened by the potential "hordes" of 50 million Tamils just across the straits in southern India. Some populist Buddhist monks buttress this defensiveness by arguing that Sri Lanka is the sacred home of Buddhism and must be protected from non-Buddhists.

Anti-Tamil chauvinism won elections, propelling more rabid politicians into positions of greater power. But these politicians did nothing to address the continued frustrations of the Sinhalese youth in the south. Once again tapping into this discontent, the JVP launched its second rebellion in 1987, this time combining antigovernment sentiment with its own virulent brand of anti-Tamil nationalism. The government agreed to the deployment of the Indian Peacekeeping Force (IPKF) in the north in 1987 to help control the Tamil Tigers. This move only further fueled the JVP, which labeled the IPKF an occupying force, accused the government of treason, and used anti-Indian prejudice to rally further support from Sinhalese in the south.

Unabashedly terrorist, the JVP set about eliminating any obstacle, including security forces, government politicians and sympathizers, and even competing left-wing civilian leadership. With acts of sabotage and an escalating series of ambushes and terrorist attacks on state workers and police, by 1989, the JVP had paralyzed southern Sri Lanka.

The Sri Lankan state had been developing a state terror system against Tamils for over a decade with the electoral support of the Sinhala majority. Now, facing an even stronger rebellion in the south, the government turned terror tactics against the Sinhalese population. During the February 1989 parliamentary election cycle alone, fourteen opposition candidates were killed. The JVP, in turn, assassinated ruling party (UNP) politicians, so the government authorized each UNP parliamentarian a private guard of up to 150 armed men. These legal bodyguard details later developed into private death squads.[1]

Unable to pinpoint exactly who all the JVP supporters might be, government forces struck back arbitrarily at the entire population of young Sinhalese men in the south. Army special forces officers developed clandestine "hit squads" to carry out assassinations. Although the JVP was the ostensible target, subsequent revelations showed that these squads also eliminated hundreds of activists from the largest opposition political party, among other civilian activists. Amnesty International attributed up to 30,000 killings to the government in 1988 and 1989 and quoted the government's figure of 6,517 killings by the JVP.[2] There were more killings in the south in those two years than during the entire northern war against the Tamil Tigers in the 1980s.

In August 1989, the JVP announced that it would kill the families of soldiers and police who did not desert. That same month, the army and police launched combined operations against the JVP: thousands of youths were detained, and hundreds were assassinated or disappeared. Photos of corpses in the streets, in the rivers, or under flaming tires began to appear regularly in the daily papers. Both sides were trying to win hearts and minds by simply terrorizing everyone into deserting the enemy. Out of this madness came the first accompaniment petition to Peace Brigades International.

The situation in southern Sri Lanka was so polarized in 1989 that anyone inquiring into the whereabouts of a detained person was suspected of being a JVP member. As more and more people were illegally detained, five lawyers of the Sri Lankan Bar Association took that risk, submitting literally hundreds of habeas corpus writs in 1988 and 1989. Lawyer Wijedasa Liyanarachichi was killed in police custody in late 1988. Charitha Lankapura was killed by unidentified gunmen at his home in July 1989. A third lawyer, Kanchana Abhayapala, then received the following message:

> We have killed Lankapura. We have three others in our list, especially you and Prins Gunasekera. Here after if you appear for one single Habeas Corpus application for JVPers you will be killed. Remember: one single Habeas Corpus Application. This is the final warning we are giving you.[3]

Abhayapala stopped, but he was assassinated anyway on August 28. The Bar Association contacted PBI, asking it to establish a volunteer team in Sri Lanka to accompany the remaining lawyers. In early October, the fourth lawyer, Neville Nisanka, was dragged out of a land registry office and shot to death. A three-person team of PBI volunteers arrived two weeks later, but Prins Gunasekara, the last lawyer, had already left. The habeas corpus work was silenced.

PBI wondered if it had arrived too late. Volunteers spent the first weeks interviewing many organizations and lawyers to get a clearer sense of the possibilities. In some of these meetings, they were told that since so many organizations had gone underground, they couldn't possibly use accompaniment as a protection: it would be like walking around with a big flag at their side, attracting unwanted attention from the security forces. In November, the team briefly accompanied a lawyer involved in prosecuting a police officer, but he too fled into exile.

Then, at the beginning of December 1989, lawyer Dharmadasa Gomes came forward, willing to risk preparing habeas corpus cases. PBI volunteers accompanied Gomes in his office and on his travels. He stayed in different houses each night. For security reasons, he kept away from his family. The accompaniment continued without incident until July 1990, by which time the threat was perceived to have diminished significantly, and other lawyers began habeas corpus work as well.

By early 1990, the government had captured and assassinated the entire JVP leadership. The war became a clean-up operation. The security forces continued to use dirty war tactics, at a somewhat lower intensity, purportedly to root out the remaining suspected JVP cadres.

The De Zoysa Case

On February 18, 1990, journalist Richard De Zoysa was kidnapped from his mother's home, in her presence, by unidentified armed men, some of whom were in uniform. The next day, his body was found on Mount Lavinia beach near Colombo. Police accused De Zoysa of working for the JVP to publicize false human rights reports.[4]

Richard De Zoysa came from an upper-class, politically active family. His uncle had been mayor of Colombo. It was quite shocking to Colombo's wealthy elite when the violence struck so close to home. De Zoysa's mother, Dr. Manorani Saravanamuttu, an elderly woman of mixed Tamil and Sinhala descent, felt that she could risk speaking out because she had no other children who could be attacked in reprisal, and most of her life was behind her. She hired a well-known progressive lawyer, Batty Weerakoon. Three months later, watching a television news program, Dr. Saravanamuttu recognized one of her son's kidnappers: Ronnie Wijesinghe, a high police official. She decided to prosecute.

The De Zoysa case became one of the hottest controversies in Sri Lanka. Lawyer Batty Weerakoon explained the importance of the case:

> For the first time . . . despite the death threats, a mother was willing to come forward and make public what she saw and she was prepared to go to court with the matter. In most disappearances during that period, the bodies were not found. Or . . . . people feared to come forward and identify those bodies as their relatives, because they feared the consequences for the rest of the family.
>
> De Zoysa was a threat to the image the government was trying to build of itself. . . . Our charge was that the police were carrying out a cover-up job, trying to conceal the fact that policemen themselves were involved in the abduction and the death. They did so not for their own reasons, but because politicians wanted it done.[5]

Learning of the case, PBI approached Weerakoon and Saravanamuttu to offer its services and began accompanying them both, in their homes and when they went to court. In May 1990, both Saravanamuttu and Weerakoon were threatened, anonymously, for pursuing the case.[6] Weerakoon was certain that the threats came from the police, acting on high-level orders. He immediately sent a letter to President Premadasa, demanding that steps be taken to ensure both his own and Dr. Saravanamuttu's safety. He also published both the threats and the letter in the newspapers.

Weerakoon was assigned two plain-clothes police escorts. A few days later, these policemen were threatened with death if they didn't leave their posts. Weerakoon accepted the bodyguards but wanted PBI as well.

PBI archive photo

Batty Weerakoon accompanied by PBI volunteers Yeshua Moser, USA (foreground), and Staffan Hansing, Sweden, July 1990.

These two young policeman were genuinely wanting to offer protection, but I just can't see how the police can protect me from the police. [If] anybody wanted to do something, they could be put out of the way, or even if something did happen, even with the best of intentions, no evidence would be forthcoming from them. But PBI was different. They could act independently, and say what they saw, both here and abroad. A man could trust on that.[7]

PBI's policy had generally been to accompany only those who chose non-violent means of protection, but the team made an exception in this case. According to PBI volunteer Yeshua Moser:

Batty said to us, "If I refuse a police guard it makes it easier for the government to excuse themselves when I get bumped off, by saying that they tried to protect me but I refused." . . . Shortly after he said this to me, his wife cornered me in another part of the house. After hearing that we may refuse to accompany him . . . she exclaimed with great emotion, "Guns can't protect him, but your presence is a power that must be reckoned with."[8]

Dr. Saravanamuttu pointed out a similar distinction: "The armed protection is there to protect you against an armed force. . . , but PBI is there to protect you against the *order* to use armed force."[9]

Later, looking back, both Saravanamuttu and Weerakoon felt that with so much international attention, the government would have been crazy to touch them, even without PBI. At the time of the threats, though, they were not so certain and asked for a steady presence.

Photo by Yeshua Moser

Dr. Manorani Saravanamuttu in 1990.

After six months, PBI gradually reduced its accompaniment, limiting it to Dr. Saravanamuttu's court appearances, which dragged on into 1992. The case was cut short in early 1993 when President Premadasa was assassinated in an LTTE suicide bombing. Among the dead was a member of the presidential guard, Ronnie Wijesinghe, the same police official accused by Dr. Saravanamuttu of kidnapping her son.

Dr. Saravanamuttu helped start the Mothers' Front in 1991, an organization of women who had lost family members, similar to the GAM in Guatemala. She often traveled internationally to publicize her case and Sri Lankan human rights in general. U.S. volunteer Marilyn Krysl accompanied her before one of these trips:

> She'd told me that morning that she planned to go abroad for a while, and I'd asked if she'd thought of leaving permanently. "It's what the authorities would like me to do," she said. "So I won't. Besides, what's left of my family, they're here. In spite of Richard's death, I still love Sri Lanka. For me, it's still the sweetest land there is."
>
> Now, all of a sudden, she turned to face me. Her eyes were watery, as though she might be on the edge of tears, and at the same time there was in them a sort of fierce light.
>
> "If I could have done something to save my son," she said, "I would have. But they don't come to bargain. They come in the night when you're alone, and for one purpose only. They come to murder, they like murder, they are murderers, men without mercy.
>
> "If there is justice at all today, it's a faint glimmer at the end of a dark, long tunnel. But I swear I will not give in to them. I will fight, I will crawl along that tunnel."[10]

Accompanying Venerable Baddegama Samitha

"When they kill me . . ." That's how Buddhist monk Baddegama Samitha casually began a sentence, while talking with a PBI volunteer in early 1991.[11] A monk and political activist, Venerable Samitha had worked to hide and protect young men who were fleeing the search-and-destroy missions of the government forces in 1989 and 1990.

> I felt that I had a kind of obligation to protect these youth . . . I am a monk, and I feel that life is more important than anything else. When [someone] is on the run, you just protect them.[12]

In some cases, Samitha found them hiding places. Other times, he intervened after they had been detained, using his status as a Buddhist monk to gain access. Once a young man was taken by the army from a public meeting, and other youths were killed on the spot for people to see. The young man's friends came and asked Samitha to help.

> It was not very far from my temple. . . . Everybody else tried to stop me, but I said, "I'll go and speak to these people. They are not animals."
> So I went to talk to [the army] about the youths they had taken. I spoke to them very nicely, I said, "Why are you beating them?" "We must punish them because they are traitors." I gently talked to them, and then they wanted to know who I was. Now you know the Western influences are highly respected here. And I was about maybe three months, four months back [from England]. I said, "I'm from the Temple . . . I just came from England." That always helps. Meanwhile I kept speaking to them. I told them, "Why don't you take them to court, if he has committed some crime." After a while I started speaking to the army officer in English. That worked for him. . . . We made some friendly gestures. So finally he promised me, "I will not kill this man."

Buddhist monks have an especially respected and privileged status in Sri Lanka. Samitha added his European veneer to enhance the protective effect. But his protection of others put his own life in danger. At the end of 1989, while Samitha was traveling again in Europe, an unidentified gunman came looking for him at his temple. Learning of this threat, his friends in Europe urged him not to return to Sri Lanka.

> I said, "No, no, no, I am not going to avoid this, I am not going to hide. I must go back. My presence in Sri Lanka isn't worse than my living like a refugee here." I said, "Let's take some action and try to protect me, but I must go." Some friends there then suggested that I should not be alone, that I should ask for the protection of PBI.

Two PBI volunteers met Samitha at the airport when he arrived in Colombo. He was accompanied off and on for the next several months—usually when he came to the capital, and at times at his monastery in the south. Having foreign accompaniment in a small Sinhalese village was a bit of an oddity, but Samitha felt that the other villagers understood and appreciated his need for protection.[13] For safety, he had to limit his movements and avoid certain locations. He made PBI's presence as visible as possible, taking his accompaniment at times on visits to the local police station or army base. While this went on, European embassies interested in Samitha's welfare demanded that the government protect him. Samitha took PBI volunteers to a meeting with presidential assistant Bradman Weerakoon (not to be confused with aforementioned lawyer Batty Weerakoon).

When we interviewed presidential assistant Weerakoon four years later, he remembered the case very well. Responding to European embassy pressure, President Premadasa had asked Weerakoon to investigate Samitha's situation. It had not been easy at first, since Weerakoon didn't really know who was doing the threatening. So he contacted all the different security forces and made sure that they knew of the president's concern. "PBI really protected Samitha, saved his life," declared Weerakoon, confirming that international pressure had been the determining factor in moving Premadasa to take action.[14]

Despite this high-level admonition to leave the monk alone, the surveillance did not end. At one point, a PBI team member felt that he was being followed by a car in Samitha's town, Baddegama. He got the license number. Some days later in Colombo, he noticed that he was being watched outside a European embassy. When he checked the license number, it was the same one, suggesting a coordinated surveillance of both Samitha and PBI. Samitha continued to receive threats for many months, especially over the telephone. During one such call, the speaker asked about the accompaniment, "Why are they here? For what purpose have they come here? Ask them to bugger off!"[15]

But when we asked Samitha what he would have done without accompaniment, he said that he would have had to "go underground or leave the country again. Public behavior wasn't possible, because of the death squads." The Samitha accompaniment is one of the clearest examples in our case studies of proven deterrence. Venerable Samitha boldly helped youths accused of being JVP members. As a result, an assassin was sent to his temple. Samitha turned to accompaniment and diplomatic pressure for protection, resulting in a direct presidential order to the security forces to leave him alone.

Photo by Yeshua Moser

Venerable Baddegama Samitha at his temple in April 1990.

The Sweetener and the NGOs

The key argument for accompaniment protection is based on assumptions that governments respond to human rights pressure and pay attention to NGOs. A closer look at how this worked in practice in the Sri Lankan case is particularly instructive, illustrating the complex and subtle environment within which accompaniment, and all NGOs, must function. For a government whose state terror system coexists with parliamentary democracy, in a country much larger, richer, and more educated than those in the previous studies, the subtleties of managing human rights damage control and NGO public relations require an expert—a problem solver and diplomat equally at ease with human rights NGOs and army mass murderers. In Sri Lanka, that man was Bradman Weerakoon.

In late 1988, President Premadasa and Defense Minister Ranjan Wijeratne were preparing a no-holds-barred attack on the JVP that they knew would involve thousands of premeditated civilian assassinations. Recognizing the political cost for Sri Lanka's image, Premadasa called in Bradman Weerakoon, appointing him special presidential assistant for international affairs. Weerakoon's job was to minimize these costs and placate the international diplomatic and NGO community. Weerakoon told us candidly, "I was the sweetener."[16] He defended his role, arguing that both the government and the international community needed people in high and influential places who would push "the softer line."

One of Weerakoon's first strategic moves was to convince President Premadasa to invite the International Committee of the Red Cross (ICRC) back into Sri Lanka. The ICRC had been asked to leave in 1983, and as conflicts escalated in the 1980s, subsequent offers to return had repeatedly been rejected. The change of policy in 1989 surprised the ICRC. One ICRC official told us that such invitations usually come after a change of government, when the new government is looking for a cleaner image and a way to blame prior governments for all problems. In this case, there was a change in policy without a change in government. "Probably the government was tired of receiving eggs and tomatoes in their face during their visits abroad, due to the bad human rights situation."[17]

Weerakoon described the invitation to us as damage control in advance. It was not because they were tired of eggs in their face, but rather that they knew that their escalating dirty war would result in many more eggs in the future if they didn't do something to limit the costs. At the same time, though, they had to ensure that the ICRC presence would be discreet and controllable and, above all, not get in the way of the security forces. The government authorized an initial delegation of only seventeen ICRC workers, waiting to see how their work developed before allowing an expanded presence.[18]

The first four ICRC staff arrived quietly on October 16, 1989. Delegation chief Philippe Comtesse tried to dispel any misconceptions that might inhibit their work: "We are not here to make an assessment, not here to make reports, not here to condemn anybody. We are here because it is our mandate to alleviate the suffering of people."[19]

The military grudgingly accepted, though according to Weerakoon, it frequently demanded that he "get the ICRC off our back." Weerakoon's hard-line counterpart in the government was Defense Minister Ranjan Wijeratne, a human rights activist's nightmare. Known publicly simply as Ranjan, he was a military hero credited by late 1989 with toppling the JVP and restoring order. In January 1990, Wijeratne refused entry to an Amnesty International delegation, referring to them as "terrorists" and "wolves in sheep's clothing" trying to destabilize the government. He went on to accuse the Sri Lankan Bar Association of funneling Amnesty International money to the JVP.[20] Interestingly, Wijeratne justified the exclusion of Amnesty, saying: "there are eight ICRC officers in Sri Lanka making an assessment. The government has nothing to hide." Thus, in less than three months, the ICRC presence had entered into the army's public rhetoric. The double standard was clear: the army was claiming that the ICRC would fulfill Amnesty's role, even though the ICRC had explicitly clarified that it did not do such assessments.

When Wijeratne blocked Amnesty's delegation, then-opposition leader Sirima Bandaranaike declared that she was going to invite "a team from the aid-giving nations and institutions to visit Sri Lanka and study human rights violations and to impose conditions on the government before granting more aid. . . . If that happens, the killings will stop. This should be done before it is too late." Ranjan responded immediately: "She is asking the donor countries to interfere in our internal affairs." He went on to explain: "Of course, aid donors are concerned about human rights violations. . . . Sri Lanka's aid donors who have given so generously . . . fully understand the need for effective action to counter insurrection and attempts to topple by force a democratically-elected government."[21]

Wijeratne, a military man less diplomatic than Weerakoon, expected other governments to value the right of any sovereign nation to defend itself. Nevertheless, the cards were on the table: Sri Lanka couldn't afford its aid to be conditioned on human rights. Under Weerakoon's tutelage, the government began to take more direct steps to improve its image.

In July 1990, just as the army was running out of excuses for terror tactics in the south, the LTTE initiated an extensive and protracted military campaign, attacking army positions and Sinhalese villages, extending its area of control and operations throughout the north and east. The renewed civil war cut off the north from government services, brought heavy casualties, and displaced hundreds of thousands from their homes.[22]

The Money Dance

President Premadasa and Bradman Weerakoon were now juggling the international reaction to two different wars and struggling to hold on to Sri Lanka's access to foreign aid. They had done pretty well so far, but the delayed impact of the carnage was accumulating. The fundamental issue was human rights; the key forum was the Paris Aid Group.

The Paris Aid Group is a consortium of all the principal donor countries that meets each year in Paris under the auspices of the World Bank. The consortium approved $612 million in aid to Sri Lanka in 1988, $785 million in 1989, and $1 billion in October 1990. After the 1990 decision, the twelve European Community nations noted "with regret that the enquiry into the killing in February of Mr. Richard de Zoysa has made such little progress . . . the Twelve wish to draw attention to the fact that Member States will be considering their future assistance for the development of Sri Lanka's economy with reference, among other factors, to the Government's performance in regard to human rights."[23] Weerakoon was concerned about the next meeting. Sri Lanka needed the money: industrial output had been interrupted by the conflict, tourism had been plummeting since 1983, and the military budget had multiplied 500 percent since 1982. This combination of economic need and human rights disaster made Sri Lanka a thorny case for Western donors. President Premadasa responded to European concerns with the creation of a special task force on human rights.

The aid pressure emanated from both political-ethical and economic considerations. Several of these donor nations had a certain reputation for defending human rights. Other countries were interested in a more stable economic climate for investment, especially the United States and Japan. They were also concerned about the political costs they might suffer from giving economic support to a government suspected of massive human rights violations.

The Sri Lankan government had to balance its own internal security concerns against these external economic pressures and was constantly posturing and shifting in an attempt to serve both. Some fancy footwork would be needed to ensure a lucrative aid package at the next Paris meeting, scheduled for early 1992.

Creating a completely positive image was out of the question. By 1991, Sri Lanka was one of the world's worst human rights violators. The Amnesty International report entitled "Sri Lanka: Extra-judicial Executions, Disappearances and Torture, 1987–1990" documented thousands of assassinations by security forces in the south. The report also denounced serious abuses by the LTTE in the north, but these could not justify government brutality.[24] The best the government could hope to achieve was an image of *change*. A democratic state being strangled by a terrorist guerrilla movement was bound to make some errors, or so the argument went: the government was doing its best to rectify the errors, and the situation was improving.

In January 1991, the European Parliament demanded that Sri Lanka demonstrate progress on human rights and proper law and order before further aid packages were approved.[25] In response, the government announced that it would name a commission to investigate disappearances, while delaying permission for a visit by a UN working group with the same mandate.[26] The U.S. State Department, meanwhile, assured Congress in March that it was "troubled" by Sri Lankan abuses.

Weerakoon couldn't keep all his attention on Paris and aid. There were fires to put out at home. On April 7, 1991, a UN High Commissioner for Refugees (UNHCR) convoy was caught in a cross fire while on the northwestern coast. Afterwards, the People's Liberation Organization of Tamil Eelam (PLOTE), a Tamil force allied with the Sri Lankan army,* accused the UN of allowing its trucks to be used by LTTE cadres to mount an attack. The UNHCR refuted the charge indignantly. Bradman Weerakoon tried to mend things, only to be accused by PLOTE of favoring foreigners over the Sri Lankan security forces. Weerakoon nevertheless managed to get PLOTE to clarify that it was not directly blaming the UNHCR for the incident.[27]

The Attack on Doctors Without Borders

As the war escalated, relief NGOs expanded their operations, and many new NGOs arrived to help. By mid-1991, more than forty international NGOs were working in the country.[28] Those that worked in the northern war zone needed explicit arrangements with both the army and the LTTE to cross the front lines regularly. Ironically, both sides wanted to keep the humanitarian aid flowing, even as they killed and uprooted civilians. But the high-profile work of international NGOs, serving primarily the displaced Tamil population, was interpreted by some in the army as consorting with the enemy.

On May 3, 1991, an air force helicopter fired on a truck belonging to the NGO Doctors Without Borders. Two French nurses, a French doctor, and their Sri Lankan driver got out to signal their neutrality, and an airplane flew over dropping bombs, wounding all four—one critically.

Doctors Without Borders pulled out of the war zone, threatened to leave Sri Lanka, and brought in a special delegation from its head office in Paris. The French ambassador released a strong protest and warned that if such an incident were repeated, "relations between France and Sri Lanka would be very seriously compromised."[29] The UNHCR, ICRC, and other NGOs also protested; some suspended their operations as well.

The fact that no one was killed made damage control somewhat easier, according to Weerakoon. He immediately issued a formal apology and

---

*PLOTE is one of several Tamil militant organizations that aligned themselves with the army in order to defeat the LTTE. This alignment is rooted in historic feuds among Tamil militant organizations, the vicious methods by which the Tigers "purged" other competitive Tamil organizations, and fundamental disagreements over the politics and strategies of Tamil resistance. The government encouraged these divisions and funded and armed Tamil paramilitary groups to help combat the LTTE.

established an investigatory commission. Weerakoon told us that this commission was "good diplomacy, regardless of the results."[30] The commission
report ultimately exonerated the army, and Doctors Without Borders called
it a "total whitewash." Contrary to this report, Weerakoon suggests that
the army was simply "fed up" watching these international NGOs move
freely in and out behind enemy lines and decided to "get them" this time.

Nevertheless, this same commission report defended the role of NGOs
in the conflict and called for greater respect and security. According to Phil
Esmonde of the Quaker Peace and Service, international NGOs feared that
the attack might signal the beginning of a trend to target foreigners working in the conflict regions. Ultimately, though, the attack and its aftermath
seemed to strengthen their role.[31] The army began meeting with the NGOs
regularly, with Weerakoon attempting to referee the process.[32]

The Dance Continues

On March 2, Defense Minister Ranjan Wijeratne was assassinated. Wijeratne's
ruthless but successful military tactics and outspoken accusations against
the international human rights community as "Tamil terrorists-in-exile"
had been inconvenient for the government's image campaign. After his
death, the government quickly granted Amnesty permission to visit and
evaluate the human rights situation. The Amnesty delegation arrived in
June for a two-week visit, subjected to intense security procedures. A
columnist in the *Daily News* called the visit an infringement of national
independence and accused Amnesty of provoking troubles to keep itself in
business.[33]

Amnesty then released a report based on data gathered before the June
trip, which announced that "thousands of civilians had been extra-judicially
executed or 'disappeared' in Northeast Sri Lanka after war resumed in June
last year." Weerakoon, attempting to pacify government and military hard-
liners, called it "grossly exaggerated" and quickly explained that a new
Amnesty report would soon be released: "I have been told that there will
be a whole chapter [on the LTTE's human rights violations.]"[34]

Weerakoon's damage-control work was seen by some in Sri Lanka as
taking sides with the internationals against his own army. Chauvinist sectors of the Sinhala population firmly opposed international interference on
behalf of Tamils. Later in the year, the Foreign Ministry accused unnamed
NGOs from the Netherlands of funding separatist terrorist activities.[35]

That fall, Sri Lanka signed various bilateral accords with the United
States, and Germany and Norway announced that their 1992 aid would be
conditioned on human rights. The Dutch government went so far as to uni-
laterally suspend aid. In September, Amnesty International finally released

the report from its June visit, with thirty-two specific policy recommendations to the government.

With the February 1992 Paris meeting fast approaching, Weerakoon took the initiative and made a tour of various European countries in December. That same month, he announced to the press that the government had accepted thirty of the Amnesty International recommendations.

In January 1992, just a month before the Paris meeting, a Canadian fact-finding mission concluded that the Sri Lanka government had not implemented Amnesty International's proposals. They warned that the Canadian government would have to reconsider aid to Sri Lanka if positive steps were not taken to end the bloody war.[36] The UN working group on disappearances, which had visited in October, reported that Sri Lanka remained the country with the highest number (12,000) of disappearances and abductions attributable to state security forces ever recorded by the UN working group.[37] It demanded that the government of Sri Lanka take "more effective measures to prevent disappearances and prosecute all those responsible government officials more rigorously."[38]

In a last-minute scramble, the government delivered a specially prepared booklet to the entire diplomatic corps. The booklet declared, among other things, that all the Amnesty recommendations were going to be implemented and that police and army officers accused of human rights violations would be punished. And just in time, the U.S. State Department released its report for 1991, emphasizing the efforts made by the government to improve the human rights situation and declaring an overall reduction in the number of violations from previous years.*

The February 7, 1992, Paris Aid Group meeting authorized $825 million for Sri Lanka, not far short of the expected $860 million. A few countries made their aid conditional on human rights improvement, and Norway, one of the principal donor nations, cut its support by 10 percent. This particular round of the dance was over; aid was secure for another year.

Loading the Dice

We asked Bradman Weerakoon about the interaction of this high-level international maneuvering with local-level accompaniment. He replied by confirming that the government certainly paid attention to accompaniment.

---

*As with the Doctors Without Borders report, many of the government's moves were purely cosmetic. In 1993, Amnesty International accused Sri Lanka of implementing only a few of the thirty-two recommendations ("Go Beyond Words, AI tells Lanka," Sunday Times, August 8, 1993).

He went further: a local policeman or soldier would also pay attention, even if he had no grasp of international politics. This local official is most concerned about what his superiors might hear about his behavior, and he naturally assumes that a foreigner has some power—or he wouldn't be there. The presence will make him cautious. Weerakoon suggested a moral angle as well: "These men who commit these acts, they know they are doing a bad thing, and they would prefer to do it in secret." What about death squads? "Most of them are aligned with the government: they have to get up in the morning and put their uniforms back on," he replied, suggesting that accompaniment would still have an effect.[39]

The various possible theories for accompaniment effectiveness were apparently sufficient for the different organizations that approached PBI. While the international community debated human rights and aid, PBI accompanied union struggles, families of the disappeared, lawyers, human rights activists, and community organizations in various regions of southern Sri Lanka and, briefly, the eastern region near the city of Batticaloa.

While the war raged in the north, repression eased in the south, and some legal protections began functioning again. After the precedent set by Dr. Saravanamuttu, others began the risky process of combating impunity, trying to use the court system to find justice. Marilyn Krysl tells of one of these experiences in 1992:

Peter, Francis and I went to Anaradapura, several hours northeast of Colombo, to attend a pre-trial hearing. One of our clients had brought charges against two policemen for the rape and death of his sister. Police had suspected her of involvement with the JVP, but she was never arrested and charged. Instead a group of men, including local police, arrived at the family's home, restrained her father and brothers and raped her, then took her away. Her body had not been found.

Anaradapura isn't a place where international observers put in regular appearances, and our arrival at court at 9:30, a half hour before the hearing, caused consternation. The bailiff immediately inquired why we were there. When we told him, he went off, then returned and announced proceedings had been set back to 1:00 P.M. At 1:00 I sat beside another plaintiff whose hearing had got set back. "Something drastic must have happened," he said. "This judge hasn't ever set back the time of a hearing."

Two policemen, defendants in the case we were observing, were marched into the dock. At a previous hearing the prosecution had made arguments in favor of trying them. This occasion was for hearing the defense's evidence why the case should not go to trial. Testimony was in Sinhala, but two reporters present passed notes to keep us informed.

Our presence would exert pressure on the judge to rule in favor of a trial. If he did, there was a very real possibility that these two men, whether or not they were guilty, would be found guilty, simply because the government is trying to polish its human rights image. If the trial received heavy publicity, the men would probably be given harsher sentences in order to demonstrate that Sri Lanka was indeed prosecuting perpetrators of violations. I understood our presence in that courtroom would be a factor in any loading of the dice. I also understood that given the crudeness of the state's state of mind, there wasn't much we could do about this. . . . When the judge announced his decision to hold a trial, the faces of her father and brothers shone. For them a great victory had gone forward. They'd taken a frightening chance, and their first display of resolve had succeeded.[40]

In this and other cases in Sri Lanka, where, unlike in Central America, the court system was sometimes functional, accompaniment gave victims the courage to strike a blow against impunity. But Marilyn's ambivalent reflection is relevant to all human rights pressure: accompaniment protection, as we've argued repeatedly, is about *power* as well as justice. Certainly any legal proceeding should be subject to outside scrutiny. But in postwar or postterror transitions, there is a strong tendency for governments to respond to such pressure not by doing the *right* thing but by doing *something*. That something often involves throwing the least costly scapegoats to the wolves. Accompaniment here helped facilitate a legal process, but it cannot ensure the justice of the outcome and could conceivably distort it.

Another legal case arose in 1993 when Tharmalingam Selvakumar was kidnapped and tortured by the EPDP (Eelam People's Democratic Party), a Tamil paramilitary group aligned with the army. After six days, the EPDP handed him over to the police, who held him another twenty-two days before releasing him, uncharged. Selvakumar, who had collaborated with the EPDP in previous years, was now trying to get out and decided to sue EPDP chief Douglas Devenanda and several police officers for violating his rights. He was then threatened by both.

The case, which was to be heard by the Supreme Court, was the first to formally uncover the close relationship between the government and the EPDP in violating individual rights. Selvakumar's lawyer put him in touch with PBI.

[At first] I thought it was stupid. . . . They said they were nonviolent, and not like a security service. It sounded very weak. . . . The people who are against me come with weapons. But [after PBI started] I saw a lot of people getting panicked at their presence at my house. I saw there was reduced surveillance [by the EPDP].[41]

PBI accompanied Selvakumar between April and August 1993. The violent and shadowy world of paramilitary groups like the EPDP was a less predictable terrain for accompaniment. Almut Wadle, a volunteer from Germany, described the nights at Selvakumar's home:

The scariest thing was just imagining the people who might come in and kill him. I didn't see them, but they were so full of fear at that place—I really felt their fear. They always asked us to answer the phone, and to look who is at the door. We wouldn't sleep. . . . We just sat on the balcony to see who might be coming.[42]

The case dragged on, and the threats continued. Finally, Selvakumar decided to accept political asylum in Europe and continue to fight his case from a distance. In July 1994, the Supreme Court absolved EPDP leader Douglas Devenanda but found two police officers guilty of willful infringement of Selvakumar's rights and, in a rare move, awarded damages payable by the state. The EPDP continued to work for the army, and Devenanda was subsequently elected to parliament.

The year 1994 was a hopeful one. The Popular Alliance, a coalition of opposition parties running on a platform of reconciliation and negotiation, won first the parliamentary and then the presidential elections, wresting control after seventeen years from the publicly chauvinist United Nationalist Party. Moderate President Chandrika Kumaratunga embarked on an ambitious series of negotiations with the LTTE, resulting in a cease-fire and a plan for "federalizing" the government structure to devolve more power to regional bodies. PBI accompanied election monitors in both elections and peace groups that were supporting the negotiation process. But overall, the situation relaxed to such an extent that accompaniment requests dried up almost completely, and PBI began making plans to leave.

In April 1995, sadly, the LTTE abruptly broke off negotiations and attacked the naval installation at Trincomalee and police and army bases throughout the north and east. As hostilities increased, all the rhetoric linking foreign NGOs to "Tamil terrorism" resurfaced again with greater force. Despite a moderate government, PBI experienced an increase in official harassment. Other NGOs were threatened even more seriously, and in several instances, PBI volunteers accompanied a British humanitarian activist who was being threatened every time he came into Sri Lanka.

The government responded to the LTTE's refusal to negotiate by launching several large offensives against the north and east, involving mass bombing and causing hundreds of civilian casualties and thousands of new refugees. With renewed war, PBI's accompaniment was again in demand, both in Colombo and in war-torn Batticaloa.

Notes

1. Judge J. F. A. Soza, Sri Lanka (governmental) Human Rights Task Force, interview by authors, Colombo, March 30, 1994.
2. Amnesty International, "Sri Lanka Briefing," September 1990.
3. Quoted from a memorandum from the Bar Association of Sri Lanka to Defense Minister Ranjan Wijeratne, October 1989.
4. Batty Weerakoon, *Extra-judicial Execution of Richard de Zoysa*.

5. Batty Weerakoon, tape-recorded interview by Patrick Coy, Colombo, October 6, 1993.
6. Batty Weerakoon, *Extra-judicial Execution of Richard de Zoysa*.
7. Batty Weerakoon interview by Coy.
8. Yeshua Moser, letter to authors, January 4, 1995. The topic of armed versus unarmed protection is discussed further in chapter 16.
9. Dr. Manorani Saravanamuttu, tape-recorded interview by authors, Colombo, April 1, 1994.
10. Krysl, "Deeper Darkness."
11. Ed Kinane, tape-recorded telephone interview by author, January 12, 1995.
12. Venerable Baddegama Samitha, tape-recorded interview by authors, April 6, 1995. "Venerable" is the accepted respectful manner of referring to a buddhist monk in Sri Lanka. Although we often shorten this to simply "Samitha" in the text, no disrespect is intended.
13. Samitha interview.
14. Bradman Weerakoon, (special presidential assistant for international affairs), interview by authors, Colombo, April 1994.
15. Samitha interview.
16. Bradman Weerakoon interview.
17. ICRC staff/Sri Lanka (name withheld), interview by authors, Colombo, April, 1994.
18. Bradman Weerakoon interview.
19. "Red Cross Here," *Lanka Guardian* 12, no. 13 (November 1, 1989).
20. *The Sun*, January 19, 1990.
21. *Daily News*, January 19, 1990.
22. Movement for InterRacial Justice and Equality (MIRJE), 1991 annual report.
23. PBI Sri Lanka Newsletter, November/December 1990.
24. *The Island*, September 19, 1990.
25. *PBI Project Bulletin*, February/March 1991.
26. *PBI Project Bulletin*, February/March 1991.
27. "Who Is for Whom?" *Sunday Times*, June 16, 1991; *PBI Project Bulletin*, April 1991.
28. Foreign Ministry statistics, cited in *The Island*, July 2, 1991.
29. *Daily News*, May 11, 1991.
30. Bradman Weerakoon interview.
31. Phil Esmonde (former Sri Lanka program director, Quaker Peace and Service), tape-recorded interview by authors, Colombo, April 1994.
32. "Total Whitewash," *Sunday Island*, June 30, 1991.
33. *Daily News*, June 13, 1991.
34. *The Island*, July 12, 1991.
35. *The Island*, July 2, 1991.
36. "Canada to Review Aid," *Sunday Times*, January 26, 1992.
37. *Inform*, February 1992 (Colombo).
38. *PBI Project Bulletin*, March 1992.
39. Bradman Weerakoon interview.
40. Krysl, "Deeper Darkness."
41. *PBI Project Bulletin*, September 1993, p. 2.
42. Almut Wadle, tape-recorded interview by authors, Colombo, April 1994.

13

The Clout Factor: The United Nations, the International Red Cross, and the NGOs

ALTHOUGH MOST OF THE accompaniment work we've studied has been carried out by NGOs, similar protection is sometimes offered by intergovernmental organizations such as the United Nations or the Organization of American States (OAS). Likewise, the International Committee of the Red Cross (ICRC), occupying a historically unique position among NGOs, can provide protective accompaniment, either explicitly or as an implicit by-product of the other services within its mandate.

We cannot do justice here to the vast global UN and ICRC efforts in human rights protection. Instead, we briefly compare the accompaniment protection of these large, "establishment" organizations with that of smaller NGOs, using examples from our country case studies.

The ICRC, UN, and other intergovernmental organizations run up against problems of sovereignty when confronting how to intervene to prevent violence in other countries. Modern human rights law is widely accepted among nations: a state that does not protect its citizens' rights is violating international law. Nevertheless, an absolute respect for state sovereignty remains in the UN Charter. Without the approval of the host government, the UN will rarely intervene—the ICRC, never.

United Nations High Commissioner for Refugees

The UNHCR has accompanied and protected millions of refugees in their initial flights, temporary shelter, and eventual resettlement. Charged with the mission of responding to refugee crises all over the world, the UNHCR is a huge yet inadequately financed body. The UNHCR has developed a significant infrastructure and experience related to refugee protection, although the human needs of a rapidly increasing refugee population often overwhelm its resources.

In conflict zones, the UNHCR usually resolves security concerns by negotiating agreements with the armed parties. Although these agreements give added clout to the UN's protection, they can also have the effect of allowing the host governments or warring parties to determine the living conditions and political futures of the refugees. Regrettably, empowerment of the refugee population is not always part of the calculation.

Refugees often view the UNHCR as inflexible and too closely allied with official government policies. Host governments, by withholding consent, can indirectly control the UNHCR's significant resources or simply prevent the UNHCR from acting. In addition, the UNHCR's task-oriented, directive approach is frequently criticized as paternalistic and lacking in cultural sensitivity, adding to distrust. Small NGOs, free of the UN's political baggage and less constrained by the quantitative demand of responding to the entire population, can often earn trust more easily in the field.

The refugee populations resettled in El Salvador and Guatemala were atypical. They were organized and self-controlled, and they were tough negotiators: the UNHCR learned from the process. Thus, the UNHCR initially resisted Guatemalan refugee demands for accompaniment. As the return got under way, it developed a working relationship and respect for NGO accompaniment, which was fulfilling a need that the UNHCR could not meet. In a complementary fashion, the physical presence of NGO volunteers and the political clout of the UNHCR together contributed to the refugees' safety.

Usually, the UNHCR mandate covers only "international" refugees—those who flee across national borders. The often far-more-numerous internally displaced have no such internationally recognized "protector." In 1993, the UNHCR and the International Council of Voluntary Agencies (ICVA) initiated a process called Partners in Action (PARINAC)—a series of conferences aimed at better coordination between the UNHCR and NGOs. PARINAC called attention to the needs of the internally displaced in a series of recommendations, supported by UNHCR participants.

Such an expansion of service is logical for the UNHCR, since most refugees are internally displaced before crossing international borders. Serving the internally displaced effectively can thus limit refugee flows. Using this rationale, the UNHCR implemented an innovative program in Sri Lanka: the Open Relief Centers (ORCs).

In 1990, increasing combat between the Tamil Tigers and government forces led to an exodus of refugees out of the villages in the conflict zones of the north and east. After a series of negotiations with both armies, the UNHCR created several decentralized and temporary camps known as ORCs. The basic idea was to offer safety in remote areas while still permitting those in danger of displacement to remain close enough to home to maintain their vital agricultural or socioeconomic activities.

These relief centers were located in both government- and LTTE-controlled zones. They provided temporary protection to the populations displaced by incursions of one force or the other. A key military factor that contributed to their effectiveness was that these incursions did not usually cause any permanent shift in control of a territory, so once the fighting died down, the temporary refugees could return to their homes. If the fighting was prolonged, and their homes were not too far from the ORC, people often continued to work their fields or businesses in the daytime but stayed in the ORCs at night for safety. These camps gave the displaced population a secure option that was less drastic than long-term flight to more distant refuges. The ORCs thus effectively decreased refugee flows to nearby India.[1]

Several international NGOs collaborated in providing services and foreign staff in the ORCs. Although these staff had technical roles, protective accompaniment was implicit, and according to UNHCR staff, it was fundamental in ensuring the fulfillment of the accords and the safety of the camps.[2]

According to one confidential source who had worked with both the UN and large international humanitarian NGOs in Sri Lanka, this sort of "implicit" protection was an even more important service to Sri Lanka than the actual material aid offered by either the UN or the NGOs. In his opinion, "humanitarian aid" is acceptable in the eyes of the authorities, whereas protection is politically controversial; most massive NGOs are aware that they are providing protection with their presence but do not make this claim publicly.

UN Unarmed Peace Missions

In recent years, the United Nations has implemented an increasing number of unarmed peace efforts, including human rights monitoring missions in El Salvador (ONUSAL), Haiti (MICIVIH), and Guatemala (MINUGUA). Although never naming protective accompaniment as an explicit task, these missions have gradually opened up to experimentation in this work.

ONUSAL was a direct result of the UN-brokered San Jose accord on human rights signed in 1990 by the Salvadoran government and the guerrilla FMLN. ONUSAL's human rights work was formally limited to reporting on abuses after they occurred and offering human rights education to the military and the general public. Human rights organizations criticized ONUSAL for not responding to requests for a "preventive" presence at events where abuses were feared. ONUSAL saw such requests as attempts to politicize its presence; that is, the popular organizations were looking to strengthen their own clout by having ONUSAL at their events.

However, ONUSAL, as well as subsequent similar missions in other countries, consciously provided a different type of preventive presence: on a broad and visual scale, it deployed hundreds of easily identified vehicles in populated areas and traveled around the country ostentatiously in white helicopters. Although the overall expense of ONUSAL's activities became another point of criticism from the impoverished NGO community, this lavish display was designed to create an omniscient image: "ONUSAL is here!" The function of this image was to deter human rights abuse and reinforce the accords.

MINUGUA was also installed after a similar human rights accord, but with a broader mandate. Aware of criticisms of the recent ONUSAL experience, MINUGUA leadership responded flexibly to different requests. Dispersed throughout the rural highlands and jungles, MINUGUA workers developed working relationships with popular organizations as well as local government and military officials. In addition to human rights monitoring and education, they helped in local mediation and conflict resolution and attended events where participants feared violence.

The clout of the UN did not always protect MINUGUA workers from violence. In late 1995, a Mexican woman was killed in an apparent highway robbery in Guatemala just after she left MINUGUA service. Although no political motive can be proved, the gang accused of the crime was directed by former military officers. More blatantly, Raul Martinez, a local civil patrol leader who opposed the refugee return to the Ixcán region, seemed to take pleasure in harassing foreigners: twice he kidnapped MINUGUA workers for brief periods.

International Committee of the Red Cross

The ICRC, a Swiss organization founded in 1863, is arguably the most influential international NGO in the history of human rights and humanitarian law in armed conflicts. Although probably most well-known for its role in drafting, advocating, and enforcing the various Geneva protocols protecting the treatment of noncombatants in wartime, the organization has also helped draft most of the other major international human rights conventions. It has earned a powerful reputation for organizing international responses to natural and man-made disasters. Since World War II, the ICRC has developed certain other areas of expertise, including visiting and monitoring the rights of political prisoners and negotiating hostage situations and prisoner exchanges.

The ICRC's firm commitment to impartiality and its strict adherence to a limited mandate earn it privileged access to governments and conflicts all over the world. Known for its discretion and confidentiality, the organization never publicly denounces abuses, a policy that is attractive to governments. Instead, the committee produces reports that are shown only to the host government and relies on ad hoc diplomacy to promote changes in abusive practices. Although fear of ICRC withdrawal could be a pressure on a government, the ICRC doesn't use this threat as a bargaining tool, and thus it has no explicit deterrence strategy. As a result, the International Red Cross is frequently allowed where other NGOs are excluded.

Fiasco in Guatemala

The ICRC offered to install a delegation in Guatemala as early as 1983, but General Mejía wanted no outsiders meddling with his war. Both President Cerezo and General Gramajo insist that they did everything possible to help the ICRC, but that the resistance of the oligarchy and the military traditionalists continued. According to Gramajo:

> Even before they [the ICRC] were established, they were talking about recognizing the "combatant" status of the insurgents. So we saw that as too belligerent on their part. Then they talked of going to the Ixcán and setting up a presence to verify the existence of prisoners. That idea alone delayed them two years in getting in. The ICRC was stuck between military orthodoxy and the dogma of the insurgents. They were screwed! So our task was to try to loosen up the orthodoxy of the military, so that it would start to cede some of its sovereignty. But military orthodoxy is very hard to overcome when the opponents are subversives, not soldiers of another nation. It was a huge dilemma. It was military orthodoxy that kept the International Red Cross out for five or six years.[3]

Additional resistance in Guatemala came from the Guatemalan National Red Cross, which, according to President Cerezo, was controlled by the oligarchy and directed by an "extremely conservative man" who saw the ICRC as direct competition.* Cerezo added:

> There was an agreement between the military government and the oligarchy to oppose the entrance of the International Red Cross. All international human rights organizations were seen as foreign intervention. They didn't really understand the ICRC. Most of the officials didn't even know about its policy of confidentiality.[4]

---

*The international Red Cross/Red Crescent federation is actually a complex and loosely knit array of autonomous national organizations. The ICRC is an entirely Swiss organization with the unique mission described earlier. It has no jurisdiction over national Red Cross societies, which tend to be focused solely on medical services and disaster relief. These national societies are frequently quite conservative in nature and and often presided over by ex-military officers. Competitive resistance to the ICRC is not uncommon.

Comparing the experiences of the ICRC and PBI in the 1980s, President Cerezo argues that the ICRC met with much more resistance. PBI was more suspicious because of its close relationship with groups like the GAM, but the prestige of the ICRC was a much more palpable threat. It took Gramajo and Cerezo three years to overcome this resistance and turn the ICRC to their advantage.

After its arrival in 1988, the ICRC could hardly be accused of justifying the conservatives' fears. Taking caution to the extreme, it embarked on no projects at all in the first few years. Even so, in December 1989, a week after the knifing of PBI volunteers, a grenade damaged the ICRC offices. General Gramajo told the ICRC that it was probably the work of a conservative right-wing military faction.[5]

In most armed conflicts, the ICRC visits prisoners of war to ascertain the conditions of imprisonment. Cerezo and Gramajo told the ICRC that it was welcome to visit every prison, jail, and military base in the country. In practice, though, no visits occurred. The ICRC instead publicly echoed government propaganda, affirming that Guatemala had no political detainees or war prisoners. This was apparently true—or at least no one has been able to find them. Supposedly, the Guatemalan army has been fighting a civil war for thirty years without taking a prisoner of war. Thousands of political activists have been detained, officially and unofficially, yet there are no political prisoners either. The ICRC would not condemn the obvious conclusion: that prisoners are killed rather than incarcerated. When the ICRC renewed its request to visit prisons in 1991, President Serrano simply denied permission, explaining that the Guatemalan constitution did not allow for the existence of political prisoners.* The ICRC made no protest.[6]

The only substantive project the International Red Cross developed was in the field of educating army officers in humanitarian law. So the army, while continuing a policy of systematic human rights abuse, was able to claim publicly and internationally that it was being trained by the ICRC.

The International Red Cross frustrated Guatemalan human rights activists. In May 1990, the GAM approached the ICRC with the hope of enlisting its support in the search for the disappeared. The ICRC refused, explaining that such activity would fall outside of its limited mandate. The GAM, incensed, held a sit-in and press conference in the ICRC office, forcing the ICRC to state its refusal publicly. It was not the first time that the ICRC has been accused of legitimizing official abuse by its silent presence.[7]

---

*Note, however, that Human Rights Watch has documented the existence of clandestine detention and political torture in Guatemala. Summary execution is probably, quantitatively, the more frequent fate of political and military prisoners.

CPRs and the Red Cross

The ICRC got another chance to offer protection to threatened Guatemalan civilians in the early 1990s, when it was approached by the Communities of Population in Resistance (CPRs). These communities consist of about 10,000 people in the northern El Quiché province who were displaced during the same scorched-earth campaign that drove the Guatemalan refugees into Mexico. These communities chose not to cross the border. Instead, they stayed close to the land they owned, hiding in the jungle in provisional camps. They were constantly fleeing the army, watching their crops burn, and digging shelters to hide from aerial bombardment.

In the late 1980s, with the help of church contacts, the CPRs began to publicize their plight in international circles. Under attack and accused of guerrilla connections, they tried to convince the world that they were civilian communities deserving of protection and support.

In 1991, CPR representatives approached the ICRC for aid. CPR leader Francisco Raymundo Hernandez recalls:

> When we first started talking with them, we had to learn the principles of the Red Cross—what they meant by impartiality, what were their norms. We eventually understood that the ICRC was completely neutral, and that they don't do anything that falls outside specific rules.
>
> They're an important international group, and we were very interested in maintaining a relationship with them, as much for the sake of protection as for humanitarian aid. We eventually felt very supported by them. We proposed a program of vaccination of children. This fit well within the ICRC's principles, and they agreed.[8]

An active ICRC project and presence would have been a major step forward in the CPRs' struggle for recognition as a civilian population. Behind the scenes, the ICRC set to work to convince the army that the CPRs were indeed a population directly affected by the armed conflict and thus an appropriate recipient of ICRC support. The army eventually gave the ICRC permission to proceed. But when the guerrillas tried to use the ICRC presence in their propaganda to embarrass the government, the army reversed itself, blocking the ICRC/CPR project.

The ICRC does not proceed without governmental permission, so there was through another round of behind-the-scenes negotiation. The army eventually relented, and the project was on again. But now the army was insisting on accompanying the ICRC on every visit to the CPRs. The CPRs refused this option. The army had been chasing and bombing them for years. The CPRs wanted the ICRC to keep the army out, not bring it in. Their fear of the army far exceeded their desire for vaccinations. The

ICRC, unable to negotiate a compromise acceptable to both, dropped the project.

A few years later, the CPRs arranged for the French NGO Doctors Without Borders to vaccinate the children. At the same time, they invited volunteers from accompaniment NGOs around the world to stay in their villages. These NGOs could respond to the CPR request without any attendant risk of military collaboration.

With a slightly more confrontational posture or a more flexible interpretation of its capacity for "ad hoc diplomacy," the ICRC can be a real thorn in the side of a government that abuses humanitarian law or human rights. It can incessantly demand visiting rights to military bases and prisons and protect victimized populations. In Guatemala, it did none of these. Hog-tied by its policy of requiring formal agreement from the authorities, and unwilling to reveal the real situation, the ICRC provided neither relief nor protection in Guatemala, while its mere presence benefited the government's international image.

Sri Lanka: Putting Prestige to Work

Like Cerezo and Gramajo in Guatemala, Sri Lankan President Premadasa and his adviser Bradman Weerakoon brought in the ICRC as a public-relations and damage-control measure. But the experience was entirely different, and it illustrates some of the potential strengths of the ICRC's international clout and privileged relationship with the government.

One of the first tasks the ICRC took on was arranging visits to detention centers. Its presence eventually expanded to the point where forty ICRC workers were visiting over 300 detention centers regularly.[9] There were thousands of detainees, resulting from the massive sweeps carried out in the clean-up operations against the insurgent JVP. The ICRC maintained its own registry of detained persons, and the follow-up on this registry was a near-guarantee that those on it would not subsequently be disappeared. According to Bradman Weerakoon, the ICRC reports were also a useful feedback to the government about the behavior of its own security forces.[10]

Although the ICRC carefully asserts that nothing can be proved, this exhaustive registry may have protected thousands from disappearance. The state could not declare that it did not have someone once that person appeared on the ICRC's list. Unfortunately, the ICRC mandate did not allow for visits to "unofficial" detention centers. Even the government's own Human Rights Task Force got involved in searching out clandestine prisons after 1992 and criticized the ICRC for not doing so.[11] Task force president Judge Soza also criticized the ICRC for its policy of not making surprise visits, pointing out that the jails can always be cleaned up before the ICRC arrives. Perhaps the military could not disappear those who ended up on the ICRC registry, but it had full control over which detainees it channeled into official centers and which ones it simply kept off the registry altogether. Thus the ICRC's strict mandate allowed its registry to be circumvented, if the security forces wanted to go to the trouble.

Protecting the Jaffna Hospital

When the Tamil Tigers launched their Eelam II war in mid-1990, they took control of a wide zone of the north and northeast. With this escalation, the ICRC began another of its traditional activities: the protection of civilian populations in war zones.

In the first months of hostilities, the Jaffna Teaching Hospital in the LTTE-controlled northern peninsula suffered frequent bombardments from the military and could not function effectively. On November 6, 1990, the army, the LTTE, and the ICRC reached an accord that declared the Jaffna Hospital an "ICRC protected area," setting several conditions: no military action could be undertaken from or against the hospital area; the borders were clearly marked so as to be visible from both ground and air; and no military personnel, weapons, or equipment could be stationed within the safety zone.

Two days after the signing of the accord, the Sri Lankan air force dropped two bombs, one within the protected area and the other very near it. The ICRC publicly condemned the bombing, which left five wounded. The Northern Military Command, denying any knowledge of the security zone, claimed that it had to attack terrorists in the area. Defense Minister Ranjan Wijeratne pledged punitive action "if there had been any infringement for frivolous reasons."[12] According to one ICRC worker, the attack demonstrated that the ICRC could not offer total protection: its ability to protect was dependent on the space the two sides agreed to keep open.[13]

But both warring parties had an interest in keeping the hospital open. Both needed a civilian population with at least certain minimal necessities covered. This common interest was facilitated by the ICRC, which could witness the fulfillment of the accord and guarantee that neither side gained an undue advantage from it. The ICRC supervised the protected zone and offered some material assistance, but it did not provide medical personnel for the hospital. After the first bombing incident, the security zone around the Jaffna Hospital was respected by both parties.

Protecting Transport

With the entire northern region cordoned off by the Sri Lankan army, transport was interrupted, curtailing all basic civilian services. Local government workers in the north, mostly Tamil, could scarcely carry out their work. There were no schoolbooks, no paper, no medicines, no postal service, and no bank operations. Once again, both warring parties found themselves with a common interest: the provision of basic services to the northern population. Government leaders in Colombo, proclaiming the unity of the island, wanted the civilian Tamil population and the outside world to see that the Sinhalese government was taking care of the population's needs. To give up this obligation would be to concede in part to the LTTE's separatist claims. The LTTE, meanwhile, was in no condition to replace these services itself and benefited from having the Colombo government provide them.

Meeting this need presented a tricky logistical and political problem. A mass of supplies needed to be moved regularly from Colombo to Jaffna through hostile territory. The ICRC stepped in, offering to accompany and protect these shipments, transported mostly by boat. Thus began a unique arrangement: the Sinhalese government continued to maintain a functioning nonmilitary state apparatus in the north by sending the money and materials to the region under ICRC supervision and accompaniment.

The schools, hospitals, and other state offices started functioning again, completely funded by the Colombo government, despite the fact that Colombo had no military or police control over the region and no real control over the distribution of the materials being sent. The Colombo government was fulfilling the Geneva conventions, providing for its civilian population in the war zone, paradoxically handing over vast resources to Tamil state workers who might be either sympathetic to or easily controlled by the LTTE. The shipments continued for over four years.

According to the ICRC, the arrangement could be implemented only with the agreement of both parties that the boats themselves would not be attacked and that the beach area of unloading at Point Pedro, Jaffna, would be free from any military activity. The crew of the ICRC vessels were Sinhalese, and they would not have felt safe sailing into these waters or unloading on this beach without the protection of the ICRC.

On August 29, 1993, Sinhalese crewmen were unloading an ICRC-escorted vessel at Point Pedro. The government Tamil navy boat *Dvora* was also operating in the area, to a certain extent subtly using the ICRC vessel's presence as a "cover" from LTTE attack. Using a small fishing boat, the LTTE approached and blew up the *Dvora*. The ICRC's Sinhala crew was so shocked by the nearby explosion that they hastily steamed off, leaving ICRC personnel standing on the beach.

The ICRC crew was rescued, but the transport operation was suspended. Before shipments resumed, it took some convincing to find a Sinhalese crew willing to sail back into those waters. According to ICRC staff: "After this event and their reaction it was clearer to us that they felt our presence was essential. . . . We can let some poor foreigner sit for weeks on a boat and nothing happens, and it may seem like a bit of a waste. But then an incident occurs and it seems to have made sense after all."[14]

Flexibility: Quaker Peace and Service in Batticaloa

Although the ICRC carried out some successful large-scale accompaniment work directly with the government, it could not respond to requests for preventive protection from civilian organizations. In the northeast, for instance, civilian villages were completely held hostage by the violence of both sides. Neelan Kandasamy, a Sri Lankan activist with the Movement for InterRacial Justice and Equality approached the ICRC to ask for a protective presence for some of these groups caught in the middle. The ICRC, however, judged the circumstances of the request to be outside of its mandate. The need was instead met by Quaker Peace and Service (QPS), a smaller and much more flexible organization.

QPS has maintained a presence in Sri Lanka since 1985, becoming interested in the country after the 1983 ethnic riots. Its goal, as an international service arm of the London Religious Society of Friends, was to offer what support it could to a process of peace and reconciliation. When the Eelam II war broke out, this commitment pulled QPS into the role of accompaniment.

The war in the eastern region of Batticaloa had disrupted all aspects of daily life. One day the army was in control, the next day the LTTE. No transport vehicles could risk the trip between Colombo and Batticaloa. According to QPS staff, more than 40,000 people were displaced. At one point, tens of thousands were in sanctuary on the university grounds, trapped between the opposing forces.

Very little food was getting into the war zones, and the local bishop asked QPS representative Brin Wolfe for help. QPS began contacting all the different NGOs working on the island to organize convoys into Batticaloa. Eventually, with support from Oxfam, the local Catholic agency EHED (Eastern Human and Economic Development) began distributing food and other basic materials to temporary refugee camps, accompanied by QPS volunteers.

QPS was next approached by some of the local Tamil assistant government agents, who were afraid to travel through the nearby Muslim communities because of the increasing tension between Muslims and Tamils. For the next two months, QPS accompanied five different government workers through the war zone to their workplaces several days each week.

It was at this point that the Doctors Without Borders vehicle was bombed (see chapter 12), and the organization withdrew all its workers from the area. The ICRC and QPS responded quickly to this abrupt shortage of medical services. QPS staff and vehicles transported and accompanied government health workers to some remote areas not under government control, where people had no other access to medical services.

QPS, as a matter of principle, was committed to serving all the various ethnic communities in the region. Given the heightened tensions between these communities due to the war, accompanying government workers was quite delicate. QPS staff wanted to preserve both physical security and good relationships with all the communities. Both the government medical workers and QPS wanted to be very careful about whom they served or offered rides to, in order to keep their mission clear and avoid harassment later. QPS endeavored to ensure that no one carrying a weapon was served by the clinic.

In the process, QPS also deliberately contacted Sinhala and Muslim communities to counteract the frequent stereotype that international organizations were serving only Tamils. According to former QPS Sri Lanka director Phil Esmonde, the objective went beyond image control. QPS had supported each community in enough instances to earn credibility. While demonstrating a willingness to see the humanity of everyone in the conflict, QPS could also help break down misconceptions the various groups had of their alleged "enemies." This aspect of the work was fundamental to QPS's belief in the power of reconciliation.[15]

QPS is not an accompaniment organization per se. It took on short-term accompaniment in Batticaloa as a response to an immediate need in an extreme situation. The task was consistent with a broader commitment to conflict resolution and reconciliation, and this commitment was reflected in its implementation of accompaniment. When the need diminished in late 1991, QPS discontinued the service. But when the situation deteriorated in 1992 and again in 1996, QPS staff again offered accompaniment.

Flexibility is conditioned by both structural and political concerns. Large organizations, for instance, develop rigid bureaucracies and internal procedures that tend to have the inertial effect of slowing decisions and avoiding political risks. So just by dint of their size, one would not expect the ICRC or the UN to exhibit a great deal of flexibility.

Although QPS is smaller, its impressive history of international service has earned it a Nobel Prize and a level of clout well beyond its size. With its broad mandate based on religious principles and a delegated trust in its field personnel to act on those principles, it had the necessary flexibility to respond to the need for accompaniment in Batticaloa. The ICRC, in contrast, is inflexible in both principle and structure. Founded on legal rather than religious principles, its rigid mandate assures governments that the ICRC will do nothing unexpected or politically damaging. Governments, and especially military leaders, trust the ICRC more than they do other NGOs. This trust gives the ICRC both access and leverage.

In exchange, the ICRC is unlikely to risk anything as politically delicate as accompaniment of a political activist who says that the government is threatening him. The government would see such accompaniment as an implicit accusation. If the activist is formally detained, the ICRC mandate kicks in, because political prisoners have certain explicit rights according to ICRC-brokered international law. Sunanda Deshapriya, a journalist and activist with the Sri Lankan free media movement, made the following distinction: "The Red Cross comes to help you after it happens—they visit you in prison. But Peace Brigades [accompaniment] is the first part: they try to stop it from happening."[16]

But even this assertion is valid only if the ICRC is available, and in this respect, we reach the more fundamental distinction: both the UN and the ICRC, as a matter of principle and mandate, function at the behest of governments and with an utter respect for sovereignty. They will not be present if the host government doesn't want them. So although both the UN and the ICRC are experimenting and broadening their mandates, there will always be a demand for NGO protection in places where the UN and ICRC are nowhere to be seen.

Notes

1. Malcolm Rodgers, "Refugees and International Aid. Sri Lanka: A Case Study," UNHCR document, Geneva, May 1992.
2. Hidaeko Nakagawa (UNHCR/Sri Lanka), interview by authors, Colombo, April 8, 1994.
3. General Hector Gramajo, tape-recorded interview by authors, Guatemala, July 7, 1994.
4. President Vinicio Cerezo Arevalo, interview by authors, Guatemala, August 1994.
5. ICRC-Guatemala staff (name withheld), interview by authors, July 1994.
6. ICRC-Guatemala interview.
7. Forsythe, *Humanitarian Politics*, p. 69. The most salient case is the ICRC's silence with respect to abuse in Nazi prisoner camps. More generally, it is frequently argued that by visiting detainees and "approving" their humanitarian treatment, the ICRC is tacitly legitimizing the arbitrary detentions that got them there in the first place.
8. Francisco Raymundo Hernandez (CPR representative), tape-recorded interview by authors, Guatemala, July 15, 1994.
9. ICRC staff, Sri Lanka (name withheld), interview by authors, Colombo, April 1994.
10. Bradman Weerakoon, interview by authors, Colombo, April 1994.
11. Judge J. F. A. Soza, interview by authors, Colombo, March 30, 1994. See also Amnesty International, *Sri Lanka; An Assessment of the Human Rights Situation,* January 1993.
12. *PBI Project Bulletin*, November/December 1990.
13. ICRC staff, Sri Lanka, interview.
14. ICRC staff, Sri Lanka, interview.
15. Phil Esmonde, interview by authors, Colombo, April 1994.
16. Sunanda Deshapriya, tape-recorded interview by authors, Colombo, April 1994.

14

Steadfast in Haiti

*I*N APRIL 1993, PAX CHRISTI USA, an organization of progressive
Catholic activists, called together several organizations in Washington,
D.C., to discuss a large-scale accompaniment project in Haiti.* The objective was to support the reemergence of the civilian democratic movement.
The project was an ambitious undertaking, and Pax Christi knew from the
start that it could not do it alone. The first hurdle was to build a coalition
of organizations whose complementary experiences and skills would meet
the challenge. The result was a nine-organization coalition known as Cry
for Justice: Nonviolent Presence in Haiti.†

The Haitian republic was formed in 1804, after the only successful slave
revolution in modern history. But the slave colony of the French was replaced
by a local tyranny of rule by force by the black mulatto elite. Over the next
two centuries, systematic economic isolation and discrimination against the
hemisphere's only black republic transformed what had been a wealthy
colony into the poorest nation in the hemisphere.

With a determination reminiscent of the original revolution, the Haitian
people overthrew the Duvalier dictatorship in February 1986, but subsequent attempts at installing democratic rule were repeatedly foiled by the
military and by former Duvalier supporters. In 1990, the Haitian people
elected Jean-Bertrand Aristide, a radical priest active in poor people's movements, to the presidency by an overwhelming margin. His presidency lasted
nine months.

On the night of September 30, 1991, tanks rolled through the streets of
Port-au-Prince, Haiti. The army surrounded the presidential palace, while
loyal supporters spirited President Aristide into hiding, followed by exile in
the United States. Soldiers controlled strategic locations throughout the city
to prevent any popular response. To further minimize the risk of a popular
revolt, the military initiated a campaign of systematic repression. In the

---

*The first accompaniment requests actually arose in Haiti in late 1992, when the Papaye
Peasant Movement asked Peace Brigades International to send a team to the central plateau
region. PBI was unable to marshal the resources to initiate its own project, so instead it helped
Cry for Justice the following year.
†The Cry for Justice coalition steering committee included Pax Christi USA, Christian
Peacemaker Teams, Fellowship of Reconciliation, Global Exchange, Haiti Communications
Project, PBI, Sojourners, World Peacemakers, and the Washington Office on Haiti.

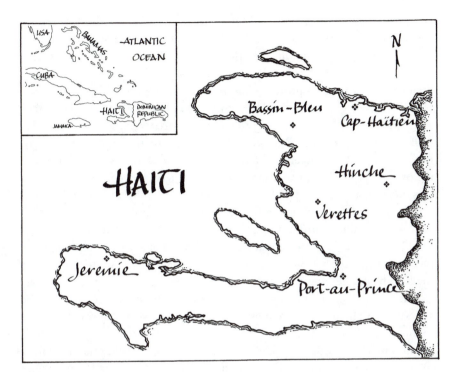

next few months, thousands of people were killed, and democratic civilian organizations were forced into hiding.

The Haitian experiment with democracy had inspired many in the international community. In particular, Aristide's eloquent espousal of the Haitian brand of liberation theology had galvanized Christian churches globally. The Haitian people had overcome dictatorship and military control through a steadfast and unarmed commitment to democracy. The coup dashed hopes around the world. But although most nations immediately refused diplomatic recognition to the coup leaders,* tangible action was a long time coming. During 1992 and 1993, different organizations began sending investigatory delegations to Haiti, informing the world about the repression and building a constituency for political pressure. The Cry for Justice coalition brought several of these organizations together.

From the beginning, the Cry for Justice had multiple objectives: to diminish violence; to educate people in the United States; to show solidarity and offer hope to frustrated and disillusioned Haitian activists; and to pressure and embarrass the UN, OAS, and diplomatic community into taking stronger

---

*With the notable exception of the Vatican, whose diplomatic representative supported the coup to the bitter end.

actions against the de facto military government. When the Governors Island accords were signed in June 1993, the UN and OAS sent in a civilian human rights monitoring mission (MICIVIH), and the return of President Aristide was set for October 30. Cry for Justice wanted to be in place by then to encourage and protect Haitian activists who would use Aristide's return to reactivate their organizations. A launch date of late September 1993 was set, with a commitment to stay for three months.

Between July and September, each member organization scrambled to find money and volunteers. Subcommittees were formed to develop funding proposals, budgets, training plans, and security procedures. Everything was done on a shoestring budget. The steering committee, dispersed around the United States, never held a face-to-face meeting: planning and decision making were done during biweekly conference calls. At the last minute, a local coordinating committee made up mostly of Haitians was pulled together in Port-au-Prince to handle field preparations and give political advice to the U.S.-based steering committee.

But as the launch date approached, the Haitian military reneged on the accords and clamped down in an ever-worsening cycle of repression. Just saying Aristide's name in Haiti was grounds for a beating or extrajudicial execution. The reversal climaxed with the public killings in mid-September of Antoine Izmery, a friend and financial supporter of Aristide, and Guy Mallory, the justice minister named by Aristide from exile. The possibilities for Aristide's return were looking slim. The military was spreading antiforeigner propaganda and calling the UN/OAS monitors "invaders."

By the time the first Cry for Justice volunteers arrived on September 25, the situation was so bad that the question was not whether they could protect Haitian activists during a democratic transition but whether a foreign presence might actually endanger Haitians, who might be better off remaining in hiding. The military government was flouting high-level political pressure from the UN, the OAS and the U.S. government,* so why would it be sensitive to an international presence? In fact, contrary to the expectation that Aristide's return would bring a "political opening," democratic activists were being forced deeper into hiding. Few Haitians felt that accompaniment could offer any real protection under these circumstances.† The rug had been pulled out from under any rationale that accompaniment would either deter violence or encourage political activity.

Based on advice from its Haitian advisers, the Cry for Justice steering committee decided that even if "protection" was unachievable, the other

---

*In fact, U.S. influence was contradictory: the CIA and the Defense Department consistently supported and funded the coup and its leaders, while the Clinton administration spoke out firmly against them.

†For example, Haitian contacts told volunteers in Jeremie, "You can do nothing if you can't protect yourself! The attachés won't care that you are white."

objectives still justified the presence. Moral solidarity with Haitians and education of the international community were still vital. Without overt democratic organizing to protect, there was still some hope that the mere presence of foreigners in rural villages might diminish the ambient violence. So, with the safety of the foreign volunteers themselves as a paramount concern, the Haitian coordinating committee on the ground worked through the churches to set up housing for volunteers in five rural communities and Port-au-Prince.*

The Haitian military authorities were never informed of the project's existence nor of its commitment to respond to violations the volunteers witnessed. Had there been a deterrence strategy, such communication might have strengthened its effectiveness, albeit at considerable risk. But with so many doubts about the deterrence possibility, the project's Haitian advisers urged that the presence be low-key and anonymous—almost clandestine. Overt identification with "justice" would be, they felt, provocative and too dangerous for Haitians and foreigners alike. Instead, in each community, a different cover was devised. In one village, volunteers lived in the rectory and, when asked, claimed to be missionaries interested in supporting a sewing project through the church. In others, they simply claimed to be interested in learning about Haiti, or they came in as "personal friends" of the local priest.

Many of the volunteers were motivated by deep Christian or nonviolent beliefs and found the necessity for blatant lying or even half-truths to be discomforting and nerve-wracking. The priests who hosted them were generally already suspect in the eyes of the military, so it was doubtful that their visitors would be perceived as "innocent," regardless of their disguise. In the village of Verrettes, the military's local thugs circled the volunteers' home three nights in a row, firing guns in the air. In Jeremie, volunteers were told to get out of town and accused of being the "communist" priest's armed bodyguards.

On October 15, citing security concerns, the UN/OAS abruptly pulled its human rights monitors out of the country. Cry for Justice volunteers watched as the Haitians' hearts sank. After a huge promise, many Haitians felt that the international community was deserting them in their hour of greatest need. From that moment forward, the driving force that kept the project going was a steadfast refusal to contribute to the abandonment of Haiti.

It wasn't easy. By the end of October, all but one of the project's Haitian advisory committee members had fled into exile, and President Aristide had not returned. The remaining Haitian staff forced themselves onward, dealing

---

*The church was about the only civilian institution that was still operating publicly, and the Catholic Justice and Peace organization had continued to report on human rights abuses since the coup.

with inexperienced volunteers' medical problems, language limitations, and personality disputes, as well as financial and communication problems. Money was short, gas was being cut off by the international embargo, and the telephones seldom worked. But they somehow held it together.

Over a period of twelve weeks, Cry for Justice sent seventy-one volunteers to Haiti. Most stayed two weeks; others stayed the whole three months. They strolled around Haitian villages, chatted with people about the weather in the market, attended mass, and in general made themselves as innocently visible as possible, hoping with no certainty that their presence was lessening the fear and violence. For most, their service was without major incident, but they lived with the tension of "waiting," knowing that war was all around them, admiring the courage of the Haitians who lived with the tension perpetually. The volunteers returned home motivated to continue working for Haitian solidarity.

In rare instances, the volunteers actually found themselves accompanying local priests on dangerous human rights investigations. One local priest brought Cry for Justice volunteers with him to inquire about a group of men they had seen arrested. In another situation in Jeremie, the volunteers intervened after seeing a man abducted by the FRAPH (the Front for the Advancement of Haiti, a well-armed pro-military paramilitary organization).

While this abduction was in progress, Canadian volunteer Joel Klassen tried to talk the FRAPH members out of taking the man. The man's mother also intervened but was beaten to the ground. The whole Cry for Justice team then went to the FRAPH office to see what they could do. A line of armed men blocked their way, yelling at them and taunting them. The Cry for Justice volunteers just stayed there, holding vigil, sometimes trying to communicate, sometimes praying.

At this point, an influential local pastor with military connections came by and offered to help. With a few of the volunteers, he approached the FRAPH men, asking them to calm down and let them in. "We can't let foreigners see us acting this way," he argued. At this they relented. After half an hour inside, the pastor emerged with the prisoner, who had been beaten badly.

It was the pastor's influence that succeeded in getting the man released, but it seemed to be the foreign presence that prompted him, or embarrassed him, into intervening with the extremist FRAPH faction. Once he decided to act, he used the same sense of nationalist pride and embarrassment to pressure the taunting FRAPH gang to relent. It is one of the only instances in our case studies of an accompaniment intervention freeing someone from a paramilitary abduction.

This incident points to the potential of accompaniment as moral-political persuasion, rather than as direct deterrence. It is unlikely that either the local pastor or the FRAPH feared any direct international consequences if they had not acted as they did. This is not to say that they acted altruistically. More likely, they were each seeking credibility and legitimacy: the pastor from the foreign volunteers and popular groups he knew they were allied with; the FRAPH from the pastor. Such concerns for legitimacy are where the moral and the political intersect.

In December 1993, the Cry for Justice steering committee got together in Washington to evaluate and end the project. Lack of resources, miscommunication, and political pressures beyond their control had taken a toll. The project ended in debt, with several key activists utterly burnt out. Given the continued repression in Haiti, the group discussed briefly whether it could continue the presence for the long term but dismissed the idea quickly. It was beyond their means. The meeting was dominated by exhaustion and sadness. The terror had taken its toll.

Despite the dejection with which the project ended, the Cry for Justice fulfilled many of its objectives, within a much more dangerous context than had been foreseen. The Cry for Justice did not apparently expand the space for democratic activism nor limit the space for army impunity (see figures 8.1–8.7). But it definitely educated North Americans, thus contributing to international pressure for human rights in Haiti. Each organization in the coalition returned to its ongoing work. Several continued to send regular short-term educational delegations to Haiti. Others broadened their lobbying campaigns in Washington.

Perhaps most importantly, Cry for Justice offered a base-level encouragement and solidarity to Haitians. Under the circumstances, this solidarity could not reach the threshold necessary to prompt political activity. But Haitians were still grateful for the presence and saw it as one of the only signs of hope coming from the international community.

One coalition member, Christian Peacemaker Teams (CPT), maintained a long-term accompaniment presence. A project of the North American Mennonite and Brethren churches, CPT was formed in 1993 to field volunteers in the service of peace. For the next two years—through the uncertainties of the last year of military control and the transitions after the September 1994 arrival of U.S. and later UN troops—CPT volunteers walked the streets of St. Helene, a poor neighborhood in Jeremie, getting to know the people and their struggle and writing reports for their churches and for the Haitian solidarity movement.*

In January 1995, when CPT volunteers were leaving St. Helene, their host, Father Samedi, told his congregation:

*Christian Peacemaker Teams went on to start a project in Hebron, Israel, offering protective accompaniment to Palestinians who felt threatened by Israeli settlers and security forces.

Today we give thanks to God for the presence of the whites in our midst for almost two years. . . . Their presence gave us much security. Anywhere we were, they were there. If we were in prison, they were there. If we were held by the FRAPH, they were there. Every night and every day they were one with us. . . . They have left their beautiful countries, left their jobs and money, and come and shared their lives with those in distress. They came in solidarity, because they believe in God. Now they are going home to their families, and so that we can be even more in solidarity with one another. They will help people learn about Haiti, help them understand the situation that we are living in.[1]

Note

1. Christian Peacemaker Teams, "Closing Week of CPT's Long Term Presence in Jeremie, Haiti." CPT public document, February 6, 1995, pp. 3–4.

15

Deterrence Up Front in Colombia

A N EFFECTIVE DETERRENCE STRATEGY can be hindered by an inability to communicate with the state. Salvadoran officials dismissed accompaniment groups as "subversives"; thus PBI and others were hesitant to identify themselves publicly. Likewise, it took years in Sri Lanka and Guatemala for PBI to build up a relationship with the government; many other accompaniment NGOs never did.

As we discussed in chapter 8, deterrence is demonstrably effective only if the potential attacker knows who the accompaniment is and what it will do—that is, what the political consequences of an attack will be. Without clear communication, the proof of deterrence is little more than supposition.

Similarly, a deterrence strategy requires access to information—a clear analysis of who the attacker is and what political pressures he is sensitive to. Finally, for this deterrence to encourage democratic activists, the activists must be willing to take the risk of acting with accompaniment. When PBI was asked to go to Colombia in 1991, it made a careful investigation to determine whether these conditions were fulfilled.

Colombia is a vast and rich country. Its history boasts one of the most stable parliamentary systems in Latin America, with a notable absence of coups. It has an image of democracy and a progressive foreign policy. But these traits coexist with other, more disturbing realities. Drug traffic captures world headlines. Less noticed are the facts that most Colombians live in poverty, and the country has one of the worst human rights records in the world. It is host to numerous paramilitary organizations. There are separate, armed conflicts among three independent insurgent groups and the army.

One cannot speak of a single Colombian conflict, but rather of various types of conflicts, with markedly different dynamics in different regions. The Colombian NGO Justice and Peace registered 37,842 political assassinations in Colombia between 1988 and 1992. Overall, according to the Andean Commission of Jurists, most human rights violations are committed by the security forces or by state-related paramilitary groups.[1]

During the 1980s, attention on Colombia's drug-related scandals kept the human rights situation off the international agenda, despite the efforts of Colombian NGOs. In the late 1980s and early 1990s, however, a series

of reports and resolutions from the UN, the OAS, the European Parliament, and various human rights NGOs began to publicize the human rights problem.[2] By 1996, the international human rights movement was pressuring the UN to name a special human rights rapporteur to Colombia.

The government responded actively to these campaigns, instituting various measures for the promotion and protection of human rights. Colombia's recently approved constitution is one of the most progressive in Latin America. The government ratified the 1977 Geneva Conventions on International Humanitarian Law and named both a people's ombudsman and a special counsel to the president for human rights.

In June 1994, President César Gaviria called together all his ambassadors to Europe and North America to give them explicit instructions about improving Colombia's external image.[3] When President Ernesto Samper took office later that year, he declared, "we accept the challenge of proving to the international community that our nation is working without rest towards the respect of human rights. . . . [Colombia] is not afraid to open itself to intense scrutiny of international governmental and non-governmental organizations."[4] Samper also clarified the economic ramifications: "the fulfillment of policies of human rights has become a pre-condition for the opening of new markets, investments, and access to strategic materials."[5]

But human rights violations continued unabated, leading numerous analysts and NGOs to criticize the inefficiency of the application of protective measures, the existing state of impunity, and the lack of productive investigation or prosecution of human rights violators.* Among the targets of repression were Colombia's independent human rights organizations, several of which solicited PBI accompaniment.

Given the variety of actors and conflicts involved in the Colombian scene, before risking an accompaniment project, PBI needed to ascertain which ones were sensitive to international pressure—and could thus be expected to be responsive to an accompaniment presence. The armed forces are under government control, and most analysts believe that many of the paramilitary organizations do not operate without the consent of the army. Consequently, given government sensitivity to international pressure, there was a strong case for accompaniment when the threat came from these sources. Effective protection against threats from guerrilla organizations, landowners' private armed groups, or drug-cartel paramilitary groups was less certain.

PBI established its initial presence in the capital, Bogotá, to work with national human rights organizations and build direct relationships with the government, local NGOs, and diplomats. Shortly after its arrival, PBI set up a satellite team in Barrancabermeja, the largest city of the Magdalena Medio, a region with strong local human rights organizations that had been denouncing abuses clearly tied to state security forces.

When the first PBI team arrived in Bogotá in October 1994, there were no other significant international NGOs providing a protective presence in Colombia except for the ICRC, so PBI could expect to stand out. Although the international community was now paying attention to the Colombian human rights situation, there was no broad solidarity movement such as the one that had supported PBI in Central America. So, from the start, the project sought collaboration with other international organizations interested in Colombia and committed itself to strengthening this incipient issue-area network. This was a long-run strategy to increase the

---

*During a visit to the country, Amnesty International general secretary Pierre Sane described Colombia sardonically as having "the biggest human rights bureaucracy in the world." PBI-Colombia, *Informe Quincenal*, November 20, 1994.

pressure that could be brought to bear when PBI's deterrence capacity was challenged.

The government considered a PBI presence to be consistent with its own stated commitment to human rights and its strategy to improve its image. Within a few weeks, unlike any previous PBI project, the team was authorized special "courtesy" visas. A few months later, the organization was duly registered and legally recognized—a process that had taken years for PBI's projects elsewhere.

In Bogotá, in the Magdalena Medio, and in any other region where PBI subsequently ventured, the work always started with a round of visits to national and local authorities, both civilian and military. On each visit, PBI explained the function and methodology of accompaniment. In PBI's deterrence strategy, these meetings communicated both the existence and the possible political consequences of the accompaniment. PBI also recruited support from the diplomatic corps, which was kept closely informed of the work. The Colombian groups formally notified the government of the accompaniment they were now receiving.

PBI's work in Colombia proceeded in a fashion similar to that of its previous projects. Within a short time accompaniment was extended to no fewer than six human rights organizations, with regular visits to their offices and personal escorting of activists, sometimes twenty-four hours a day. In one noteworthy case, ASFADDES, an organization of families of the disappeared, was campaigning against a government proposal to rewrite the military code of laws, a proposal that the group believed legitimized impunity. As a result, ASFADDES members were threatened in late 1994. They considered fleeing into exile but changed their minds when PBI accompaniment became available.*

In the Magdalena Medio, PBI faced its first serious challenge only a few months after installing a team. On April 9, 1995, two PBI volunteers accompanied a delegation, including several local human rights organizations and two representatives of the U.S.-based Human Rights Watch–Americas, to investigate recent abuses in rural areas of Sabana de Torres. As evening approached, the group received a false report of a massacre, urging them to travel immediately to a nearby area of considerable paramilitary activity. Suspicious of its veracity, the delegation did not respond. After subsequent investigation, police sources confirmed "a presumed ambush that paramilitary

---

*At the end of 1994, the Colombian congress debated a legislative proposal dealing with forced disappearances. The government maintained that these cases fell within the jurisdiction of military courts—a stand that garnered considerable criticism internally and externally. ASFADDES, the Colombian national organization of families of the disappeared, led a public campaign opposing the government's position. This confrontational stand coincided with several ongoing cases in which military men were being brought before the courts.

organizations had been planning for a national and international commission visiting the area."[6]

The abortive ambush attempt represented a direct challenge to PBI's deterrence commitment and to Human Rights Watch's international clout. Human Rights Watch cut its visit short, leaving the next day. The PBI team embarked immediately on a series of interviews with embassies and government officials. PBI chapters around the world communicated their concern to their own governments and their embassies in Colombia. On May 19, a special delegation of diplomatic representatives from three European embassies went to Barranca-bermeja and met with the regional civilian and military authorities to emphasize their support for PBI's work in the region and their concern for the physical well-being of the volunteers.[7] This high-level intervention made it clear to local authorities and, presumably, through internal military channels, to the paramilitary groups that had allegedly planned the ambush, the potential political consequences of attacking PBI. It had the further effect of increasing PBI's locally perceived clout. PBI noted a different reception in its subsequent meeting with local officials.[8] Thus the application of a deliberate deterrence strategy, in the context of a responsive government and a cooperative diplomatic corps, rapidly gained PBI a credibility that might otherwise have taken years to develop.

One of the organizations with PBI on that delegation was CREDHOS, the Regional Human Rights Commission, which had originally invited PBI to the region. Prior to 1993, six CREDHOS activists had been assassinated, and most of the surviving directorate had fled into exile. When the organization started to revive in 1993 and 1994, the government provided the CREDHOS office with armed guards of the Administrative Security Department (DAS), although some CREDHOS members were reluctant to accept it.

In May 1995, only a month after the ambush scare, CREDHOS published a report naming the armed forces as a major violator of human rights in the Magdalena Medio region. Immediately, its staff began to notice suspicious vehicles following them, and its office received numerous telephone threats. CREDHOS sent an open letter of protest to President Samper, demanding guarantees of safety.[9] The threats continued, and armed men began hanging around the neighborhood of the CREDHOS office. Up to this point, PBI's accompaniment had been sporadic. CREDHOS now asked for a constant presence in its office.

On June 30, CREDHOS president Osiris Bayter denounced the military in a speech commemorating the third anniversary of the assassination of a CREDHOS worker. That afternoon, the office received a series of telephone threats. An unknown man lingered outside the office all day. When a PBI volunteer approached and asked him what he was doing there, the man refused to answer and left. At the end of the day, a CREDHOS staff member was descending the stairway outside the building when an armed man with a walkie-talkie and military boots stopped her and asked if there was anyone else inside. Terrified, she lied and said no, and the man left. An hour later, a man identifying himself as a journalist telephoned, asking for PBI. When a PBI volunteer took the telephone, the man asked how long he planned to stay in the office. It seemed clear to PBI that someone was verifying whether the office was accompanied.[10]

From the moment PBI's accompaniment became continuous, however, the suspicious men disappeared from the neighborhood, and the harassment declined significantly.[11] Now, the infrequent telephone threats sometimes alluded to the accompaniment, saying things like "They won't always be protecting you" or "As soon as they leave you alone, we'll take care of you in fifteen minutes!"[12] This series of events suggests that PBI's presence in the CREDHOS office, reinforced by the recent supportive visit of European diplomats, succeeded in deterring the threats and harassment.

The nascent accompaniment work in Colombia rapidly achieved a remarkable coherence, in part because it was so enthusiastically embraced and understood by Colombian human rights organizations. They not only saw its potential but also understood the tactical steps necessary to maximize its deterring effect. Thus, in January 1995, when PBI had only just arrived in Barrancabermeja, CREDHOS officially notified the government of its intention to use accompaniment, adding:

> PBI workers will be permanently accompanying CREDHOS personnel in our daily work. In spite of this, we wish to clarify that the Colombian state continues to be directly responsible for the lives and safety of the members of the organization.[13]

According to CREDHOS president Bayter:

> On one occasion, a battalion commander came here and asked me if I felt safe with the international presence. I told him yes, and that it gave us considerable peace of mind.[14]

This transparent communication is an effective element of a deterrence strategy. Nevertheless, in our case studies, such direct communication between a threatened group and the state about the role of accompaniment is surprisingly rare, with the notable exceptions of the massive refugee returns.

Even more remarkable were the decisions of ASFADDES and CREDHOS to forgo the option of armed protection. Both organizations had been offered armed escorts by the DAS in 1994, and both accepted. In ASFADDES's case, the government never came through on its offer. Finding itself still unprotected when PBI arrived, ASFADDES told the government that it no longer desired DAS bodyguards.

CREDHOS had DAS bodyguards for some time before PBI arrived. For PBI, the combination was problematic, if not contradictory, since the simultaneous presence of armed guards weakened both the clarity and the credibility of the deterring presence of PBI volunteers. While providing a sporadic presence at the CREDHOS office, PBI refrained from accompanying individual activists who traveled with DAS bodyguards. Not long afterwards, CREDHOS decided to dispense with the DAS protection altogether.

> We have always told the government and DAS that human rights work is incompatible with weapons; much less so with having them right in your office, where people would come, full of fear, to lodge their complaints and testimonies about abuses. After a while the people stopped coming—seeing the police there, and we had to start going to their houses to take testimony. We're doing completely legal work. But the police were inspecting everything—right up to the newspapers which arrived at the door. It caused a lot of mistrust in the people.[15]

The decision was practical, moral, and strategic, and we discuss the interaction of these aspects further in the next chapter. From PBI's perspective, the decision allowed for a more coherent application of an unarmed accompaniment deterrence strategy. In a society where armed protection is widely accepted, the CREDHOS and ASFADDES decisions demonstrated the powerful encouraging effect of the accompaniment option.

Notes

1. See "Balance de un quinquenio," *Justicia y Paz* 5, no. 4 (October– December 1992). According to a study of life-threatening attacks between January 1991 and June 1992 by the Andean Commission of Jurists, 49.3 percent of those cases in which a responsible party could be identified were the work of state agents; 33.5 percent were committed by paramilitaries, and 13.2 percent by guerrilla forces. Andean Commission of Jurists, "¿Las ilusiones perdidas? Derechos humanos y derecho humanitario en Colombia en 1992," Bogotá, January 1993.
2. "Los derechos humanos en Colombia en 1995: violaciones a granel e impunidad," document series no. 1, International Office for Human Rights—Colombia Action (OID-HACO), February 1996; "Nuevas agendas en derechos humanos," *Boletín Informativo de Justicia y Paz* (1995), p. 8. As a result of pressure, for example, four Colombian military officers were denied visas to visit Germany in 1993, and Colonel Alfonso Plazas was refused by Germany when he was named as consul, because of his record as a human rights violator. *El Espectador*, June 6, 1995.
3. Diego Pérez, *Cien días*, no. 27 (August–November 1994).
4. "Política del Gobierno del Presidente de la República de Colombia Ernesto Samper Pizano en materia de derechos humanos," government document, Bogotá, February 1995.
5. Presidential document, September 9, 1994, cited in "Nuevas agendas en derechos humanos," *Boletín Informativo de Justicia y Paz*, p. 9.
6. *El Colombiano*, June 21, 1995.
7. *La Vanguardia Liberal*, May 20, 1995.
8. Javier Zabala, tape-recorded interview by authors, Bogotá, December 1995.
9. *La Vanguardia Liberal*, June 19, 1995.

10. PBI internal report, July 1995.
11. Osiris Bayter, tape-recorded interview by authors, Barrancabermeja, Colombia, December 1995; Zabala interview; Edurne Almirantearena, interview by authors, Bogotá, November 5, 1995.
12. Bayter interview; Zabala interview; see also Julián Alberto Lineros, "Bajo amenazas," *Cambio 16: Colombia*, no. 121 (October 2, 1995).
13. Letter from CREDHOS directorate to the Barrancabermeja director of DAS, January 24, 1995.
14. Bayter interview.
15. Bayter interview.

PART III

16

Principles in Action

ORGANIZATIONAL DECISION MAKING and planning can be broken down into four stages: principles, objectives, strategies, and tactics. Different accompaniment organizations may seem to be implementing the same tactic, but they start from a wide range of basic principles and objectives. The strategies chosen to implement the accompaniment are in turn conditioned by varying political analyses and by resource constraints. Faced with a difficult situation in the field, two different organizations, or even two individuals, frequently make different—even contradictory—tactical choices.

For example, PBI arrived in Guatemala with certain principles, including nonviolence, nonpartisanship, and a belief in local empowerment. Its objective, in broadest terms, based on those principles, was to aid in the development of nonviolent movements for social justice. It chose an overall strategy of sending small peace teams into conflict zones. At a critical moment in 1985, accompaniment burst into being as an immediate tactical response to external events. But PBI's lack of money, people, and political clout made it difficult to implement.

But accompaniment is much more than an immediate tactic, and over time, it was transformed into a broad objective requiring a long-term strategy. It required substrategies for communicating with the army, building political clout, making diplomatic contacts, recruiting and training adequate volunteers, finding funding, and developing an emergency response network. These substrategies are conditioned by basic principles but are also designed to alleviate resource limitations and actively change the political context.

Consider the International Red Cross: its principles include a fundamental commitment to working within the framework of international law. The ICRC has multiple objectives, and its strategy is one of collaborating with military authorities. Its resource limitations are of a different magnitude than most NGOs, and its clout is enormous. In this context, when accompaniment is chosen as a tactic, the implementation is unique.

The intersection of different organizational choices with varying conflict situations yields scenarios too numerous to analyze exhaustively. We limit ourselves here to a discussion of some of the more controversial variances in principles and strategy.

Nonpartisanship, Independence, and Noninterference

Nonpartisanship is a widely misunderstood issue facing all humanitarian organizations working in conflict situations. Larry Minear and Thomas Weiss of the Humanitarianism and War Project have attempted to codify the concept in their "Providence Principles" for humanitarian action: "Humanitarian action responds to human suffering because people are in need, not to advance political, sectarian, or other extraneous agendas. It should not take sides in conflicts." They go on to argue that humanitarian action must serve victims rather than causes and should not embrace political parties or religious or cultural ideologies. "When multiple objectives exist, humanitarian considerations are frequently crowded out."[1]

Minear and Weiss distinguish, however, between nonpartisanship and *impartiality*. Most humanitarian organizations affirm a partiality for the poor, the suffering, and the marginalized while maintaining a nonpartisan position with respect to the armed parties in conflict. Semantically, the words nonpartisanship and impartiality are almost identical, but the distinction in practice is essential. Nonpartisan service responds to demonstrable objective and external criteria rather than to alignments in the conflict. Categories such as the poor, the suffering, and those in need are criteria that cross boundaries of specific political conflicts. To be partial but nonpartisan, then, is to say, "We will be *at your side* in the face of injustice and suffering, but we will not *take sides against* those you define as enemies."

Many organizations serve a specifically defined population. The UNHCR, for instance, has an externally defined mandate to serve refugees. If all Sri Lankan refugees at a given moment are Tamil, the UNHCR's service is still nonpartisan, as long as it is available in the event of a Sinhala refugee situation. Quaker Peace and Service in Batticaloa established an objective criterion that it would not transport anyone carrying a gun. The criterion is nonpartisan, even if all armed individuals requesting transport happened to come from one group.

With respect to accompaniment, then, we define nonpartisanship as a refusal to condition accompaniment according to political alignment or ideology and a refusal to support any side in an armed conflict. Using Minear and Weiss's terminology, all accompaniment is *partial* to those it protects, supporting their right to live and work free from attack. But not all accompaniment organizations are nonpartisan.

Peace Brigades International maintains a strict commitment to nonpartisanship, refraining from any advocacy role. Accompaniment is made available to groups and individuals from varying political factions, the only criteria being that the accompanied group be committed to unarmed struggle for human rights and justice. However, in situations of state terror, it is invariably the activists with strong political agendas opposed to the state who come under threat. PBI accompanied groups in Central America because they were in danger, not because they were opposed to the government. The fact that nearly all of them *were* opposed to the government was not coincidental, but this does not contradict the nonpartisanship—although it may be impossible to convince the government of this commitment.

The concept of *independence* in international humanitarian work generally means avoiding being controlled by local actors, including local government authorities. Although accompaniment organizations might desire such independence, if they raise the ire of the host government, they can be expelled at any moment. To the extent that an organization must measure its actions against the threat of expulsion, as PBI did in the Olga María incident, its independence from government manipulation is circumscribed. Yet if it ignores such diplomatic concerns, expulsion is much more likely, resulting in an end to the protective service altogether.

International organizations must accept the reality that local actors may try to exert influence over them. Accompaniment organizations frequently encounter pressures to act outside their mandates; often the pressures come from the very people being accompanied. Although such influence can never be completely avoided and is not necessarily damaging, organizations committed to independence try to control such manipulation. One method is for an organization to define strict limits on what it will or will not do and resist pressure from local activists to extend these limits.

Independence, as such, is not sought by all accompaniment groups. Many individual volunteers and smaller organizations attach themselves to a particular civilian organization as helpers and accompaniment, offering any type of assistance within their means and ceding decision making and independence to the local group. The Marin County group's accompaniment was managed by the Salvadoran Human Rights Commission. The GAM and the CERJ in Guatemala each recruited its own multipurpose volunteers for short periods, specifically in response to PBI's unwillingness to provide other services beyond accompaniment. Sometimes the strategy of local control is the only available option: the Cry for Justice, for instance, would have ground to a halt without Haitian guidance and management.

Ceding accompaniment control to local activists can be defended firmly on the grounds of supporting the *self-determination* and *empowerment* of indigenous organizations and avoiding the risk that the foreigner, or the foreign organization, is being manipulative in setting conditions of service. This principled choice has strategic costs. Independence and nonpartisanship tend to give an organization credibility in the eyes of both local governments and the international community. Dispensing with both concepts weakens the clout of the deterrence. Organizations that choose this option must build clout in other ways.

In practice, accompaniment projects managed by the local activists frequently suffer functional problems. The activists, overwhelmed with their own local struggles, have neither the inclination nor the time to fulfill all the administrative and decision-making needs of the volunteers. The volunteers, in turn, face a decision-making void that they have not been given the authority to fill. Their role is often vaguely defined, with multiple objectives, and they lack the guidance to know when they are doing something inappropriate until it is too late. Although some volunteers adapt well to these conditions, frustration and confusion are frequent. If the accompanied organization or community is itself involved in internal power conflicts (a common occurrence), a nonindependent accompaniment status becomes almost untenable, since it is no longer clear who has legitimate authority.

From a different perspective, an accompaniment organization's commitment to independence and nonpartisanship is consistent with respect for the activists' empowerment and self-determination, based on the related concept of *noninterference*. Volunteers are naturally curious and are usually inspired by and committed to the causes of those they accompany. Without a clear role definition, they often gradually get more involved in the internal workings of the accompanied group, sometimes reaching the point of giving strategic advice or helping with policy making. This shift may not be actively opposed by the accompanied group—it may even be invited—but it may be resented later as inappropriate interference. Some accompaniment organizations believe that both organizational independence and a clearly defined and limited role (such as accompaniment) help avoid this tendency.

Similarly, some accompaniment groups studiously avoid any material aid relationship (providing funds, supplies, or technical expertise) with local groups to minimize the risk of long-term dependency. This stance minimizes the risk that activists may cultivate accompaniment not for protection but for the material advantage of the relationship. It also presents an unambiguous message to the host government, which cannot use the material relationship to discredit the objectivity of the accompaniment as witness.

This skepticism about the decision-making role of foreigners in the third world is one of the things that draws many people to an accompaniment model based on nonpartisanship and noninterference. They are looking for a way to serve in the third world while avoiding the paternalistic trappings of missionary and development work, which often dominate such international relationships. The volunteers are proud of "not doing for them what they can do for themselves," and they frequently point out, "We don't tell anyone what to do."

Short of "telling someone what to do," there is still the gray area of giving advice. Advice from external NGOs may be heeded because it is good advice or because of unspoken, even unconscious, pressures. Based on other experiences with foreign NGOs, an activist may assume that the accompaniment service will be withheld if advice is not heeded, or that this outsider is an "expert" and should be listened to. It is often difficult to assess the competence of "expertise" from a different cultural context. Thus the mere offering of advice might be a type of interference, even when it is explicitly requested. The paradox is that accompaniment deterrence, as we saw in Colombia, may be more effective when it is a *joint* strategy implemented in a coordinated fashion by both the activists and the accompaniment organization. Developing a joint strategy inevitably involves a give-and-take of mutual advice; thus a strict adherence to noninterference might limit the construction of an effective strategy.

Nonviolence

Nonviolence as a guiding principle is common to many, but not all, accompaniment organizations. Principled nonviolence usually implies a commitment to reconciliation, a basic respect for life, and a refusal to recognize violence as a legitimate method of struggle. In the field, the principle is generally interpreted conservatively to mean that accompaniment should be limited to those who do not use violent means of struggle and do not collaborate with armed groups.

Activists sometimes have to choose among different modes of protection. Some activists never ask for accompaniment, counting on their own ability to defend themselves—sometimes with weapons. Others opt for both accompaniment and armed protection. PBI accompanied Batty Weerakoon in Sri Lanka and Rigoberta Menchú in Guatemala while each had armed police escorts, although the protection of the police in both cases was at best ambiguous. An organization might have a constant accompaniment presence, but when its office is surrounded or attacked, machetes, batons, or even Molotov cocktails might come out of the back room.

When the Colombian Association of Familes of the Disappeared (ASFADDES) refused armed protection, it wrote to the government, "Conceptually this humanitarian option of accompaniment is absolutely coherent with our own principles: as family members, the negative psychological impact of the idea of armed escorts is unacceptable."[2]

When Osiris Bayter explained CREDHOS's similar decision, she emphasized the practical disadvantages of having armed men hanging around a human rights office, but added: "The psychological tension of having an armed man at your side is unbearable, especially when you believe that it is not weapons that save lives. That's why the possibility of PBI accompaniment appealed to us."[3]

Although neither CREDHOS nor ASFADDES explicitly espouses nonviolence in its rhetoric, their comments demonstrate a repugnance of weapons and a deep understanding of nonviolence as both principle and strategy.

Nonviolence is consistent with struggles for human rights and social justice, but it is interpreted in many different ways. Many of the groups asking for accompaniment use nonviolent tactics and strategies as a matter of necessity but have no principled commitment to nonviolence. Many people, including many of the individual volunteers doing accompaniment, endorse the right to use violence in self-defense, as punishment, or simply as a useful tactic when necessary.

For a brief period in Guatemala, the GAM advocated the death penalty for those responsible for disappearances. PBI continued to accompany but found this espousal of an obviously violent policy quite unsettling. In Sri Lanka, volunteers accompanied a labor struggle in which the workers they were ostensibly protecting initiated a violent action against the police. PBI withdrew, despite the fact that the police might have retaliated with even greater violence against the workers in PBI's absence. These are extremely difficult decisions, since, given the often unequal correlation of forces, all violence cannot be considered equal. Guatemalan soldiers in the returned refugee village of La Aurora (see chapter 10) may have been provoked and intimidated in a way that some would characterize as violent. An accompaniment volunteer, had one been present, would have had a hard time explaining a withdrawal on those grounds, given the massacre that followed.

In the context of popular insurgency, some argue that a commitment to nonviolence is neither necessary nor desirable, and that solidarity with an oppressed people should not try to dictate that people's tactics. The Salvadoran FMLN guerrilla movement built a vast array of international contacts and alliances, including mass-based U.S. organizations such as CISPES and various European solidarity groups. Through such organizations, it encouraged many foreigners to come support the "people's struggle." Accompaniment of popular mobilizations was combined with direct material aid to the FMLN. A commitment to nonviolence or nonpartisanship in this case would be contradictory. But given the political clout of groups such as CISPES and the indiscriminate animosity of the Salvadoran military toward foreigners, it would be difficult to claim that volunteers committed to nonviolence provided any greater protective value than those who were not.

Organizations trying to maintain a commitment to nonviolence are often on thin ice, politically. In Guatemala or El Salvador, for instance, most accompanied groups promoted political platforms almost identical with those of the guerrilla movements. This coincidence was logical, given the governmental policies that both opposed, but accompaniment groups could never really know the extent to which those they accompanied consciously collaborated with the guerrillas. Since even the hint of such collaboration was dangerous, it could not be investigated. The guerrilla movements were both military and political, so such collaboration was not a priori violent. But politics is a continuation of war, as much for a guerrilla army as for a government, so there was always some risk that nonviolent tactics were being used strategically for military ends. Nonviolent accompaniment could thus be indirectly facilitating a violent military strategy.

Any policy, however principled, in which outsiders place conditions on access to an important resource risks being a manipulation or an interference with the self-determination of the population being served. One of the primary arguments against making nonviolence a condition for access to accompaniment is that such a policy influences people's choices and thus interferes inappropriately. A completely noninterfering accompaniment policy, by this argument, would be available to any threatened activist regardless of whether he or she espoused guerrilla warfare or any other violent tactic.

This is but one of numerous examples in which basic principles collide in practice. Each accompaniment organization has to prepare for these collisions by establishing priorities among principles, with an understanding of the flexibility necessary for applying them in practice.

Education

The concept of empowerment works in both directions: a key objective of some accompaniment projects is the empowerment and education of the volunteers themselves, and the *movement-building* impact of the work they can do upon their return. This objective, which we refer to here as *education*, might be considered a secondary objective of a deterrence strategy, since over the long haul, movement building strengthens the global support network backing up the accompaniment and expands the financial and human resources available for the work. Education can also be an objective in and of itself. The Canadian Project Accompaniment confronted the paternalistic assumption that volunteers are "doing a favor" for accompanied activists with a commitment to *mutuality*: accompaniment as a relationship of mutual encouragement and empowerment. On this basis, a significant portion of its strategic planning revolved around empowerment and movement building in Canada, a process that simultaneously fulfilled the mutuality principle and strengthened the protective value of the presence.

Whether principled or strategic, the education objective affects how the accompaniment is implemented. If it is given a high priority, it has two particularly controversial potential drawbacks. One is that it can reinforce a natural curiosity and inquisitiveness that can easily go beyond the bounds of discretion or safety. The volunteer, after all, wants to go back home with the best possible stories and information to educate the home community and may not be aware of how intrusive this "research" can be. Human rights activists operating under state terror and frequent surveillance are suspicious of people who ask too many questions, even well-intended ones. Even if the questions are not a security risk, they can be an annoyance, distracting the activist from the work at hand.

The second drawback is that a high priority on education usually leads to very short stays for volunteers, frequently as little as two weeks. The tendency is logical: allowing short stays makes accompaniment service possible for many more people who may not have time for longer periods of foreign service. This allows numerous volunteers to serve for short periods and return home, speeding up the movement-building process.

The risks of such short-term service should be obvious, but they had to be learned the hard way by most organizations. Inexperienced volunteers, without time to adapt and "learn the ropes," make mistakes that can be dangerous or costly to the reputation of the organization—and to that of other organizations as well. Cultural ignorance results in offensive behavior, damaging the relationship of trust with the accompanied groups. The hurry to get the most out of a short stay exacerbates the inquisitiveness problem. Accompanied activists, meanwhile, live through a stream of volunteers whom they watch make the same errors over and over. But even if the deportment of short-term volunteers were impeccable, the accompanied activists must constantly expend valuable energy orienting and relating to them.

In contrast, a project without a movement-building component can find itself with insufficient support. PBI after 1989, for instance, prioritized discretion and security concerns far above education and allowed only long-term volunteers. But PBI was supported by a Central America–focused solidarity network built largely by other organizations. When PBI expanded to Sri Lanka, there was no such network to depend on, and the organization had no strategy or capacity to build one. This weakness led to consistent resource and personnel shortages. Many of those volunteers who were recruited had little prior knowledge or analysis of Sri Lanka's politics, as there were no local organizations to nurture their interest.

Different models have met with varying success in confronting these pitfalls. Witness for Peace sent long-term volunteers to both Nicaragua and Guatemala, where they stayed anywhere from nine months to several years. A key part of their work was organizing and supervising "delegations" of ten to twenty people who visited for two or three weeks on carefully guided tours. Delegation members were given a participatory role in certain decisions, and the long-term team controlled those aspects that could not be handled responsibly by newcomers. These delegations lived—and thus accompanied—in rural villages for part of their stay but were also given the opportunity to attend educational sessions with local leaders or authorities. Such meetings with authorities served to demonstrate—numerically—the force of the movement behind the accompaniment.

Canadian Project Accompaniment, the Holland Accompaniment Project (HOLACOM), and others used a system of sending long-term paid staff to Guatemala to supervise a steady flow of volunteers. These volunteers accompanied returned refugee villages for six weeks or more. Although six weeks is still relatively short, the permanent staff could maintain a constant relationship with the Guatemalan groups being accompanied and help the other volunteers avoid pitfalls.

Other combinations exist, and the ones that work all involve some level of supervision of short-term volunteers by either staff or longer-term volunteers who can provide continuity of analysis and build long-term relationships with the various groups. This supervision is usually combined with explicit behavioral guidelines, clear role definitions, and careful screening of volunteers. The all-too-common system that doesn't work at all is for an organization to simply send short-term volunteers without guidelines or rigorous supervision, or for inexperienced volunteers to come without any organization at all. Although many of these volunteers do excellent accompaniment, the exceptions wreak havoc, damaging the credibility and effectiveness of all other accompaniment groups working in the conflict. The risk can be reduced through supervision or training but never entirely eliminated.

Tactics in the Field: Two Camera Incidents

Even when principles, objectives, and strategies are clear and consistent, accompaniment demands a constant contextual reevaluation of tactics. A decision as simple as taking a picture, for instance, has complex ramifications.

In 1987–88, Peace Brigades volunteers maintained a twenty-four-hour-a-day, thirteen-month presence on the sidewalk outside the Lunafil factory in Guatemala, which was occupied by striking workers. The workers feared retaliation because they knew of union activists who had been killed at the owner's other factories. Using more subtle tactics, the owner threatened to close the factory permanently. One day, a caravan of trucks arrived with a police escort to remove the raw materials from the factory buildings, ostensibly to be auctioned elsewhere. After one such incident, the strikers built a concrete barricade a few feet high in the entranceway to prevent trucks from entering again.

That night, while union activists and a PBI volunteer slept on the sidewalk, thirty armed men in civilian clothes showed up with attack dogs. After threatening everyone present, they destroyed the barricade with picks and shovels. The PBI volunteer got out her camera to record the event. The other union members quietly motioned for her not to take the picture: they were afraid that the camera flash in the dark would be too provocative and might upset the men with guns. Thus the logical, almost textbook, response for a human rights observer—to take photos to document a threatening event—was deemed inappropriate. The photo was not going to stop the men who had come so prepared to carry out their task. The benefit of documentary evidence was not worth the risk of angering them.

In early 1993 in Sri Lanka, PBI observed a labor demonstration at the entrance to the free trade zone north of Colombo. The police demanded that the demonstrators disperse. In response the demonstrators sat down peacefully, and the police began dragging them away by force. One of the PBI volunteers attempted to photograph a plain-clothes police officer who was wielding a long wooden switch at a woman in the crowd. The police detained the volunteer, removed the film, and exposed it to sunlight. A second PBI observer also had her camera taken and film destroyed. The officer in charge told them that he found PBI's action provocative and that he did not want his men to be portrayed in an unsavory light.

This time, the union activists urged PBI to take legal action against the police for taking the cameras and destroying the film. They argued that if PBI let them take the cameras and didn't denounce it, the police would think that they could get away with it again, or perhaps take further advantage. According to the activists, such acquiescence would weaken the strength of the accompaniment. PBI chose to let the matter drop rather than initiate an additional confrontation.

Taking the whole progression as a single event, one might argue that the deterrence commitment represented by the camera was weak. The threat of taking a picture is not much of a threat if you simply acquiesce when they take your camera. The police might assume from such weakness that the organization cannot follow through on its commitments. Since the aggressor's belief in such follow-through is a crucial factor in the effectiveness of deterrence, this perception weakens the future protective value of the camera and perhaps even of the volunteers' presence.

However, one can also look at the incident as an unfolding series of events that called for a series of tactical decisions as the context changed. Thus, as the demonstration progressed, the volunteers had their cameras visible, as always. When the police began beating the demonstrators, the act of taking photos was a necessary follow-through on the commitment implied by the presence of the cameras. What would be the point, after all, of having a camera but refraining from using it to document the moment of violence you had hoped to deter? At the same time, the very use of the camera might be an effective intervention to calm the violence. It might either prompt the police to consider the political consequences of the attack or distract them into the more benign pastime of detaining the volunteers and their cameras.

In this analysis, the photo taking may have served its deterring purpose. The photos themselves might be less important than the interruption caused by the act of taking them. So, when later faced with the expropriation of the cameras by police officers who may have needed a face-saving conclusion to the episode, PBI acquiesced to lessen the tension and polarization of the situation. The benefits of ending the conflict outweighed the cost of losing the film.

These contradictory analyses coexist side by side. We do not know whether those police officers, in the end, felt that PBI made a reasonable compromise or simply displayed weakness. In any case, the camera is not an end in itself but rather a tool in a complex strategy. These incidents illustrate the importance of understanding in advance the functions and objectives of any such tool. Accompaniment organizations must try to prepare volunteers for the decisions they may be faced with.

To implement any humanitarian work in conflict zones, one must deal with competing principles, strategies, and tactics under conditions of considerable uncertainty. Organizations may work from different principles and multiple objectives, but the clarity of their work depends on their understanding of the strategic and tactical implications of those principles and objectives. Given the complexities in the field, even the most thorough analysis will not suffice without a heavy dose of tolerance for paradox and ambiguity.

Notes

1. Minear and Weiss, *Humanitarian Action*, p. 23.
2. ASFADDES, letter to Carlos Vicente de Roux, Presidential Counsel for Human Rights, December 16, 1994.
3. Osiris Bayter, tape-recorded interview by authors, Bogota, December 1995.

17

Looking Ahead

A Brief Assessment

A CCOMPANIMENT HAS ACHIEVED some notable successes in human rights protection. In addition to saving lives, this international presence has helped catalyze the formation of new human rights organizations, enabled their growth, added to their stability, and strengthened their international credibility. Death squads and governments alike have been forced to take notice.

Despite numerous successes and considerable expansion and flexibility, accompaniment projects have been dogged by chronic weaknesses. The accompaniment movement is young and is still learning by trial and error. Because the work arose largely from grassroots nonviolence and solidarity movements, there is an unfortunate reticence to learn from the more experienced, established humanitarian organizations already working in conflict zones, such as the ICRC, Doctors Without Borders, and others. The reticence is in some cases ideological, but it is also based on simple ignorance of prior relevant experience and lack of time for adequate investigation. Accompaniment organizations spend a lot of time and effort learning some of the basic realities of functioning in conflict zones—realities that other organizations have been experiencing for decades. The volunteers themselves are usually young and often lack prior experience working in conflict zones or even in NGOs. The result is often an amateurish and nonrigorous application of a delicate tool.

Yet the grassroots nature of accompaniment is one of its greatest strengths. In the field, the accompaniment movement's steadfast recognition that the local activists must be the protagonists in their own search for solutions is something that some of the more establishment humanitarian interventions could learn from. And even if dependence on volunteers poses a risk of amateurism, accompaniment challenges average citizens to take risks in the struggle for human rights and creates opportunities for volunteers to put their beliefs into action. The long-term empowering effect of the accompaniment experience on the volunteers has added global strength to the worldwide grassroots movements for nonviolence and human rights, as volunteers return home and continue their activism.

Asking the Right Questions

The lessons of any limited experience must be viewed with careful skepticism when they are applied to new situations. The implementation of accompaniment, as we have seen, is extremely context specific. The future will bring countless new conflicts with many different causes and dimensions. Bluntly projecting a lesson or rule into a different conflict can result in grave errors. Dismissing past lessons, though, can be equally risky, condemning an accompaniment project to repeat the errors of the past. The challenge is to distinguish which aspects of these experiences are solely dependent on context and which are transferable.

Accompaniment does not by itself end wars or resolve conflicts. It is but one tool for pressure in a complicated interaction of many players. International presence affects power relationships, or, as we have described it, it shifts perceptions of available political spaces. But since there are always other factors conditioning the political reality, accompaniment cannot guarantee safety. The inherent risks run by both activists and volunteers demand that accompaniment organizations carefully analyze their own political space. We believe that an understanding of deterrence theory, state terror, psychological encouragement, trust, and certain basic concepts of political psychology is essential to this analysis. This framework, and these case studies, should be helpful in determining the relevance of accompaniment in many possible future contexts.

We have, by and large, come up with more questions than answers. But there are no simple rules of thumb for accompaniment. If we can learn from the past what the right questions are, we have come a long way. Consider a hypothetical future request for an accompaniment project in a country in conflict. What does the accompaniment organization need to know to respond?

A first set of basic questions concerns the scenario where the tool is being considered:

- What is the conflict, and who are the actors involved?

- What exactly is the perceived threat, and what is expected from the accompaniment?

- Are the available information and analysis on the conflict trustworthy and thorough?

- Is there reason to believe that the aggressor party would be susceptible to international pressure and, thus, sensitive to the accompaniment presence? What are the lines of communication for this pressure? What are the aggressor's international strategies and relationships to external actors such as other states, NGOs, foreigners in general?

- What is the ideological and cultural context? What are the biases and stereotypes of both the aggressor and the group requesting accompaniment that might affect their attitudes toward the accompaniment organization?

- Who are potential allies? What other foreign NGOs are on the scene, and what has their experience been? Is there an existing global network of organizations, individuals, and politicians who are interested in the particular conflict? Does the organization have access to this network?

To develop the accompaniment strategy, other questions need answering:

- Which types of human rights abuses are going to constitute the focus of attention and protection? What types of conduct by the aggressor will be defined as unacceptable?

- What is the deterrence commitment? That is, what will the accompaniment organization do to "punish" the aggressor in the event of unacceptable human rights abuse? What international bodies can be counted on to apply pressure? How frequently can such pressure be applied? Is it credible and sufficient to deter?

- How will the accompaniment organization inform the aggressor of its deterrence commitment?

- What is the aggressor's cost-benefit analysis? Are there external benefits to attacking that outweigh the costs the international community can inflict?

Other questions deal with the relationship with the accompanied party:

- How are the activists measuring the danger? What other protective tactics are they using? What experiences have other threatened activists had in this context?

- What relationship and communication do the activists have with the aggressor? Does this relationship in any way constrain or aid the potential communication between the accompaniment organization and the aggressor?

- Do the activists expect anything more than accompaniment from the volunteers?

- Is there any risk of building a dependency relationship?

Finally, these answers should lead the accompaniment organization to question itself:

- What is the organization's position with respect to the principles of non-partisanship, independence, noninterference, and nonviolence? How will these positions influence the implementation of the accompaniment?

- What will be the selection criteria for volunteers in this accompaniment situation? What are the linguistic and physical demands? Do they have the political analysis and judgment, cultural sensitivity, patience, humility, and diplomacy necessary to carry out the task safely and effectively? What security measures must volunteers follow?

- Can the organization find and train enough qualified volunteers and generate the resources and political support to meet the need on a continuing basis? Does the organization have the political maturity and administrative capacity to take on the challenge?

- Is the organization capable of evaluating its own effectiveness and recognizing when its presence is no longer needed?

We are not suggesting that it will ever be possible to find satisfactory answers to all these and other questions before embarking on an accompaniment mission. Sometimes there is not enough information or too much ambiguity. The urgent demands of a pressing human rights crisis sometimes leave little time for adequate investigation. But the organization must be sensitive to the risks involved in proceeding without answers. At the very least, a clear understanding of where the uncertainties lie can help in the development of fallback plans in case of surprises.

Challenges

There are still some critical problems that have not been sufficiently addressed in practice by accompaniment groups. One of these is the development of strategies for accompanying those who are not threatened by governments or state-controlled groups. Human rights activists in Sri Lanka, for instance, were threatened and killed by both the JVP guerrillas and the Tamil Tigers. PBI in Colombia consciously targeted its accompaniment in regions where state security forces were the major force, avoiding areas where the key players were either drug cartels or "independent" paramilitary groups. In other conflicts, such as the southern Sudan or Chad, accompaniment has been considered, but not implemented, where nonstate forces commit serious human rights abuses.

The general models developed here, as well as the specific lists of questions above, should be useful in analyzing the possibility of deterring nonstate aggression as well. The basic objective is the same: to exert enough external pressure to change behavior. But how does one exert this pressure? Most international law applies only to states. Governments have explicit and unique mechanisms for transmitting and absorbing international pressure, and to the extent that economic and trade policy is controlled by the same entity as human rights policy, there is a built-in reason for sensitivity. A guerrilla or other clandestine organization, in contrast, is difficult to communicate with and is generally dependent on deliberately concealed sources of support.

Consider, for example, the Liberation Tigers of Tamil Eelam. We discussed the idea of accompaniment as protection against the Tigers with one courageous Sri Lankan activist who has repeatedly condemned the Tigers' abuses in print. He dismissed it as foolishly ideal; his security choice is clandestinity.

In theory, a coherent pressure campaign might investigate all the Tigers' international sources of support, all its clandestine businesses and trade partners, and so forth to find potential points of pressure. It could also pressure the Tamil exile community. If possible, direct meetings with Tigers leadership might help clarify their sensitivity to pressure. The ICRC experience has shown that the Tigers are open to communication with NGOs when it is in the Tigers' interest. It has also shown the utility of reaching clear agreements with such parties before taking the risk of placing people in the field.

There is no reason to assume a priori that a rebel terrorist group is not susceptible to pressure or open to communication. When Amnesty International issues a report criticizing the Tigers' human rights abuses, the Tigers' moral legitimacy is questioned, and international support of its cause is weakened. Simultaneously, the Sri Lankan government uses the criticism to strengthen its own international legitimacy, improving its chances of obtaining military aid—clearly a negative consequence for the Tigers.

Human rights activists who attempt to take on nonstate aggressors with accompaniment protection are exploring uncharted territory. Even if an accompaniment strategy is possible in theory, the uncertainties present huge risks. Who wants to be a test case? Still, human rights activists are constantly testing limits, and the global human rights movement must develop strategies to support them. A protection limited to only one source of danger is at best incomplete.

A second problematic area for accompaniment work is related to the fact that most volunteers come from the so-called first world, and most projects operate in the third world. PBI has fielded a few volunteers from Argentina, Brazil, Chile, Colombia, Japan, and India. Christian Peacemaker Teams in Haiti included volunteers of African American and Caribbean descent. But these are exceptions. Most accompaniment volunteers have been Western European or North American and white. The primary explanation for this is that all these NGOs were conceived and based in Northern countries, but this tendency is compounded by the common perception that the supposed immunity and protective power of the volunteers is based on their skin color or national background.

There are several interrelated but distinct dynamics at play here: the imbalances of political-economic power among nations, the influence of colonial traditions and history, and stereotypes or prejudices connected to physical characteristics such as skin color. Thus, some Salvadorans we interviewed insisted that because of U.S. political influence, the protection offered by a U.S. citizen would be greater than that of a European; one stated that the protection of a Latin American volunteer would be inadequate. Colonial histories—and the resulting shared languages—lead to a different reception of Spaniards in Central America or English volunteers in Sri Lanka than of volunteers from other nations. Sri Lankans repeatedly stated that the protection was dependent on the "white face" and that a volunteer from another South Asian country would do no good, despite the fact that India is the regional superpower. Likewise, although Mexico wields far more clout in Guatemala than does, for instance, New Zealand, a white New Zealander is symbolically more powerful than a Mexican accompaniment volunteer. The dynamic is further complicated by the fact that different actors will respond to different influences—a high-level policy maker, for instance, may be more affected by global politics, whereas a local thug may exaggerate visual or cultural biases.

Evidence in some cases has shown that Northern volunteers are less frequently mistreated by authorities than those from southern countries with less clout.* Although this differential treatment of different foreigners does not automatically imply a difference in the protective clout of their accompaniment, the factors involved are similar. Any deterrence analysis has to be done within the context of these dominant political perceptions and local attitudes, regardless of their subjective character. If some Salvadorans

---

*We have already discussed the differential treatment in El Salvador. In Sri Lanka, a PBI volunteer of partial Indian descent was the only foreigner to be struck by a policeman during the violent break-up of a demonstration.

or Sri Lankans feel more protected by a Western or a white-skinned volunteer, their attackers might share the same perception.

Accompaniment organizations often suggest that, in a kind of moral jujitsu, they turn global structural inequities and prejudices against the oppressors by protecting the victims. But any tactic that relies for its effectiveness on a system of unequal worth may, to a certain extent, lend an unintended but insidious credence to that very inequality.[1] A protective presence may be encouraging, but the constant physical reminder of global social inequities may be a heavy, and disempowering, burden for the activists who live with it.

Yet African Americans in Haiti, Colombians in El Salvador, and Japanese in Sri Lanka have often sensed a deeper connection with those they accompany than their Northern or white teammates, with a correspondingly enhanced ability to empathize and encourage. Linguistic and cultural proximity, or a sense of shared oppression, can overcome trust barriers. A multicultural organization may have more credibility with the protected activists than one that is a mirror image of the globally dominant white power structure.

The objective of multinational, multicultural accompaniment requires a strategy to address both the stereotypical perceptions and the potentially real differences in security for different volunteers. One obvious step is building organizational credibility and power, such that the volunteer's symbolic clout is respected regardless of ancestry, origin, or skin color. A corollary step is a system of identification so that the volunteer is clearly and visibly associated with the clout of the organization.

The United Nations, for instance, sends multinational unarmed missions into conflict zones. These UN workers generally wear some sort of identifying clothing—in some cases, as simple as a blue cap clearly labeling them "UN." The label calls attention to the inherent clout of their organizational affiliation rather than to the volunteers' physical traits. The International Red Cross, although using primarily Swiss foreign staff, hires many workers in country. It uses the universally recognized white vehicle with a red cross to protect them. Gene Stolzfus of Christian Peacemaker Teams has suggested that peace teams and accompaniment groups learn from the Red Cross example and adopt a uniform symbol or logo for their volunteers to use in conflict zones. In time, this symbol would become, like the red cross/red crescent, universally recognized and respected.[2]

PBI has experimented with various types of markings. The Guatemala volunteers have ID cards that they sometimes wear on their chests. At other times, they have used colored armbands to separate themselves visibly while accompanying mass events. Members of the Sri Lanka PBI team wear bright yellow vests at public events, identifying them as international observers. But for the most part, accompaniment organizations have not attempted to distinguish themselves visually.

Variations, Expansion, and Enhancement

Many efforts have expanded the accompaniment experience, sometimes transforming it significantly. In the early 1990s, for instance, after several violent confrontations between native people and the Canadian government, PBI began a project that aimed to provide a pacifying presence based on the models it had developed in other conflicts. But the geographic and cultural context demanded something quite different. Sometimes, PBI found itself training local human rights watch groups near native reserves where conflicts were likely; in other cases, PBI volunteers were a conciliatory third-party presence in intracommunity conflicts with no easily identifiable villains. In addition, the project worked on antiracist education and building cultural sensitivity to native concerns—in particular, the harsh political and economic pressures native people face. Thus, an initial accompaniment impetus expanded into much broader strategies for reconciliation and social justice, reclaiming the broad mandate of nonviolence work upon which PBI had been founded.

In 1994, the Balkans Peace Team International placed volunteer teams in Zagreb and Split, Croatia, and in Belgrade, Serbia. These teams, supported by a coalition of European and international organizations, offer accompaniment in some situations, for example, to protect ethnic Serbs against a policy of systematic eviction in Croatia. Volunteers also directly collaborate with local human rights organizations, offering services such as language classes and translation. They try to serve as a channel of independent and nonpartisan information and analysis of what is going on in these extremely complex conflicts.

Most accompaniment organizations are small, with severe resource limits. The larger organizations generally take on accompaniment only sporadically, as a collateral effect to other higher-priority work, or, like the UNHCR, with a mandate limiting the population they can serve. Accompaniment may not help in all conflicts, but the demand has consistently exceeded the capacities of existing organizations. If, as we suggest, accompaniment is a promising tool for human rights protection, the international community should work toward an expanded and improved implementation.

Unfortunately, given the heart-wrenching and unanswered demands of human rights victims, the drive for expansion can sometimes be a detriment. Accompaniment results are not measured by the number of warm bodies sent out into the field. It must be implemented carefully and rigorously.

Bigger is not necessarily better. All accompaniment would benefit from clearer strategies and planning, more extensive analysis and training, and more critical selection of volunteers. Organizational effectiveness also depends on building both grassroots and high-level political clout, strengthening existing issue-area networks, and improving information flow. Each of these demands requires investments of resources and time. Humanitarian organizations and volunteers, however, are so driven by the immediacy of the vulnerable activists' plight that such long-term investments often fall by the wayside.

Part of the necessary rigor must be supplied by the research community. It has been a privilege to do this study, as much for the chance to meet so many courageous and dynamic people as for the opportunity to study the pioneering texts in human rights research and analysis that pointed our way. We cannot help but think, however, that given the monumental importance of the issue of human rights to both world politics and human dignity, there is a vast need for more study and analysis, both empirical and documentary. Such study helps activists learn from the past and improve their analyses, strategies, and chances for survival.

There are several ways that the utilization of accompaniment might be expanded. The first is that existing or yet-to-be-formed groups will expand their grassroots organizing and funding and gradually extend their range of operation. The strategies and tactics of this process are as varied as the organizations. A second possibility is that large organizations that already have both resources and political clout will adopt accompaniment as a method of humanitarian intervention. This might include human rights groups, such as Amnesty International,* or progressive development organizations that recognize that respect for human rights is a precondition for development.

Intergovernmental and governmental bodies may also incorporate more accompaniment in their work. Recent UN peace missions were discussed in chapter 13. The newly established UN High Commissioner for Human Rights might be another mechanism. Regional bodies, such as the Organization of American States, the Organization of African Unity, or the European Community, also have the resources and political motivation to include accompaniment in their range of responses to conflict. The European Parliament, for instance, invited accompaniment organizations to a series of consultations in 1995 and 1996 on a proposed Civil Peace Corps that would include protective accompaniment as a possible area of work.[3]

---

*A working group at the May 1996 Amnesty International conference on the protection of human rights monitors in Latin America recommended accompaniment to AI as a tactic for serious consideration. (See the conference document: "Propuestas en torno a campañas, publicidad y mecanismos de protección," Amnesty International, Santa Fe de Bogotá, Colombia, May 22–25, 1996.)

Individual governments may consider accompaniment as a potential complement to their existing foreign aid programs. Many already support human rights and "democracy enhancement" efforts. German churches and NGOs, for instance, are proposing that their government fund a Civilian Peace Service. Citing PBI and the Balkan Peace Team as precedents, the German proposals suggest that volunteers work in a variety of capacities, including as international observers and protective accompaniment for refugee repatriations.[4]

The groups being accompanied may react quite differently to government-aligned protection than to independent NGOs. We've already seen that the UN is sometimes mistrusted. Regional or single-government efforts might suffer an even greater alienation, as they would be suspected of hidden agendas motivated more by bilateral political or economic relations than by the genuine needs of the people. Threatened activists should be suspicious of political strings attached to accompaniment. The entire strategy of deterrence can easily be distorted. For instance, for extraneous political reasons, a governmental organization may be unwilling to exert punitive pressure just when accompaniment strategy calls for it. Despite these limitations, governments undeniably have clout and resources that the NGO community lacks, and threatened activists have the right to choose from every possible protective option.

An intermediary possibility is the development of collaborative projects between existing accompaniment organizations and some of the larger organizations already mentioned. Informally, collaboration already occurs, for instance, between UN monitors and accompaniment volunteers in Guatemala and Haiti. In creative collaborations, different organizations' strengths and weaknesses can complement one another, thus meeting vital needs that might otherwise go unmet. But, as the previous chapter suggests, even apparently minor differences in mandates can lead to tensions and dilemmas in the field. Collaboration should be carefully strategized in advance, and it requires a high level of trust, clarity, flexibility, and mutual respect.

Aside from the obvious physical risks—which any foreign service work in a conflict entails—accompaniment presents political risks to organizations that do it. The difficulty accompaniment groups have convincing governments of their commitment to nonpartisanship or noninterference might well scare off many "establishment" organizations concerned about their image. An activist's claim of being threatened is often an unprovable allegation, and accompaniment can be interpreted as a direct accusation against the alleged threatener. Many organizations are loath to put their names even indirectly behind such accusations without proof. But accompaniment is preventive. If you wait for proof of the threat, it may be too late.

The fledgling and impoverished accompaniment movement could gain a lot from collaborations with larger and more established organizations. Political clout should logically increase the protective power of accompaniment, so protected activists should also benefit. But the net gain is questionable if a by-product of establishment clout is political temerity. Bureaucratic, political, or image concerns cannot be allowed to constrain the availability of accompaniment to the activists who most need it. These concerns, though, are a cost of doing business for international organizations, and the resulting constraints are often directly related to organizational size and political influence. There will always be a role for small NGOs willing to risk their own credibility to protect the activists that others are unable to help.

In the mid-1990s, Nineth Montenegro and Amilcar Mendez in Guatemala, Humberto Centeno in El Salvador, and Venerable Baddegama Samitha in Sri Lanka are all either running for office or serving in congress or parliament. Nineth's daughter, Alejandra, accompanied in her infancy, is now a healthy teenager, but Humberto Centeno's son was brutally murdered in 1996, four years after the Salvadoran civil war officially ended. Guatemala, El Salvador, and Haiti are struggling through difficult transitions, speaking of "democracy" and "postwar" development. Sri Lanka and Colombia are still mired in conflict.

Meanwhile, as new conflicts erupt around the world, new requests for international accompaniment arise, from Turkey to the former Soviet republics to the Sudan. The "internationalism" that so confused General Gramajo's army ten years ago is now stronger than ever, and the previously inviolable "sovereignty" argument can no longer justify state human rights abuses. Human rights activists around the world are communicating more efficiently, discussing options for solidarity and protection. When a new threat arises, a request for accompaniment can now be transmitted around the world in moments on the Internet.

But will anyone respond? The human rights movement has grown remarkably in the last two decades, and accompaniment has steadily matured as a method of protection. But most new requests for accompaniment still go unanswered. The international community has thus far been unable to effectively marshal the necessary resources and commitment to meet the ever-increasing need.

Accompaniment extends the boundaries of the "international community." The international community goes beyond governments, beyond the UN, beyond the establishment humanitarian agencies and the existing human rights NGOs. Accompaniment has helped connect grassroots efforts for justice and human rights around the world with these larger international structures. The accompaniment volunteers are a living bridge between the threatened activists and the outside world, and also between their own home communities and the reality of the global struggle for human rights.

These links may help overcome the seemingly impossible challenge of human rights protection. In the final analysis, the international community's response to human rights abuse is not a question of resources but one of hope and empowerment. Accompaniment volunteers experience a rare privilege of standing at the side of some of the world's most courageous and committed activists. This courage injects immeasurable energy into the international community's efforts.

A request for human rights protection should never fall on deaf ears. Like the GAM in Guatemala, the international community must redefine the possible. We can take the lead from these threatened activists who are asking for our support. They do the impossible every day.

Notes

1. Coy, "Protective Accompaniment."
2. Gene Stolzfus, presentation at the Global Peace Service conference, New York City, December 1993 (author's notes).
3. Ernst Gulcher (European Parliament member), memo on Civilian European Peace Corps, Brussels, December 20, 1995; David Phillips (European Parliament), European Centre for Common Ground, conference report on "Establishing a European Civil Peace Corps," Brussels, November 6, 1995.
4. Forum Ziviler Friedensdienst (Civilian Peace Service Forum), proposal to German parliament, January 12, 1996; Forum Ziviler Friedensdienst brochure: "Civilian Peace Service: 18 Questions, 18 Answers."

Appendix 1

Field Interviews

Guatemala

Nineth Montenegro de García, former president, Mutual Support Group for Families of the Disappeared (GAM), Guatemalan Congress, 1996–

Amilcar Mendez, former president, Council of Ethnic Communities (CERJ), Guatemalan Congress, 1996–

Diego Perebal, CERJ member

Rosalina Tuyuc, president, National Council of Guatemalan Widows (CONAVIGUA), Guatemalan Congress, 1996–

Alfonso Bauer Paiz, lawyer for refugees returning to Guatemala from Mexico

Miguel Angel Albizures, labor activist, columnist

Francisco Raymundo Hernandez, Communities of Population in Resistance (CPR)

Nery Barrios, union leader, Unidad de Acción Sindical y Popular

Frank LaRue, Guatemalan labor and human rights lawyer, member of Unified Representation of the Guatemalan Opposition (RUOG), founder of the Guatemalan Center for Human Rights Legal Action

Byron Morales, Labor Unity of Guatemalan Workers (UNSITRAGUA), Guatemalan Congress, 1996–

Sergio Guzman, UNSITRAGUA

Ester de Herrarte and Blanca de Hernandez, Families of the Disappeared of Guatemala (FAMDEGUA)

Oswaldo Enriquez and Anantonia Reyes, Guatemala Human Rights Commission (CDHG)

Factor Mendez, Center for Investigation and Education for Human Rights

Lunafil Thread Factory Union (names withheld)

Committee for Campesino Unity (CUC) (name withheld)

General Hector Gramajo, Guatemalan minister of defense, 1986–89

General Oscar Mejía Victores, de facto president of Guatemala and minister of defense, 1983–86

Marco Vinicio Cerezo Arevalo, president of Guatemala, 1986–90

Rodriguez Weaver, Special Commission for Attention to Repatriates (CEAR)

Armando De La Torre, political science professor and adviser to the military academy

Arnoldo Ortiz Moscoso, former minister of the interior, 1993

Father Andres Girón, Guatemalan Catholic priest, land activist, and congressman

John Contier, Norwegian Popular Aid

Beate Thorensen, International Council of Voluntary Agencies

Benjamin García, U.S. embassy human rights attaché

Manuel Piñiero, Spanish ambassador to Guatemala

UN High Commissioner for Refugees (name withheld)
International Committee of the Red Cross (name withheld)

El Salvador

Celia Medrano, Nongovernmental Human Rights Commission (CDHES)
Mirna de Anaya, widow of Herbert Anaya, assassinated leader of the
CDHES
Jorge Villatoro, representative of the repatriated community of Ciudad
Romero
Carlos Bonilla, representative of the repatriated community of Santa Marta
Father Luis Serrano, Episcopal priest
Edgar Palacios, Baptist minister and leader of the Permanent Commission for
the National Debate
Alicia de García, Committee of Mothers of the Disappeared and Assassinated
(COMADRES)
Humberto Centeno, National Unity of Salvadoran Workers (UNTS)
Felix Ulloa, founder and president of the Salvadoran Institute for Juridical
Studies and lawyer for the UNTS
Christian Committee for the Displaced of El Salvador (CRIPDES)
General Juan Orlando Zepeda, retired
General Mauricio Vargas, Salvadoran foreign affairs ministry adviser
Jorge Martinez, former vice-minister of the interior
Kirio Waldo Salgado, conservative ideological leader, Institute for Liberty and
Democracy
Julia Hernandez, Tutela Legal (Catholic Church legal support office)
Reed Brody, International Human Rights Law Group and UN Mission to El
Salvador (ONUSAL)

Sri Lanka

Negombo United Peoples Organization
Dr. Manorani Saravanamuttu
Batty Weerakoon, lawyer for Dr. Saravanamuttu
Britto Fernando, labor union organizer
Sunanda Deshapriya, journalist, activist with the Free Media Movement
Baddegama Samitha Thero, Buddhist monk
Kumadini Samuels, human rights activist
Neelan Kandasamy, Movement for InterRacial Justice and Equality (MIRJE)
Kalyananda Thiranagama, Lawyers for Human Rights and Development
Bradman Weerakoon, presidential adviser for international affairs, 1989–94
Judge J. F. A. Soza, Governmental Human Rights Task Force
Swedish embassy attaché (name withheld)
U.S. embassy attaché (name withheld)
Hidaeko Nakagawa, United Nations High Commissioner for Refugees
(UNHCR)

International Committee of the Red Cross (name withheld)
Doctors Without Borders (name withheld)
Phil Esmonde, Quaker Peace and Service

International Accompaniment Volunteers *

United States

Anne Aleshire
Toby Armour
Sharon Bernstein
Karen Brandow
Suzanne Bristol, Marin
  County Interfaith Task Force
Christine Clarke
Edith Cole
Diane Harder, Cry for Justice
Bill Hutchinson, director, Marin
  County Interfaith Task Force
Edward Kinane
Meredith Larson
Carolyn Mow

Phil Pardi
Anne Marie Richards
Winifred Romeril
Janey Skinner
Jeff Smith
Pablo Stanfield
Hazel Tulecke
Curt Wands, National
  Coordinating Office for Refugees
  and Displaced (NCOORD)
Paul Weaver
Sara Wohlleb, Witness for Peace
Anonymous volunteer, Marin County
  Interfaith Task Force/CDHES

Spain

Ramon Ballester
Jose Luis Blanco
Cristina Casado
Carmen Diez
Ester Domenech
Rosa Maria Garcia Gutierrez
Luis Miranda
Fernando Nicosio

Luis Perez
Clemen Pulet
Fermin Rodrigo, PBI in 1992,
  independent accompaniment
  volunteer with CPR in 1994
Maria Gabriela Serra
Javier Zabala

Canada

Rusa Jeremic
Andrew Kendle

Barbara MacQuarrie
Karen Ridd

Germany

Gerd Büntzly, German accompaniment organization CAREA
  (Guatemala refugee return)

Heike Kammer
Almut Wadle

*Organizational affiliation is PBI unless otherwise noted.

England

Bue Alred
Peter Gordon

Brent Horner

Japan

Tomoko Ishigawa, independent
  accompaniment of
  CONAVIGUA

Futoshi Sato

Other

Georgina Areneda (Chile)
Christina Banzato (Italy)
Francoise Denis (Belgium)
Eric Pedersen, International
  Forum (Denmark)

Alain Richard (France)
Marcela Rodriguez (Colombia)
Gabriela Schonbrun (Switzerland)
Susana van der Meij, coordinator,
  Netherlands Accompaniment
  Project

Letters, Journals, and Personal Documents

United States

Chris Corry
Patrick Coy
Steve Dudley
Jack Fahey, Seva Foundation
Virginia Flagg
Ryan Golten, Seva Foundation
Susan Greenblatt
Marilyn Krysl
George Lakey

John Lindsay-Poland
Yeshua Moser
Aaron Perry
Raynor Ramirez, Seva Foundation
Debra Riklan
Barbara Scott
Carol Stuart
Terry Vandiver, Seva Foundation

Other

Carminia Albertos (Spain),
  Seva Foundation
Martin Kulldorff (Sweden)

Eric Robinson (Canada)
Sel Burroughs (Canada)

Appendix 2

Accompaniment Organizations

If you are interested in finding out about ongoing accompaniment work, you can get more information from the following:

In the United States

Peace Brigades International–USA
2642 College Ave.
Berkeley, CA 94704 (USA)
tel: 1-510-540-0749
fax: 1-510-849-1247
e-mail: pbiusa@igc.apc.org

Christian Peacemaker Teams (CPT)
P.O. Box 6508
Chicago, IL 60680
tel: 1-312-455-1199
e-mail: cpt@igc.apc.org
http://www.prairienet.org/cpt/
(CPT currently has programs in Haiti and Israel/Palestine.)

Witness for Peace
110 Maryland Ave. NE, Suite 304
Washington, DC 20002
tel: 1-202-544-0781
fax: 1-202-544-1187
e-mail: witness@w4p.org
http://www.w4p.org/wfp

National Coordinating Office on Refugees and Displaced of Guatemala
(NCOORD)
Guatemala Accompaniment Project
59 E. Van Buren St., Suite 1400
Chicago, IL 60603
tel: 1-312-360-1705
e-mail: ncoord@igc.apc.org

In Canada

Peace Brigades International–Canada
192 Spadina Ave., Suite 304
Toronto, Canada M5T 2C2
tel: 1-416-504-4429
fax: 1-416-504-4430
e-mail: pbi@web.net

Canadian Project Accompaniment
1618 Preston St.
Halifax, Canada, B3H 3V1
tel: 1-902-423-3820
e-mail: accatl@web.net

In Europe

Peace Brigades International
5 Caledonian Rd.
London N19DX England
tel: (44)-171-713-0392
fax: (44)-171-837-2290
e-mail: pbiio@gn.apc.org
(For information on PBI chapters and contacts in France, Germany, Spain,
Netherlands, Switzerland, Italy, Sweden, Belgium, and other countries,
contact the London office.)

Balkans Peace Teams International
Marienwall 9
D-32423 Minden
Germany
tel: (49)-571-20776
fax: (49)-571-23019
e-mail: Balkan-Peace-Team@bionic.zerberus.de

CAREA (Cadena por un Retorno Acompanado)
Glashüttenstr. 106
20357 Hamburg
Germany
tel: (49)-40-438256
e-mail: zapapres@cl-hh.comlink.de
(Accompaniment in Guatemala)

HOLACOM
Proyecto Holandes de Acompañamiento
Domstraat 29
3512 JA Utrecht
Netherlands

tel: (31)-30321112
fax: (31)-30317278
e-mail: GKN@Antenna.NL
(Accompaniment in Guatemala)

Entrepueblos
Plaza Ramón Berenguer el Gran n° 1, 3ª-1°
08002 Barcelona
Spain
tel: 34-3-268.33.66
fax: 34-3-268.49.13
e-mail: epueblo@pangea.upc.es
(Development and accompaniment work in Guatemala, El Salvador,
Nicaragua, Colombia, Ecuador, and Haiti)

Associació d'Amistat amb el Poble de Guatemala
Calle Vistalegre nª 15
08001 Barcelona
Spain
tel: 34-3-443.43.92

Mugarik Gabe
Calle Zapatería nª 9, 1°
Pamplona, Spain
tel: 34-48.210.822
fax: 34-48.212.758

Abbreviations

AEU	Association of University Students
ARDE	Anticommunist Revolutionary Action for Extermination (El Salvador)
ARENA	Nationalist Republican Alliance of El Salvador
ASFADDES	Association of Families of the Disappeared (Colombia)
CAVISA	Central America Glass Company
CCPP	Permanent Commissions of the Guatemalan Refugees in Mexico
CDHES	Nongovernmental Human Rights Commission of El Salvador
CDHG	Guatemala Human Rights Commission
CEAR	Special Commission for Attention to Repatriates (Guatemala)
CEJIL	Center for Justice and International Law
CERJ	Council of Ethnic Communities "Everyone Equal" (Guatemala)
CHRLA	Center for Human Rights Legal Action
CIA	Central Intelligence Agency (United States)
CISPES	Committee in Solidarity with the People of El Salvador (United States)
CNR	National Coordination for Repopulation (El Salvador)
COMADRES	Committee of Mothers of the Disappeared and Assassinated (El Salvador)
COMAR	Mexican Refugee Commission
CONAVIGUA	National Council of Guatemalan Widows
CONDEG	Council of Displaced Guatemalans
CONFREGUA	Conference of Religious of Guatemala
COSCO	Committee for Eastern Solidarity (El Salvador)
CPR	Communities of Population in Resistance (Guatemala)
CPT	Christian Peacemaker Teams
CREDHOS	Regional Human Rights Commission (Colombia)
CRIPDES	Christian Committee for the Displaced of El Salvador
CUC	Committee for Campesino Unity (Guatemala)
DAS	Department of Administrative Security (Colombia)

EGP	Guerrilla Army of the Poor (Guatemala)
EHED	Eastern Human and Economic Development (Sri Lanka)
EPDP	Eelam People's Democratic Party
EPICA	Ecumenical Program on Central America and the Caribbean
FAMDEGUA	Families of the Disappeared of Guatemala
FDR	Revolutionary Democratic Front (El Salvador)
FENASTRAS	National Federation of Salvadoran Workers
FLACSO	Latin America Faculty of Social Sciences
FMLN	Farabundo Marti National Liberation Front (El Salvador)
FRAPH	Front for the Advancement of Haiti
G-2	Guatemalan Military Intelligence Agency
GAM	Guatemalan Mutual Support Group for Families of the Disappeared
GRICAR	International Group for Consulting and Support of the [Guatemalan] Return
ICRC	International Committee of the Red Cross
ICVA	International Council of Voluntary Agencies
IDHUCA	Human Rights Institute of the University of Central America
JVP	People's Liberation Front (Sri Lanka)
LTTE	Liberation Tigers of Tamil Eelam (Sri Lanka)
MICIVIH	Combined UN and OAS Civilian Mission to Haiti
MINUGUA	United Nations Mission to Guatemala
MIRJE	Movement for InterRacial Justice and Equality
NCOORD	National Coordinating Office on Refugees and Displaced of Guatemala (United States)
NGO	nongovernmental organization
OAS	Organization of American States
ONUSAL	United Nations Mission to El Salvador
ORC	Open Relief Center
OXFAM	Oxford Committee for Famine Relief
PAC	Guatemalan civil patrol
PARINAC	Partners in Action
PBI	Peace Brigades International
PLOTE	People's Liberation Organization of Tamil Eelam (Sri Lanka)
QPS	Quaker Peace and Service

RUOG	Unified Representation of the Guatemalan Opposition
UCA	Universided de Centro America
UN	United Nations
UNHCR	United Nations High Commissioner for Refugees
UNP	United Nationalist Party (Sri Lanka)
UNSITRAGUA	Labor Unity of Guatemalan Workers
UNTS	National Unity of Salvadoran Workers
URNG	National Revolutionary Unity of Guatemala
USAID	U.S. Agency for International Development

Bibliography

Agosin, Marjorie. *Surviving Beyond Fear: Women, Children and Human Rights in Latin America*. Fredonia, N.Y.: White Pine Press, 1993.

Aguilera Peralta, Gabriel. *Seguridad, funcion militar y democracia*. Guatemala City: FLACSO, 1994.

Aguilera Peralta, Gabriel. *Violencia y contraviolencia: La violencia y el regimen de legalidad en Guatemala*. Guatemala: Editorial Universitaria, 1979.

Amati, Silvia. "Aportes psicoanaliticos al conocimiento de los efectos de la violencia institucionalizada." In Horacio Riquelme U., ed. *Era de Nieblas: Derechos Humanos, terrorismo de Estado y salud psicosocial en America Latina*. Caracas, Venezuela: Editorial Nueva Sociedad, 1990.

Americas Watch. *Civil Patrols in Guatemala*. New York: Americas Watch, 1986.

Americas Watch. *Closing the Space—Human Rights in Guatemala, May 1987–Oct. 1988*. New York: Americas Watch, 1988.

Americas Watch. *The Group for Mutual Support, 1984–1985*. New York: Americas Watch, 1986.

Americas Watch. *Human Rights in Guatemala During Pres. Cerezo's First Year*. New York: Americas Watch, 1987.

Americas Watch. *Messengers of Death: Human Rights in Guatemala, Nov. 1988–Feb. 1990*. New York: Americas Watch, 1990.

Americas Watch. *The More Things Change: Human Rights in Haiti*. New York: Americas Watch, 1989.

Americas Watch. *Persecuting Human Rights Monitors: The CERJ in Guatemala*. New York: Americas Watch, 1989.

Amnesty International. *El Salvador: Death Squads—A Government Strategy*. New York: Amnesty International, 1988.

Amnesty International. *Peacekeeping and Human Rights*. London: Amnesty International, 1994.

Armstrong, Robert, and Janet Rubin. *El Salvador: El rostro de la revolucion*. San Salvador: UCA Editores, 1986.

Aron, Adrianne, Shawn Corne, Anthea Forsland, and Barbara Zelwer. "The Gender-Specific Terror of El Salvador and Guatemala: Post-Traumatic Stress Disorder in Central America." *Womens Studies International Forum* 14, no. 1/2 (1991): 37–47.

Bahbau, Bishara. *Israel and Latin America: The Military Connection*. New York: St. Martin's Press, 1986.

Baranyi, Stephen. "Ampliando los limites de lo posible: Mision de paz de Naciones Unidas en America Central." *Estudios Internacionales* 5, no. 9 (1994): 105–24.

Barry, Tom. *El Salvador: A Country Guide*. Albuquerque: Inter-Hemispheric Education Resource Center, 1990.

Becker, David, and Hugo Calderon. "Traumatizaciones extremas, procesos de reparacion social, crisis politica." In Horacio Riquelme U., ed. *Era de Nieblas: Derechos Humanos, terrorismo de Estado y salud psicosocial en America Latina*. Caracas, Venezuela: Editorial Nueva Sociedad, 1990.

Beristain, Carlos, and Francesc Riera. *La Comunidad Como Apoyo: Salud Mental*. San Salvador: Universidad CentroAmericana, 1992.

Biegbeder, Yves. *The Role and Status of International Humanitarian Volunteers and Organizations*. Dordrecht: Martinus Nijhoff, 1993.

Blake, Samuel W. *Guarding the Guards: General Hector Gramajo and the Guatemala Army*. Cambridge, Mass.: JFK School of Government, 1994.

Blondel, Jean-Luc. "Assistance to Protected Persons." *International Review of the Red Cross* 260 (1987): 451–68.

Blondel, Jean-Luc. "Getting Access to the Victims: Role of the ICRC." *Journal of Peace Research* 24, no. 3 (1987): 307–14.

Boutros Boutros-Ghali. *An Agenda for Peace*. New York: United Nations, 1995.

Bryans, Michael. "The Banality of Deterrence." *Peace and Security* 3, no. 1 (1988): 4–5.

Burger, Andrea. "Changing Civil-Military Relations in Sri Lanka." *Asian Survey* 32, no. 8 (1992): 744–56.

Cahill, Kevin M., ed. *A Framework for Survival: Health, Human Rights and Humanitarian Assistance in Conflicts and Disaster*. New York: Council on Foreign Relations and Basic Books, 1993.

Chandraprema, C. A. *Sri Lanka: The Years of Terror; The JVP Insurrection 1987–1989*. Colombo, Sri Lanka: Lake House, 1991.

Chopra, Jarat, and Thomas G. Weiss. "Sovereignty Is No Longer Sacrosanct: Codifying Humanitarian Intervention." *Ethics and International Affairs* 6 (1992): 95–117.

Christian, Shirley. "Guatemalan Defense Patrol: Force in Its Own Right." *New York Times,* June 2, 1991.

Cohen, Roberta. *Human Rights Protection for Internally Displaced Persons*. Washington, D.C.: Refugee Policy Group, 1991.

Comision de la verdad [El Salvador Truth Commission]. "De la locura a la esperanza: La guerra de doce anos en El Salvador." *Estudios Centroamericanos* 533 (1990).

Compher, Vic, and Betsy Morgan. *Going Home: The Story of Repatriation*. New York: Apex Press, 1991.

Corradi, Juan E., Patricia Weiss Fagen, and Manvel Antonio Garreton. *Fear at the Edge: State Terror and Resistance in Latin America*. Berkeley: University of California Press, 1992.

Coy, Patrick G. "Cooperative Accompaniment in Sri Lanka with Peace Brigades International." In Charles Chatfield, Ron Pagnucco, and Jackie Smith, eds. *Solidarity Beyond the State: The Dynamics of Transnational Social Movements*. Syracuse, N.Y.: Syracuse University Press, in press.

Coy, Patrick G. *Going Where We Otherwise Would Not Have Gone: Nonviolent International Accompaniment by PBI in Sri Lanka,* forthcoming dissertation, Syracuse University, Syracuse, N.Y.

Coy, Patrick G. "Protective Accompaniment: How Peace Brigades International Secures Political Space and Human Rights." In V. K. Kool, ed. *Nonviolence: Social and Psychological Issues*. Latham, Md.: University Press of America, 1993.

Dunkerley, James. *Power in the Isthmus: A Political History of Central America*. London: Verso, 1988.

ECA. *La Guerra de Baja Intensidad*. San Salvador: ECA, 1989.

Ennals, Martin. "Amnesty International and Human Rights." In Peter Willetts, ed. *Pressure Groups*. London: F. Pinter, 1982.

EPICA/CHRLA. *Out of the Shadows: The Communities of Population in Resistance in Guatemala*. Washington, D.C.: Ecumenical Program on Central America, 1993.

Faber, Jan. "On Bounded Rationality and the Framing of Decisions in International Relations: Towards a Dynamic Network Model of World Politics." *Journal of Peace Research* 27, no. 3 (1990): 307–19.

Falk, Richard. *Human Rights and State Sovereignty*. New York and London: Holmes and Meier, 1981.

Falla, Ricardo. *Historia de un Gran Amor*. N.p., n.d.

Falla, Ricardo. *Masacres De La Selva*. Guatemala City: Editorial Universitaria, 1992.

Farina, Juan Jorge. "El Terror de Estado como Fantasma." In Horacio Riquelme U., ed. *Era de Nieblas: Derechos Humanos, terrorismo de Estado y salud psicosocial en America Latina*. Caracas, Venezuela: Editorial Nueva Sociedad, 1990.

Faundez, Hector. "El lenguaje del miedo: Dinamicas colectivas de la comunicacion bajo el terror en Chile." In Horacio Riquelme U., ed. *Era de Nieblas: Derechos Humanos, terrorismo de Estado y salud psicosocial en America Latina*. Caracas, Venezuela: Editorial Nueva Sociedad, 1990.

Figueroa Ibarra, Carlos. *El recurso del miedo: Ensayo sobre el estado y el terror en Guatemala*. San Jose, Costa Rica: Editorial Universitaria Centroamericana (EDUCA), 1991.

Fogelman, Eva. *Conscience and Courage: Rescuers of Jews During the Holocaust*. New York: Anchor Books, 1994.

Forsythe, David P. *Human Rights and Development: International Views*. New York: St. Martin's Press, 1989.

Forsythe, David P. "Human Rights and the International Committee of the Red Cross." *Human Rights Quarterly* 12 (1990) 265–89.

Forsythe, David. *Humanitarian Politics*. Baltimore: Johns Hopkins University Press, 1977.

Friedlander, Robert A. "Human Rights Theory and NGO Practice: Where Do We Go From Here?" In Ved P. Nanda, James Scarritt, and G. Shepherd Jr., eds. *Global Human Rights: Public Policies, Comparative Measures and NGO Strategies*. Boulder, Colo.: Westview Press, 1981.

Galtung, Johan. "Cultural Violence." *Journal of Peace Research* 27, no. 3 (1990): 291–305.

Galtung, Johan. "Some Factors Affecting the Local Acceptance of a UN Force." In *Peace, War and Defence: Essays in Peace Research*. Oslo: International Peace Research Institute, 1976.

Galtung, Johan. "Three Approaches to Peace: Peacekeeping, Peacemaking and Peacebuilding." In *Peace, War and Defence: Essays in Peace Research* (Vol. 2). Oslo: International Peace Research Institute, 1976.

Gandasegui, Marco A. "Militares, Democracia y Desarrollo." In Gabriel Aguilera Peralta, ed. *Reconversion Militar en America Latina*. Guatemala City: FLACSO, 1994.

Garreton, Manuel Antonio. "El miedo y las dictaduras militares." In Ignacio Martin-Baro, ed. *Psicologia Social de la Guerra*. San Salvador: UCA Editores, 1990.

Gettleman, E., P. Lacefield, L. Menasche, and D. Mermelstein, eds. *El Salvador: Central America in the New Cold War.* New York: Grove Press, 1987.

Goldberg, Ana. "Efectos psicologicas del exilio y del retorno." In Ignacio Martin-Baro, ed. *Psicologia Social de la Guerra.* San Salvador: UCA Editores, 1990.

Golden, Renny, and Michael McConnell. *Sanctuary: The New Underground Railroad.* Maryknoll, N.Y.: Orbis Books, 1986.

Goodwyn, Lawrence. *The Populist Moment.* Oxford: Oxford University Press, 1978.

Gramajo Morales, Hector Alejandro. *De la Guerra, a la Guerra.* Guatemala City: Fondo de Cultura Editorial, S.A., 1995.

Green, Linda. "Fear as a Way of Life." *Cultural Anthropology* 9, no. 2 (1994): 227–56.

Griffin-Nolan, ed. *Witness for Peace.* Louisville, Ky.: Westminster/J. Knox, 1992.

Handy, Jim. *Gift of the Devil; A History of Guatemala.* Boston: South End Press, 1984.

Handy, Jim. "Resurgent Democracy and the Guatemalan Military." *Journal of Latin American Studies* 18 (1987): 409–23.

Herman, Edward. *The Real Terror Network.* Boston: South End Press, 1982.

Horowitz, Donald. *Coup Theories and Officer's Motives: Sri Lanka in Comparative Perspective.* Princeton, N.J.: Princeton University Press, 1980.

Human Rights Watch. *Slaughter Among Neighbors: The Political Origins of Communal Violence.* New Haven, Conn.: Yale University Press, 1995.

IDHUCA (Instituto de Derechos Humanos and Universidad Centroamericana). *Los derechos humanos en El Salvador en 1989.* San Salvador: IDHUCA, 1990.

Jamail, Milton, and Margo Gutierrez. *It's No Secret: Israel's Military Involvement in Central America.* Belmont, Mass.: Association of Arab-American University Graduates, 1986.

Jay, Alice. *Persecution by Proxy—The Civil Patrols in Guatemala.* New York: Robert F. Kennedy Memorial Center for Human Rights, 1993.

Jonas, Susanne. *Battle for Guatemala: Rebels, Death Squads and U.S. Power.* Boulder, Colo.: Westview Press, 1991.

Keyes, Gene. "Force Without Firepower: A Doctrine of Unarmed Military Service." *CoEvolution Quarterly* (1982): 4.

Kinzer, Steven. "Guatemalans Organize to Find Missing Kin." *New York Times,* July 21, 1984.

Kinzer, Steven. "Killings Chill Rights Groups." *New York Times,* April 19, 1985.

Kinzer, Steven. "1000 Marchers in Guatemala Call Attention to Abduction." *New York Times,* April 14, 1985.

Kinzer, Steven, and Stephen Schlesinger. *Bitter Fruit.* Garden City, N.Y.: Doubleday, 1981.

Klare, Michael, and Peter Kornbluh, eds. *Low Intensity Warfare: Counterinsurgency, Proinsurgency, and Antiterrorism in the Eighties.* New York: Pantheon, 1988.

Korten, David C. *Getting to the 21st Century: Voluntary Action and the Global Agenda.* West Hartford, Conn.: Kumarian Press, 1990.

Kriesberg, Louis. "Non-coercive Inducements in International Conflicts." *Peace and Change* (Fall 1981): 37–47.

Krysl, Marilyn. "A Deeper Darkness." *Manoa, A Pacific Journal of International Writing* 7, no. 1 (Summer 1995): 168–79.

Larson, Meredith. "Model Mugging Graduate Defends Herself Against a Knife Attack." *D.C. Model Mugging Newsletter* 2 (March 1990): 2.

Leary, Virginia, and Suriya Wickremasinghe. *An Introductory Guide to Human Rights Law and Humanitarian Law*. Colombo, Sri Lanka: Nadesan Center, 1993.

Lebow, Richard Ned, and Janice Gross Stein. *When Does Deterrence Succeed and How Do We Know?* Occasional Paper 8. Ottawa: Canadian Institute for Peace and International Security, 1990.

LeoGrande, William, and Carla Anne Robbins. "Oligarchs and Officers: The Crisis in El Salvador." In Brian Loveman, ed. *The Politics of Antipolitics: The Military in Latin America*. Lincoln: University of Nebraska Press, 1989.

Lichbach, Mark Irving. "Deterrence or Escalation: The Puzzle of Aggregate Studies of Repression and Dissent." *Journal of Conflict Resolution* 31, no. 2 (1987): 266–97.

Lindsay-Poland, John. "Unwelcome in El Salvador: For Those Who Come to Help, Threats, Deportation, Even Death." *Progressive* 53, no. 5 (May 1989): 32–4.

Lira Cornfeld, Elizabeth. "Guerra Psicologica: Intervencion politica de la subjetividad colectiva." In Ignacio Martin-Baro, ed. *Psicologia social de la Guerra*. San Salvador: UCA Editores, 1990.

Lira Cornfeld, Elizabeth. "Psicologia del miedo y conducta colectiva en Chile." In Ignacio Martin-Baro, ed. *Psicologia social de la guerra*. San Salvador: UCA Editores, 1990.

Livesey, Lowell. *Nongovernmental Organizations and the Ideas of Human Rights*. Princeton, N.J.: Center for International Studies, 1988.

Loveman, Brian, and Thomas M. Davies Jr. *The Politics of Antipolitics: The Military in Latin America*. Lincoln: University of Nebraska Press, 1989.

Manz, Beatriz. *Refugees of a Hidden War: The Aftermath of Counterinsurgency in Guatemala*. Albany: State University of New York Press, 1988.

Manz, Beatriz. *Repatriation and Reintegration: An Arduous Process in Guatemala*. Washington, D.C.: Hemispheric Migration Project, Georgetown University, 1988.

Martin-Baro, Ignacio, ed. *Psicologia social de la guerra*. San Salvador: UCA Editores, 1990.

McConahy, MaryJo. "The Well-Meaning American." *Image* (February 1988).

Milburn, Michael A. *Persuasion and Politics: The Social Psychology of Public Opinion*. Pacific Grove, Calif.: Brooks/Cole, 1991.

Minear, Larry, and Thomas Weiss. *Humanitarian Action in Times of War*. Boulder, Colo.: Lynne Rienner, 1993.

Minear, Larry, and Thomas G. Weiss. *Mercy Under Fire: War and the Global Humanitarian Community*. Boulder, Colo.: Westview Press, 1995.

Mitchell, Christopher R. "Como poner fin a guerras y conflictos: Decisiones, racionalidad y trampas." *Revista Internacional de Ciencias Social* 127 (1991): 35–58.

Nairn, Allan. "Behind the Death Squads." *Progressive* (May 1984): 20.

Nairn, Allan. "CIA Death Squad." *The Nation* (April 17, 1995): 511.

Nairn, Allan. "Confessions of a Death Squad Officer." *Progressive* (March 1986): 26–30.

Nairn, Allan. "The Country Team." *The Nation* (June 5, 1995): 22.

Nairn, Allan. "Exchange." *The Nation* (May 29, 1995): 742, 772.

Nairn, Allan, and Jean-Marie Simon. "Bureacracy of Death: Guatemala's Civilian Government Faces the Enemy Within." *The New Republic* (June 30, 1986): 13.

Nanda, Ved P., James R. Scaritt, and George W. Shepard Jr., eds. *Global Human Rights: Public Policies, Comparative Measures and NGO Strategies.* Boulder, Colo.: Westview Press, 1980.

Painter, James. *Guatemala: False Hopes, False Freedom: The Rich, the Poor and the Christian Democrats.* London: Catholic Institute for International Relations, 1987.

Patterson, Franklin. "The Guatemalan Military and the Escuela Politecnica." *Armed Forces and Society* 14, no. 3 (1988): 359–90.

Payeras, Mario. *El Trueno en La Ciudad.* Mexico City: J. Pablos, 1987.

Peace Brigades International. *PBI Project Bulletin* (all issues). London: PBI, 1981–96.

Pelento, Maria Lucila, and J. B. de Dunayevich. "La Desaparicion: Su repercusion en el individuo y en la sociedad." In Ignacio Martin-Baro, ed. *Psicologia Social de la Guerra.* San Salvador: UCA Editores, 1990.

Pion-Berlin, David. *The Ideology of State Terror.* Boulder and London: Lynne Rienner, 1989.

Plant, Roger. *Abandoning the Victims: The UN Advisory Services Program in Guatemala.* New York: Lawyers Committee for Human Rights, 1990.

Poe, Steven C. "Human Rights and the Allocation of U.S. Military Assistance." *Journal of Peace Research* 28, no. 2 (1991): 205–16.

Power, Jonathan. *Amnesty International: The Human Rights Story.* New York: McGraw-Hill, 1981.

Preston, Julia. "Dwindling Protest Group." *Boston Globe*, August 4, 1985.

Pritchard, Kathleen. "Human Rights: A Decent Respect for Public Opinion." *Human Rights Quarterly* 13 (1991): 123–42.

Riquelme U., Horacio. "America del Sur: derechos humanos y salud psicosocial." In Horacio Riquelme U., ed. *Era de Nieblas: Derechos Humanos, terrorismo de Estado y salud psicosocial en America Latina.* Caracas, Venezuela: Editorial Nueva Sociedad, 1990.

Riquelme U., Horacio. "Lo real espantoso: Efectos psicoculturales del terrorismo de Estado en America del Sur." In Horacio Riquelme U., ed. *Era de Nieblas: Derechos Humanos, terrorismo de Estado y salud psicosocial en America Latina.* Caracas, Venezuela: Editorial Nueva Sociedad, 1990.

Rodgers, Malcolm. *Refugees and International Aid. Sri Lanka: A Case Study.* Geneva: UNHCR, 1992.

Rodriguez Beruff, Jorge, and H. Garcia. "Cambio estrategico global y nueva politica militar de EEUU: Su impacto en America Latina y el Caribe." In Gabriel Aguilera Peralta, ed. *Reconversion Militar en America Latina.* Guatemala City: FLACSO, 1994.

Rodriguez Elizondo, Jose. *Democracia y derechos humanos en America Latina.* Madrid: Ediciones de Cultura Hispanica, 1989.

Rosa, Herman. *AID y las transformaciones globales en El Salvador.* Managua, Nicaragua: Coordinadora Regional de Investigaciones Económicas y Sociales (CRIES), 1993.

Rozitcher, Leon. "Efectos psicosociales de la represion." In Ignacio Martin-Baro, ed. *Psicologia Social de la Guerra*. San Salvador: UCA Editores, 1990.

Schindler, Dietrich. *The International Committee of the Red Cross and Human Rights*. Geneva: ICRC, n.d.

Schirch, Lisa. *Keeping the Peace: Exploring Civilian Alternatives in Conflict Prevention*. Uppsala: Life and Peace Institute, 1995.

Scott, Barbara Edith. *Two Years of Witness: Political Violence in Guatemala, 1987–1989*. Master's thesis, University of Connecticut, 1990.

Scott, James C. "Domination, Acting and Fantasy." In Carolyn Nordstrom, ed. *The Paths to Domination, Resistance, and Terror*. Berkeley, Los Angeles, and Oxford: University of California Press, 1992.

Scott, James C. *Weapons of the Weak: Everyday Forms of Resistance*. New Haven, Conn.: Yale University Press, 1985.

Sharp, Gene. *Making Europe Unconquerable*. Cambridge, Mass.: Ballinger, 1985.

Sharp, Gene. *The Politics of Nonviolent Action*. Boston: Porter Sargent, 1973.

Shepherd, George W. "Transnational Development of Human Rights: The Third World Crucible." In Ved P. Nanda, James Scarritt, and G. Shepherd Jr., eds. *Global Human Rights: Public Policies, Comparative Measures and NGO Strategies*. Boulder, Colo.: Westview Press, 1981.

Sikkink, Kathryn. "Human Rights, Principled Issue–Networks and Sovereignty in Latin America." *International Organization* 47, no. 3 (1993): 411–41.

Sloan, John W. "Political Terrorism in Latin America: A Critical Analysis." In Michael Stohl, ed. *The Politics of Terrorism*. New York: Marcel Decker, 1979.

Smith, Jackie, R. Pagnucco, and W. Romeril. "Transnational Social Movement Organizations in the Global Political Arena." *Voluntas* 5, no. 2 (1994): 121–54.

Snyder, Glenn, and Paul Diesing. "External Bargaining and Internal Bargaining." In Robert O. Matthews, Arthur G. Rubinoff, and Janice Gross Stein, eds. *International Conflict and Conflict Management: Readings in World Politics*. Ontario, Canada: Prentice Hall Canada, 1989.

Stohl, Michael, and George Lopez. *The State as Terrorist*. Westport, Conn.: Greenwood Press, 1984.

Stohl, Michael, and George Lopez. *Terrible Beyond Endurance: The Foreign Policy of State Terrorism*. Westport, Conn.: Greenwood Press, 1988.

Suarez-Orozco, Marcelo. "A Grammar of Terror: Psychocultural Responses to State Terrorism in Dirty War and Post–Dirty War Argentina." In Carolyn Nordstrom and JoAnn Martin, eds. *The Paths to Domination, Resistance, and Terror*. Berkeley, Los Angeles, and Oxford: University of California Press, 1992.

Tambiah, S. J. *Sri Lanka: Ethnic Fratricide and the Dismantling of Democracy*. Chicago: University of Chicago Press, 1986.

Tomasevski, Katarina. *Development Aid and Human Rights Revisited*. London: Pinter, 1993.

Torres-Rivas, Edelberto. "Guatemala: Crisis and Political Violence." In Stanford Central American Action Network, ed. *Revolution in Central America*. Boulder, Colo.: Westview Press, 1983.

Universidad de CentroAmerica (UCA). *La resistencia noviolenta ante los regimenes salvadorenos que han utilizado el terror institucionalizado en el periodo 1972–1987*. Universidad de Centro-America, Departamento de Sociologia y Ciencias Politicas, Instituto de Derechos Humanos, and Harvard University (Center for International Affairs) Program on Nonviolent Sanctions in Conflict and Defense. San Salvador: UCA Editores, 1988.

U.S. Committee for Refugees. *El Retorno: Guatemala's Risky Repatriation Begins*. Washington, D.C.: American Council for Nationalities Service, 1993.

Varas, Augusto. *Democracy Under Seige: New Military Power in Latin America*. New York: Greenwood Press, 1989.

Vertzberger, Yaacov Y. I. *The World in Their Minds: Information Processing, Cognition, and Perception in Foreign Policy Decisions*. Stanford, Calif.: Stanford University Press, 1990.

Walker, Charles C. "A World Peace Guard." In Michael Beer, ed. *A Peace Team Reader*. Washington, D.C.: Nonviolence International, 1993.

Walter, Knut, and Phillip J. Williams. "The Military and Democratization in El Salvador." *Journal of Interamerican Studies* 1 (1993): 39–77.

Weber, Thomas. "From Maude Royden's Peace Army to the Gulf Peace Team: Assessment of Unarmed Interpositionary Peace." *Journal of Peace Research* 30, no. 1 (1993): 45–64.

Wechsler, Lawrence. *A Miracle, a Universe: Settling Accounts with Torturers*. New York: Penguin, 1990.

Weerakoon, Batty. *The Extra-judicial Execution of Richard De Zoysa*. Colombo, Sri Lanka: Star Press, 1991.

Weinstein, Eugenia. "Problematica psicologica del retornado del exilio en Chile." In Ignacio Martin-Baro, ed. *Psicologia Social de la Guerra*. San Salvador: UCA Editores, 1990.

Wilkinson, Daniel. "'Democracy' Comes to Guatemala." *World Policy Journal* 12, no. 4 (Winter 1995–96): 71–5.

Willetts, Peter. "Pressure Groups as Transnational Actors." In Peter Willetts, ed. *Pressure Groups*. London: F. Pinter, 1982.

Wiseberg, Laurie. "Protecting Human Rights Activists and NGOs: What More Can Be Done?" *Human Rights Quarterly* 13 (1991): 525–44.

Witness for Peace. *Ten Years of Accompaniment*. Washington, D.C.: Witness for Peace, 1994.

Zagare, Frank. *The Dynamics of Deterrence*. Chicago: University of Chicago Press, 1987.

Index

About the Authors

LIAM MAHONY has been working with Peace Brigades International (PBI) since 1987. He has done accompaniment work in Guatemala and cofounded the Peace Brigades Haiti Project. Mahony also serves as a consultant for the Seva Foundation, training volunteers to accompany refugees returning to Guatemala, and is a freelance writer and trainer for nongovernmental organizations. He lives on Cape Cod, Massachusetts.

LUIS ENRIQUE EGUREN, M.D., served as an accompaniment volunteer in El Salvador in 1988, in Sri Lanka in 1989, and cofounded the PBI–Colombia Project in 1994. Eguren also carried out investigations on accompaniment in the Balkans. He has served in medical projects in El Salvador and with the Doctors of the World in Guatemala. He works as a doctor in the Canary Islands, Spain.

 Kumarian Press is dedicated to publishing and
distributing books and other media that will
have a positive social and economic impact
on the lives of peoples living in "Third World"
conditions no matter where they live.

**As well as books on Peace and Conflict Resolution,
Kumarian Press also publishes books
on the Environment, International Development,
Nongovernmental Organizations,
Government, Gender and Development**

To receive a complimentary catalog, request writer's
guidelines, or to order books call or write:

Kumarian Press, Inc.
14 Oakwood Avenue
West Hartford, CT 06119-2127
USA

Inquiries: 860-233-5895
Fax: 860-233-6072
Order toll free: 800-289-2664

e-mail: kpbooks@aol.com